Fresh Pond

Fresh Pond

The History of a Cambridge Landscape

Jill Sinclair

The MIT Press
Cambridge, Massachusetts
London, England

Aerial photograph of Fresh Pond to Boston, 1989.
© 2009 Alex S. MacLean/Landslides.

For information about special quantity discounts, please email special_sales@mitpress.mit.edu

This book was set in Chaparral Pro by the MIT Press and was printed and bound in Canada.

Library of Congress Cataloging-in-Publication Data

Sinclair, Jill, 1961-
    Fresh Pond : the history of a Cambridge landscape / Jill Sinclair.
        p. cm.
    Includes bibliographical references and index.
    ISBN 978-0-262-19591-1 (hardcover : alk. paper) 1. Fresh
Pond (Middlesex County, Mass.)—History. 2. Cambridge (Mass.)
—History. 3. Landscape—Massachusetts—Cambridge—History.
4. Landscape—Social aspects—Massachusetts—Cambridge—
History. 5. City planning—Massachusetts—Cambridge—
History. 6. Natural history—Massachusetts—Cambridge.
7. Cambridge (Mass.)—Environmental conditions. I. Title.
    F74.C1S54 2009
    974.4'4—dc22
                            2008031028

10 9 8 7 6 5 4 3 2 1

The author and publisher would like to thank the Hubbard Educational Foundation, the Cambridge Heritage Trust, and the Friends of Fresh Pond Reservation, whose generous financial awards made this book a reality.

. . . for the pleasure of memory, to Fresh Pond, dear to the muses of youth, the Sunday afternoons of spring, . . .

Henry James, *The American Scene*, 1907

FRESH POND
AND ITS SURROUNDINGS

ABOUT 1866

Compiled and drawn by
Charles D. Elliot

Contents

Acknowledgments   xi

1   Introduction   1

2   A Place to Play   11

3   Industry at the Pond   33

4   Social Reform and the City   57

5   Professional Design   81

6   Municipal Expansion   107

7   Citizen Involvement and the Green Agenda   141

Afterword   157

Notes   163

Index   175

Acknowledgments

This is the first book published on Fresh Pond. Until now its history has been available only in glimpses: a tantalizing photograph, an anecdote in a journal, a brief section in a larger work. I am grateful to all those who have made it possible.

Particular thanks go to Charles Sullivan, the executive director of the city of Cambridge Historical Commission, for suggesting the topic, and for his support, encouragement and wisdom throughout; Chip Norton, watershed division manager of the city of Cambridge Water Department, for allowing me access to his staff, papers, and time; Elizabeth Wylde, president of the Friends of Fresh Pond Reservation, for her unending enthusiasm about my research; and my academic advisor, Alice Ingerson PhD, for her insightful comments on drafts of the thesis from which this book has been developed.

I am also indebted to Kathleen (Kit) Rawlins at the Cambridge Historical Commission; Jean Rogers and Tim McDonald at the Cambridge Water Department; Patricia Pratt and other members of the Cambridge Plant & Garden Club; Marion Pressley and Lauren Meier, landscape architects and preservation specialists; Arleyn Levee, landscape historian and Olmsted scholar; John Furlong, the faculty and students at Harvard's Landscape Institute; Sean Fisher, archivist for the Massachusetts Department of Conservation and Recreation; Janice Snow and other members of the Fresh Pond Advisory Board; Sister Therezon Sheerin of the Boston Congregation of the Sisters of St. Joseph; Michele Clark at the Frederick Law Olmsted National Historic Site; Richard Duffy and colleagues at the Arlington Historical Society; Richard Betts, editor of the Belmont Historical Society newsletter; as well as the countless other researchers, staff and volunteers who assisted me at various libraries, archives, and historical societies. Their help and encouragement made this a better book; any errors of interpretation or judgment are my own.

For their particular help with the images I am grateful to David Cobb at the Harvard Map Collection; Diana Carey at the Schlesinger Library; Bree Detamore Harvey at the Mount Auburn Cemetery Archives; Robin McElheny at the Harvard University Archives; and Charlotte R. Morrill and colleagues at the Southwest Harbor Public Library. Changing the work from an academic thesis to a commercial publication has been both hard work and much fun, and I would like to thank Luise Erdmann and Regis DeSilva for encouraging me to publish; and the admirable team at the MIT Press, especially Marguerite Avery, Erin Shoudy, Michael Sims, and Yasuyo Iguchi.

And finally, I am grateful to my husband Mark and daughter Elin Rose, for their patience, good humor, and support.

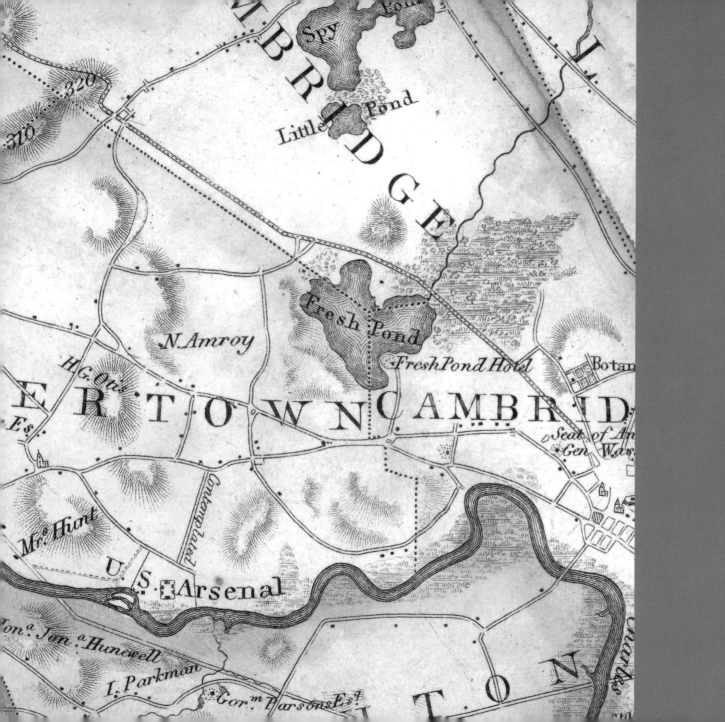

1 Introduction

Fresh Pond has been described as a "landscape loved to death."[1] It evokes fierce loyalty and even fiercer debate. A quick search on the internet will produce affectionate poems written by schoolchildren about Black's Nook; tirades about the need to tear down the fence that surrounds the water; albums of charming photographs of the scenery through the seasons; schedules and directions for organized games of soccer, softball, baseball, running, and tennis; lovingly compiled inventories of the birds and other wildlife that visit; angry criticisms of the shortcomings of the bike path; guides for grateful dog owners on how their pets can run free around the perimeter path; and much else. Everyone seems to know Fresh Pond, and to have an opinion on it. We all feel, in different ways, that we own it: the landscape is a part of our memories, a part of our lives.

Located at the northwest edge of modern Cambridge, Fresh Pond is a natural lake, nestling in a distinctively glacial landscape. Around 15,000 years ago the retreating ice age carved out its kettle lakes and rocky moraines. For thousands of years, Native Americans saw the water and surrounding woodland as a rich source of food. European settlers arrived in the 1600s and also fished and hunted there. Outside the growing centers of population in Cambridge and Watertown, Fresh Pond increasingly became home to farms and orchards and, by the early 1800s, was turning into a retreat from city life for wealthy Bostonians. Hotels, gentlemen's farms, and country estates gradually appeared on the shoreline. Working people and local students used the land for sporting activities and social picnics.

1.1 An aerial view of Fresh Pond, 2005. About half of the 317-acre reservation is formed by the natural water basin of Fresh Pond, part of the Mystic River watershed. The surrounding land is municipally owned open space and contains a mix of smaller water bodies, forest, wetlands, scrub, and meadow. The pond serves as the receiving reservoir for the city of Cambridge; on its eastern shore is the new water treatment facility, adjacent to the wooded promontory known as Kingsley Park. On the bluffs to the south is the Glacken Sports Ground while the nine-hole Thomas P. O'Neill Jr. Municipal Golf Course covers about a third of the land on the western side. Facilities for the elderly at Neville Center and Neville Place lie to the north. Around the shoreline of the pond is a 2.25-mile-long perimeter path, popular with joggers and dog owners. Office of Geographic and Environmental Information (MassGIS), Commonwealth of Massachusetts, Executive Office of Energy and Environmental Affairs.

During the nineteenth century, the area also became industrial, with clay being dug from the surrounding marshland for the local brick industry. Every winter, merchants cut the ice from the frozen pond in vast amounts and shipped it for sale as far away as England, Singapore, and India. It was a colossal and immensely profitable industry, but today it is largely forgotten.

Fresh Pond took on a different role and a different appearance when it became the drinking-water supply for the city of Cambridge. The water board acquired and completely cleared all the surrounding land, to limit the polluting effects of agriculture and industry. Major engineering work reshaped the shoreline and reworked the landscape. The social reform agenda of the late nineteenth and early twentieth centuries

1.2 This 1819 map shows how the pond at that time formed part of the boundary between the three towns of Cambridge, Watertown, and West Cambridge (now Arlington). It became fully a part of Cambridge in 1880. By the time of the map, there were roads leading to the pond (notably the Concord Turnpike to the north) and a few nearby farms. The Fresh Pond Hotel was already well established on the promontory. To the northeast, around the Alewife Brook, the Great Swamp was later to become the site of the brick industry and, more recently, home to the T station, shopping center, and Danehy Park. John G. Hales, Map of Boston and Its Vicinity. Philadelphia, 1819 (detail).

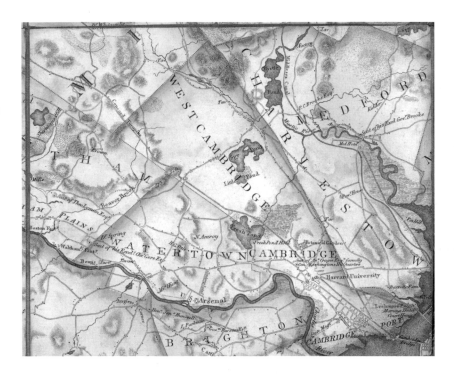

led to further new uses of the land. The water board engaged leading landscape architects Olmsted, Olmsted and Eliot to help turn Fresh Pond into a public park. Playgrounds and a municipal golf course followed. As the perceived need to use the landscape to protect the water supply diminished, so parts of the reservation were set aside for other uses, including a large infirmary, and some sections were sold for housing or commercial development.

By the early 1960s, the reservation had become neglected and overgrown, with serious soil erosion, illegal dumping, and invasive plants all causing problems. Local citizens worked with the city to try to improve the health of the landscape, and a series of projects and studies was undertaken. But it was not until the decision by the city in 1989 to replace its water treatment plant that a fundamental review began. The review brought to the surface the tensions inherent in this landscape, between the need for engineering works to preserve the quality of the water, the desire to protect its delicate ecology and perceived wild nature, the wish to retain the aesthetic appeal of the scenery, the demands for public recreational space, the pressure to retain and restore a historic designed landscape, and many more. The city, consultants, and local residents struggled and strove together to produce the Fresh Pond Reservation Master Plan (2000). Its decade-long, multimillion-dollar implementation is well underway. It aims to protect the reservation's natural resources (including water quality) while meeting the complex needs of today's public for the enjoyment of the space.

The conflicts that emerged during the master planning process reveal the sense of attachment that many people feel toward this place. It is striking how often Fresh Pond has featured in memoirs and diaries, poems, and drawings: from the myriad reminiscences of nineteenth-century Harvard students who sailed and feasted there, to fond sketches by the young Winslow Homer, to affectionate recollections by Catholic schoolgirls who were for a time educated on the shores, and to late twentieth-century pop songs about the adjacent parkway. Fresh Pond emerges from recent history as emblematic of

1.3 The first known photograph of Fresh Pond, taken from Mount Auburn Cemetery, c. 1860s. In the background (right) is the wooded promontory now known as Kingsley Park, with the Fresh Pond Hotel nestling among the trees. To the far left are some of the many large icehouses that stored the pond's winter harvest.
Harvard University Archives Call # HUV 965 1–7.

nature, of the past, of memories of childhood and friendship; it is a place viewed with great affection, with a special link to individuals: it is frequently "dear" Fresh Pond.

A number of reasons explain people's unusually affectionate and protective feelings toward this place. Its relative size as an extensive, naturalistic area within the small, closely built city is an important factor. Described a hundred years ago as "the largest open space Cambridge can ever hope to possess,"[2] Fresh Pond is particularly valued and treasured by the city's inhabitants, increasingly squeezed into Cambridge's packed six square miles. Its designation in colonial times as a "Great Pond" protected Fresh Pond from private acquisition or development; it meant that local residents saw it as belonging to them, a place where they had rights to fish and fowl, to navigate, to enjoy and use the water and the surrounding land. Its appeal has long been as somewhere secluded, intimate, and rich in natural resources: a special meeting place of land, sky, and water.

1.4 Throughout its history, local residents have enjoyed, explored, and celebrated the landscape at Fresh Pond. Today, the active Friends of Fresh Pond Reservation seek to involve the community in enhancing and protecting the landscape. Here, members brave the January snow to learn about the specimen trees growing on the golf course, including this mature weeping willow.
Elizabeth Wylde photograph, 2006.

Its location for so long on the periphery, close enough to be known and visited, but not part of the town, has also contributed to the pond's appeal. It led to its reputation as a retreat and a refuge for the ill, the old, the poor, and the persecuted, and as a haven for the wealthy—and for endangered local wildlife. Even with the surrender of Great Pond rights, its size and location meant that Fresh Pond continued to offer a special bond with its visitors, most recently for the local residents who volunteered to work with the city on the master plan. Today it represents for many the rural character that has otherwise been lost to Cambridge.

This book seeks to reveal Fresh Pond's history principally through a splendid selection of historical and contemporary photographs, maps, drawings, prints, and plans. Collected from numerous sources, the images bring the landscape's history dramatically to life, with accompanying explanations and interpretations of what the reader is seeing. Views of the landscape are described and analyzed, maps and plans are examined for continuity and change, portraits introduce the characters whose lives have profoundly affected this place. Supplementing the images is an array of vignettes that use memoirs, old newspaper articles, official reports, and personal correspondence to bring alive the thinking and attitudes of the time.

Rather than seeking neat conclusions or universal patterns, the book stays close to the stories of Fresh Pond, letting the details of this specific landscape strike their own resonances: "not privileged, just particular: another country heard from."[3] Yet it is clear that Fresh Pond also provides a case study in how changing social goals and values have affected American landscapes. From the wealth of details about this

1.5 A Works Progress Administration (WPA) Map of the Streets & Buildings of Cambridge, produced for the state planning board in 1940, shows the extent of development in the city. Apart from Fresh Pond (top left), the only remaining large open spaces in the city by that time were playgrounds and cemeteries.
Courtesy Massachusetts Archives.

particular place, it is possible to glimpse a broader history. So each chapter begins with a brief overview of selected historical themes, social trends, and events that place Fresh Pond's story in its wider context.

Readers will discover the enduring importance of the glacial origins of the area. They will be able to trace how changes in transport have affected the use, value, and perception of Fresh Pond, from the opening of the West Boston Bridge and the Concord Turnpike for carriages, to the arrival of the railroad, which supported industry and tourism at the pond, the streetcars and trolleys that were part of the speculation to create suburbs on previously undeveloped land, and then the twentieth-century advent of the automobile and the ensuing highway infrastructure.

From early annexations that moved town boundaries around and through the water, to vitriolic battles with neighboring Belmont over appropriate uses of the land, Fresh Pond has brought to the surface issues of town pride and civic stewardship. Frequent political interventions over priorities for its use and redesign have exposed deeply held views about what is best for the city, and what is likely to be most popular with its citizens. We can see too how major political events, from the Civil War and the two world wars to Roosevelt's New Deal, have all left their mark on this landscape.

The book will reveal the significant impact of the Industrial Revolution and its myriad accompanying changes, including the mass migration of people to urban areas and the ensuing growth in the scale and scope of local government. The social reform movement, which emerged to counteract the negative impacts of modern industrialized life, also plays out strongly

1.6 The water board acquired and cleared the land around Fresh Pond in the 1880s to safeguard its water supply system. This 1894 plan shows the new straightened edges of the reservoir (compared with the dashed shoreline of 1841), and the new carriage road around its edge. It was at this time that Little Fresh Pond and Black's Nook were separated from the main pond. The shaded areas indicate hills from which substantial amounts of gravel were removed to fill small coves and boggy areas nearby.
Courtesy of the National Park Service, Frederick Law Olmsted National Historic Site.

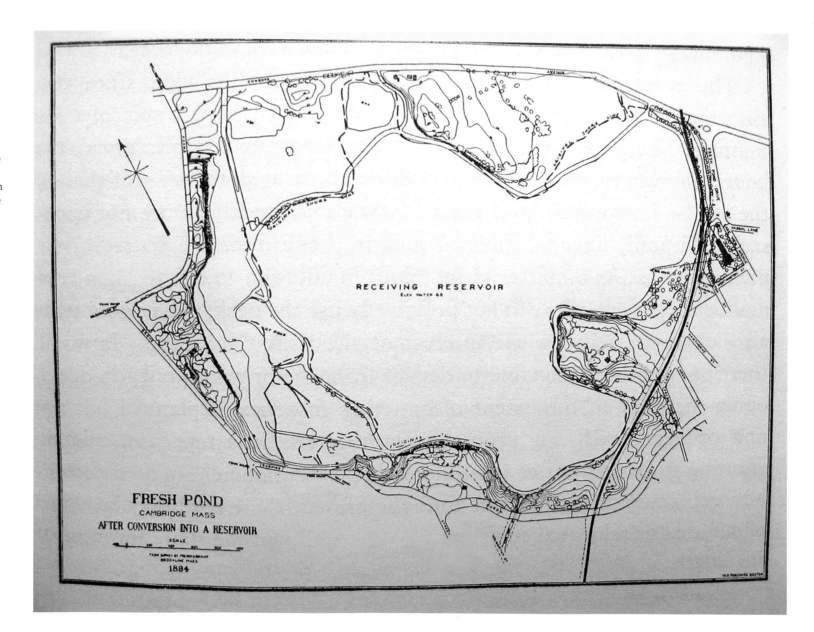

RECEIVING RESERVOIR
ELEV WATER 60

FRESH POND
CAMBRIDGE MASS
AFTER CONVERSION INTO A RESERVOIR

SCALE

FROM SURVEY BY FRENCH & BRYANT
BROOKLINE MASS
1894

at Fresh Pond, as it became the source of the city's first public water supply, and the location for a major public park, designed to provide restorative access to natural scenery. In the conflicts over the appearance of the park, readers will witness the rise of new professional classes, each jostling for the right to be considered an expert in the provision of designed landscapes.

Through the continuing developments at and around Fresh Pond emerge the wider history of the twentieth-century expansion of the city and the sustained growth of its municipal government. We see the impact of changing patterns of recreational use from pastoral, passive enjoyment of landscapes to active, organized sports. More recently, we can observe the rise of citizen activism and community-based planning, and the influence of the environmental movement.

Readers will perceive how broad shifts in public attitudes to nature have played out at Fresh Pond: from brutal wilderness to be explored and conquered by men like Oregon pioneer (and Fresh Pond ice trader) Nathaniel Wyeth, to a resource for humanity to harness: the pond as a never-ending supply of ice and water and clay. For a time nature is seen as something separate and pure, deserving protection from human activity. A symbol of universal goodness, its influence imparts a sense of morality to people living in increasingly industrialized, corrupting cities. In the early twentieth century we can perceive a major shift: now the power of technology is seen as able to subjugate nature: the purity of the water supply is controlled by treatment plants, chemicals, and other human intervention. More recently, we discern an emerging view of the natural world as irreplaceable, superior to humanity, and at risk from us. Vulnerable and damaged, nature needs to be let alone, with all signs of human intervention and human history removed or disguised.[4]

We can trace similar shifts in attitudes to water. The pond was once seen as something mysterious and powerful, its depth and the ultimate source of its water unclear. Great Pond rights enshrined a view of water as something so essential to life that it needed to be preserved for all citizens. Then, as technology meant that supplies became increasingly easily available, it was no longer something precious, hauled laboriously in a bucket, its source well known and part of everyday life. It became taken for granted, something people thought of as limitless, if they thought of it at all, theirs by rights to wash their cars and flush down their toilets. The source of the water was no longer obvious: Fresh Pond became a place of restorative water views and aesthetic scenery. Even today some visitors find it difficult to accept that it is the source of the city's water supply.

Fresh Pond seems destined to remain Cambridge's receiving reservoir under the city's prudent stewardship. It will no doubt continue to be a popular place for its myriad users, and the site of facilities for organized recreational activities and care for the elderly. Differing views and perspectives on the landscape will continue to coexist and collide. My hope is that there will also be room in Fresh Pond's future for a developing understanding and celebration of the historic value of this wonderful place.

1.7 The north shore of Fresh Pond, 1895, after the water board had completed its substantial engineering works. The edges of the reservoir were protected with riprap, and the hills behind were extensively excavated for gravel. Members of the landscape architecture firm Olmsted, Olmsted and Eliot were critical of the impact of the board's work on the landscape.
Courtesy of the National Park Service, Frederick Law Olmsted National Historic Site.

Fresh Pond, Cambridge.

2 A Place to Play

All those who prefer nature to art—all those who wish to enjoy the Serenade of the Groves—all those who delight in Fishing and Fowling—all those who are in health, as well as those who are anxious to regain so invaluable a blessing, are requested to call at his Hotel for amusement, recreation, and enjoyment.

Jacob Wyeth, advertisement for the second season of the Fresh Pond Hotel, April 1798

During the last ice age, New England and much of the northeastern side of North America was covered by the Laurentide glacier, a vast sheet of ice centered in Labrador, Canada, and extending down as far as Long Island and Martha's Vineyard. The ice sheet was thick enough to cover New Hampshire's 6,288-foot Mount Washington. The ground under the ice was compressed by its sheer size and weight into what is known as *bedrock* or *hardpan*. As the vast glacier advanced inexorably southward, it stirred up rocks and ground them into clay, gravel, and sand, which became mixed in with the glacial ice.

As the climate warmed some 15,000 years ago, the ice melted and dropped the debris it had crushed. Around Cambridge the glacier refroze and advanced again briefly, pushing the debris up into characteristic ridges, known as *glacial moraines*, around Fresh Pond. These moraines are distinctively irregular, lacking the usual lines or strata of different materials. Instead they are an unpredictable mix of sand, clay, and gravel. As the temperature warmed up again, some pieces of ice fell away from the main glacier as it melted and were buried under the debris

2.1 A modern-day (1977) conjectural map of the topography of northwest Cambridge in 1638, showing Fresh Pond (bottom left), with extensive areas of marsh and wet meadow on three sides, the Great Swamp to the north, and the glacial moraines separating it from the settlements of Cambridge and Watertown.
Survey of Architectural History in Cambridge, Report Five: Northwest Cambridge.

2.2 This detail is from *A Chart of Boston and its Vicinity, Massachusett's Bay* (sic), which was drawn about 1633 with later annotations in the hand of John Winthrop. Its orientation is unusual, with north to the left, and Boston harbor at the top of the image. Easily the earliest known map of the area, it shows Fresh Pond near the center, in what was then Watertown. Immediately above is Newtowne (Cambridge). Fresh Pond has been accidentally reversed, with the wooded promontory shown on its western side rather than its east. Between the pond and the "Mistick River" to the north runs the unlabeled Alewife Brook, with an encampment of Indian tepees on its eastern bank.
© British Library Board. All rights reserved. Additional MS. 5415.g.iii.

that was being deposited. These pieces of ice gradually melted, leaving large holes or depressions. Some of these filled with water, and are known as *kettle lakes* because of their shape. Others were slowly filled by the accumulation of vegetable matter, and became swampland. Fresh Pond is thus a distinctively glacial landscape, with the 160-acre kettle lake surrounded by large, deep pockets of swamp or marshland, and the gravely hills of the moraine forming a natural barrier to the south and east.

Early Settlers and Great Pond Rights

For thousands of years, Native Americans fished extensively in these glacial ponds and streams, cultivated crops such as maize, beans, and tobacco, and hunted wildlife in the surrounding marshes and woods. Footpaths almost certainly existed around Fresh Pond and Alewife Brook to its northeast, where fishing weirs were constructed, and the resulting catch was often smoked and saved for winter consumption. Members of an Algonquian-speaking tribe (most likely the Massachusett) probably established a seasonal settlement on the north shores of Fresh Pond, which may have survived into the contact period with European settlers.[1] Some anecdotal evidence exists of a burial ground nearby.[2]

With the arrival of the European settlers, the early colonial towns of Newtowne (soon to become Cambridge) and Watertown developed on the River Charles. Fresh Pond was well known to them (the name was appearing in town records as early as 1635)[3] but its distance from the river, the barrier formed by the glacial moraine, and the fact that much of the surrounding soil was marshland, meant that it was not settled

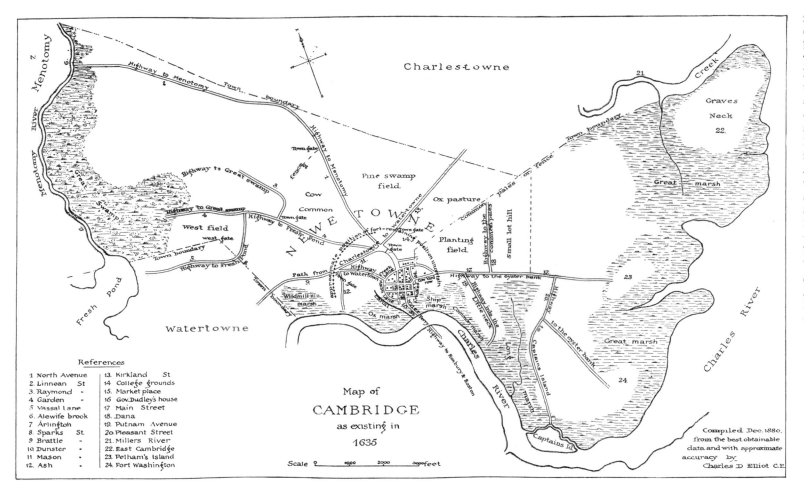

References

1 North Avenue	13. Kirkland St
2. Linnean St	14. College grounds
3. Raymond "	15. Market place
4 Garden "	16. Gov. Dudley's house
5 Vassal Lane	17. Main Street
6. Alewife brook	18. Dana "
7 Arlington "	19. Putnam Avenue
8. Sparks St	20. Pleasant Street
9. Brattle "	21. Millers River
10. Dunster "	22. East Cambridge
11 Mason "	23. Pelham's Island
12. Ash "	24. Fort Washington

Map of
CAMBRIDGE
as existing in
1635

Scale 0 __ 1000 __ 2000 __ 3000 feet

Compiled Dec. 1880,
from the best obtainable
data and with approximate
accuracy by
Charles D Elliot C.E.

2.3 Reconstructed map of Cambridge in 1635, compiled by Charles D. Elliot in 1880. The small town center, going little further northwest than the town common, was surrounded by a *pallysadoe* or stockade, built by the settlers to mark the edge of Newtowne and to protect its cattle from wild animals. A public way to Fresh Pond was in place by 1634, with spurs leading to the Great Swamp on its north side. Most of Fresh Pond at this time lay within the boundaries of Watertown. William Brewster, *The Birds of the Cambridge Region of Massachusetts* (Cambridge, Mass.: Nuttall Ornithological Club, 1906).

for many years. Like the indigenous people, the settlers found the area a rich source of food: they fished for alewives, hunted waterfowl, and also cut hay from the meadows.

In Roman times, common law had established that the air, running water, the sea, and its shoreline were the common property of every citizen. In England, the sovereign held such lands and water in trust for the public. The colonists realized the importance of establishing a similar doctrine in their new homeland. It would be essential for commerce, sustenance, and travel that settlers could use all the major waterways without fear of trespassing or appropriation by others as private property. So one of the early acts of the Massachusetts Bay Colony in 1641 was to create a colonial ordinance that protected public access to certain unique natural resources. Included in this was the concept of "Great Pond rights." Great Ponds were defined as inland bodies of water that in their natural state were ten acres or more in size. Under the ordinance, which applied to Fresh Pond as well as hundreds of other water bodies in the new colony, householders had legal rights for fishing, fowling, and navigation on any Great Pond in their town, as well as the right to cross undeveloped land to gain access to the water. Although the ordinance was not reenacted after the Revolutionary War, Great Pond rights remained part of the state's common law and were eventually codified into the Massachusetts General Laws.[4]

Fresh Pond Farm

With new waves of settlers arriving, the land around the pond was soon divided into lots but, even by the 1700s, it was still considered too far outside town for many people to establish dwelling houses there; the Coolidge homestead (see figure 2.4) was one of the few exceptions. Instead, many of the lots were given over to pasture, orchards, and farms. One of the most significant of these was Fresh Pond Farm, built in the 1630s on the northern shore, close to the current site of Neville Place (see figure 2.5). The estate was first owned by Nathaniel Sparhawk, and then by Justinian Holden and his descendants.[5] It was to play a major role at Fresh Pond in the nineteenth century, although little evidence remains about its early history.

A Refuge and Retreat

Fresh Pond soon gained a reputation as a tranquil and undeveloped place. In 1660, its "beautiful woods" were the site for quiet walks by two of Oliver Cromwell's followers, who had fled England after the restoration of the monarchy, hoping to escape possible retribution in the largely sympathetic colonies.[6] (Cromwell had signed the death warrant of King Charles I of England and led the country as Lord Protector for five years.)

By the 1730s, a Watertown scholar was publishing poetry in Fresh Pond's praise:

> Of ancient streams presume no more to tell,
> The famed Castalian or Pierian well.
> Fresh pond superior must those rills confess,
> As much as Cambridge yields to Rome or Greece:
> More limpid water can no fountain show,
> A fairer bottom, or a smoother brow;
> A painted world its peaceful gleam contains,-
> The heavenly arch, the bord'ring groves and plains.[7]

2.4 This colonial homestead was established, probably in the last years of the seventeenth century, on Grove Street to the southwest of Fresh Pond. For much of the eighteenth and nineteenth centuries it was owned by the Coolidge family.
Watertown Free Public Library, n.d.

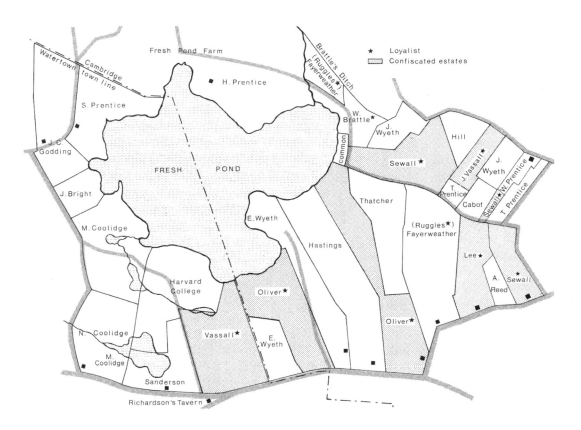

2.5 By the time of the Revolutionary War, more buildings were appearing on the land bordering the pond, but, as can be seen on this modern (1977) map of land ownership, they tended to be at the very edge of the narrow lots to the south: the area closest to the centers of Cambridge and Watertown. Fresh Pond Farm, owned by the Prentice (or Prentiss) family since about 1729, is shown on the north shore; to the west is a farmhouse built by John Holden in the 1660s, which had also passed to the Prentice family. *Survey of Architectural History in Cambridge, Report Five: Northwest Cambridge.*

A Place to Play **15**

Two Revolutionary War stories also illustrate the way that Fresh Pond was seen at this time as a refuge or retreat from town. One is told by Hannah Winthrop, whose writing provides a vivid contemporary account of the fighting in Massachusetts. In a letter to a friend, she describes the noise, confusion, and fear the day war broke out in Cambridge in April 1775. It soon became clear that women and children should "retire to some place of safety" from the "British barbarity," and so they "were directed to a place called Fresh-Pond, about a mile from town." Women from all over Cambridge had been sent to the same place and she recalled: "what a distressed house did we find there, filled with seventy or eighty weeping and agonizing women, whose husbands had gone forth to meet the assailants."[8]

Within a few months, George Washington was also to see Fresh Pond as somewhere safely distant from the inhabitants of Cambridge. He was fighting not just the British troops but also a major outbreak of smallpox in the area that threatened to engulf the Continental Army. Consequently a dedicated smallpox hospital was set up at Fresh Pond and everybody still healthy was told to keep clear: on July 4th, 1775, Washington ordered that "No Person is to be allowed to go to Fresh-water pond a fishing or on any other occasion as there may be a danger of introducing the small pox into the army."[9]

So Fresh Pond's history up until the creation of the United States is as a wooded lake some distance outside town. Protected as a Great Pond, it was used for fishing, fowling, and gentle recreations by the local inhabitants. Some of the surrounding land was dedicated to grazing and farming. Its reputation was as a place of natural beauty and as something of a refuge.

Country Seats and Gentlemen's Farms

Cambridge became attractive to wealthy Bostonians as a place for summer homes. A French visitor described the town in 1788 as "surrounded by delightful country houses used by Boston merchants for vacations . . . the air is infinitely pure, the environs are charming and offer a vast space for the exercise of young men."[10]

The appeal of Cambridge increased when the West Boston Bridge (now the site of the Longfellow Bridge) was built in 1793. This development "completely re-oriented the relationship between Boston and Cambridge."[11] Instead of making the eight-mile-long journey to reach Cambridge through Roxbury and Brookline via the 1662 Great Bridge, Bostonians could now simply cross the water from the center of town and be in what soon became Cambridgeport. From there, good roads led to Harvard Square and beyond. Outlying areas such as Fresh Pond became easily accessible and land there was soon being bought by affluent Bostonians.

Probably the first such purchase was in 1798, when William Tudor acquired Fresh Pond Farm from Henry Prentiss. Tudor was a Boston attorney who, at the age of twenty-five, had served as Washington's judge advocate general during the Revolutionary War. Having inherited a good fortune, Tudor planned to live a life of leisure on the proceeds of his investments. For whatever reason, however, he decided to sell Fresh Pond Farm within a few weeks of acquiring it.

Charles Storer bought the estate from Tudor and sold it to Colonel John Apthorp three years later. By 1811, the property was being described as a "country seat."[12] In 1816 the estate was for sale again, the auction notice describing it as:

That much admired and intrinsically valuable Estate, FRESH POND FARM, consisting of about 100 acres of land, well wooded and capable of the most productive cultivation for the Boston market, as well as the highest style of ornamental farming. There are upon it a large convenient Dwelling House, beautifully situated upon the banks of the Pond, a Farm House, Barn, and other out buildings, a spacious Ice House, and extensive Garden, stocked with good Fruit, and enclosed by a handsome fence. But few situations possess more of the requisites for a gentleman's country seat.[13]

Despite this appreciative description, it seems it did not sell at auction, as the following month Apthorp was advertising the House for rent.[14] Later the same year the estate was finally sold to C. C. Foster,[15] and was bought in 1838 from one of the Foster family by William Tudor's son, Frederic.[16]

Throughout much of this time, it was not the various owners of the property who were enjoying its beautiful situation and extensive garden. Instead, it was leased to Apthorp's cousin, Anna Bulfinch, and her husband George Storer (the son of Ebenezer Storer, treasurer of Harvard).[17] They used Fresh Pond Farm as a summer residence from about 1811 to 1830, and they frequently invited family members and friends to stay at the house. "To all the young people he was known as 'Uncle Storer,' and the house at the Pond came to fill a large place in their affections, associated as it was with the country freedom so dear to city children."[18]

One of those young visitors was Susan Bulfinch Coolidge (later to become Mrs. Joseph Lyman), who wrote in great detail about the house and its grounds, with the beauty of the pond

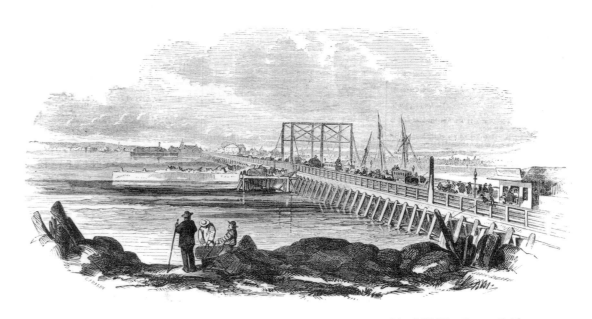

2.6 The 1793 West Boston Bridge over the Charles River was three quarters of a mile long. Funded by private investors, it made travel between Cambridge and Boston dramatically easier. Image c. 1855. *Ballou's Pictorial Drawing Room Companion* 8 (1855): 12.

and the woods on the far shore. She described the bowling alley that was situated between the house and the water, and the rowboat that was available for entertainment. The Storers kept cows and grew fruit and vegetables, with help from farmhands and a foreman. People frequently came to stay, or just visited for tea. In 1830, Mrs. Storer's brother, the noted architect Charles Bulfinch, and his wife Hannah spent some time at the house. Both were now elderly, but Mrs. Bulfinch wrote affectionately about "this sweet and pleasant spot,"[19] although she noted that the Storers did not stay there during the winter as "the Pond is too remote and inaccessible at times for anyone, almost, who has not a hardy constitution."[20]

Undoubtedly the best-known country estate linked with Fresh Pond was one built about half a mile to its west. Indeed, in its day, landscape architect Charles Eliot thought it was "the most famous seat near Boston."[21] This was the home of China

2.7 In 1808 Seth Hastings erected a new Federal-style mansion on his estate to the southeast of Fresh Pond. This house and thirty-eight acres of land were soon acquired by William Gray, a wealthy Salem merchant, who called it The Larches and used it as his summer residence. He added ornamental gardens and hothouses, to make it a traditional country seat. In 1915 the house was moved slightly, to its current location on Larch Road, as seen in this 2005 photograph.
Jill Sinclair.

trader John Perkins Cushing who, on returning to Boston at the age of forty-four, married and, in 1834, chose as his new home a 117-acre estate in Watertown. Apparently he was attracted to the estate at least in part because, from a central knoll, it offered grand views of Fresh Pond and the Mystic River valley. As a result, he called his new home Bellmont.

Cushing spent the rest of his life developing the house and grounds. At its peak, Bellmont boasted a fenced deer park, a vast conservatory and fourteen greenhouses, a grand three-acre walled garden, orchards, and open lawns and glades. The influential writer Andrew Jackson Downing included Bellmont in his first book as a model estate. As a result, Cushing opened the grounds to the public one day a week, and visitors from all over America and Europe arrived to see the estate that had become locally and nationally famous.[22]

With such estates establishing themselves in the nearby countryside, Fresh Pond had become a very different place from the distant retreat of the Revolutionary War. One writer captures the feel of Fresh Pond in the mid-1830s, with its "well-cultivated farms and a number of gentlemen's country seats, forming a picture of rural beauty and plenty . . . rich pasturage, numerous dairies and profitable orchards, the luxuriousness of well-cultivated gardens of all sorts of culinary vegetables."[23]

Hotels on the North Shore

While the wealthy had invested in property so that they could enjoy the delights of Fresh Pond for themselves, others were concentrating on how to make money by marketing its attractions. The pond was not just for those who could afford a country retreat. Local residents, students, and visitors also enjoyed the area, and some businessmen and women began to see the opportunity to turn such enjoyment into a profit for themselves.

One of the first people to attempt this was Richard Richardson who, in 1784, at the age of thirty-three, bought a piece of Fresh Pond Farm from Joseph Holden. He invested heavily in the planned construction of the Concord Turnpike, the first road to be built directly across the Fresh Pond moraine. The road was to cross his land and he decided to build a hotel "in anticipation that the Turnpike would be a great thoroughfare for travel."[24]

Unfortunately for Richardson, neither the investment in the proposed Turnpike (which was not completed until 1803) nor the hotel made him any money, and he lost much of the property as a result of his debts. In 1792, he surrendered ownership of the hotel to the town of Cambridge.

Others could still see potential, however, in hotels or places of entertainment at Fresh Pond. In the same year that Richardson gave up his business, John and Mary Burke were advertising in local newspapers the attractions of their house on Fresh Pond Farm. The Burkes described the food and wine on offer, the excellence of the service they provided, and the fishing and fowling available in and around the water. Their advertisements also mentioned the opportunities for rural walks, and the "good and improving" roads that led to the hotel.

One 1795 visitor, probably to this establishment, wrote of her "most agreeable jaunt to Fresh Pond" to take tea. She found it to be "a most enchanting place—it is beyond description charming" and explained how the design of the building made

MARY BURKE

BEGS leave to inform her Friends and the Publick in general, that she shall continue to improve that commodious and agreeably situated House on said Farm the present season—where she proposes as far as is in her power, to accommodate those who please to favour her with their company.

Her House will be open every ay in the week except the Sabbath—She is under the necessity of saying, that on that day it will be shut up, and no company entertained, which she hopes her friends will excuse.

Her Larder will be constantly furnished with the choicest and most suitable Provisions—her Cellar with Liquors of the best quality—her House with the best attendants she can procure—her Stable with the best Hay and Provender—And the favours of her guests studied to be gained, and always gratefully acknowledged.

Fresh Pond is six miles from *Boston*; the Roads good and improving; the Pond well stored with Fish, Boats, and all necessary fishing apparatus for Ladies and Gentlemen provided. The adjacent country furnishes Game—and the walks in its vicinity are rurally agreeable.   (1 a w. 8 w.)
April 11, 1792.

2.8 Mary Burke's newspaper advertisement for the hotel on the north shore of Fresh Pond. *The Columbian Centinel*, May 5, 1792.

it ideal for large groups to visit: "the front of the house which is erected on its margin presents in its centre an octagon, which furnishes a large Hall, ample enough to dine commodiously those pleasurable parties political, and civic associations, with which this Metropolis abounds, and which frequently retire there for the laudable purpose of enjoying their convivial meetings with the highest zest. . . . This charming recess is the resort of the fashionable, and the gay, in their happiest hours . . . it is a resort of our gentry."[25] Despite such praise, the Burkes' business venture did not endure.

In 1811 the Fresh Pond New Hotel was launched on the north shores of the pond.[26] It was run by a Mr. R. Wrightson, the owner of Boston's Union Coffee House. With the Turnpike now established, Wrightson sought to capitalize on his hotel's location and advertised its "delightful situation" as well as its fine wines and spirits and the "best and most seasonable Provisions which the market affords." The hotel also provided bowling alleys, promenades, and boarding for six or eight gentlemen. As an incentive, Wrightson offered free dining at the Union Coffee House for anyone who stayed at the hotel. Like Richardson and the Burkes before him, he failed to make a success of the venture, and very soon the house became a summer home for "Uncle Storer" and his family.

The Fresh Pond Hotel

It was to be elsewhere at Fresh Pond that a hotel was to flourish and make a great fortune for its owners. Located on the woody promontory to the east of the pond, the Fresh Pond Hotel became one of the area's best-known landmarks. Both the hotel, and the Wyeth family who established it, were to have a significant impact on Fresh Pond.

Ebenezer Wyeth was the first member of this influential family to settle at Fresh Pond. He was a brick-maker and his son, Jacob, born at Fresh Pond in 1764, followed him into that business. At the age of about twenty-four, Jacob decided to further his education and managed to gain entry to Harvard, where he graduated with distinction.

On return from working briefly in Europe, Jacob married Betsey Jarvis and set up business with a partner, Phineas Stone, in Littleton, Massachusetts. The business, however, was unsuccessful and Jacob returned to Cambridge penniless.

2.9 On his marriage in 1751, Ebenezer Wyeth bought farmland extending from what is now Mount Auburn Street to Fresh Pond. Here in the same year he built a new farmhouse, which still stands today, albeit in a different place and probably unrecognizably altered. It can be found next to William Gray's The Larches, to which it was attached for a time as a service wing.
Jill Sinclair, 2005.

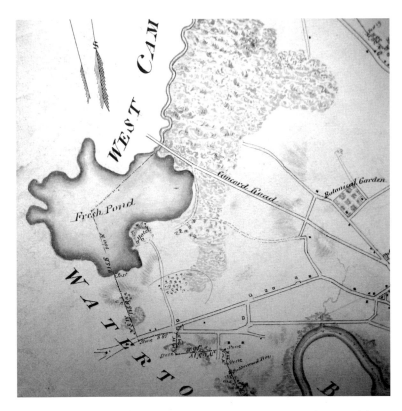

2.10 The Fresh Pond Hotel, built on the promontory to the east of the pond, shown on the John Hales map of Cambridge, 1830 (detail). Courtesy Massachusetts Archives.

In 1796, Ebenezer gave eight acres of Fresh Pond farmland to his son, and Jacob embarked on a "pioneering venture"[27] to establish a hotel there, hoping no doubt to succeed where Richardson and the Burkes had already failed. He employed housewrights John Walton (or Walter) and Joseph Moore to erect a large Federal-style hotel on the wooded promontory, their investment secured by a mortgage on the property.[28]

For whatever reason (maybe the greater proximity of the hotel to Cambridge, or its position overlooking the water, or the greater skill of its owner), the Fresh Pond Hotel seems to have been an immediate success. It opened for the 1797 season and within eighteen months Jacob had earned enough to be able to pay back his housewrights all that he owed them.[29]

FRESH POND HOTEL.

THE Subscriber requests that his Friends and the Public will receive his warmest acknowledgments, for the patronage afforded him the last season, at his Hotel. He is sensible that thanks are a poor return for favors—he hopes his will be received as the Widows' mite, having no king else to give. All those who prefer nature to art—all those who wish to enjoy the Serenade of the Groves—all those who delight in Fishing and Fowling—all those who are in health, as well as those who are anxious to regain so invaluable a blessing, are requested to call at his Hotel for amusement, recreation, and enjoyment. He assures them that very delicacy of the season shall be provided—everything calculated to satisfy a keen, as well as to sharpen a dull appetite. If striving to please will insure approbation, he feels confident of success: Those who expend a *Mill*, or those who expend an *Eagle*, will be equally intitled to his warmest gratitude.
JACOB WYETH.
Cambridge, April 25, '98.

2.11 Jacob Wyeth's advertisement for the second season of the Fresh Pond Hotel.
The Columbian Centinel, May 26, 1798.

To attract patrons, Jacob Wyeth made full use of the resources that were available at Fresh Pond. As well as the fishing and fowling that had long been the right of any local citizen, he provided bowling alleys, swings, and opportunities for sailing and rowing on the pond. The hotel also became famous for the splendor of the meals it provided, and the range of wines and other alcoholic drinks available. He laid on orchestras to play dance and orchestral music, and even college songs when groups of well-to-do Harvard students came to dine.

So for escaping the heat of the Boston summer, or for indulging in lavish food and wine, the Fresh Pond Hotel soon became famous as a resort. It began to feature regularly in diary entries, guidebooks, and memoirs. Two separate descriptions of visits by Harvard students in the 1820s are typical: one describes how "after breakfast . . . we went to Fresh Pond. . . . We amused ourselves in the morning in bowling at nine pins. Some took to rowing, some to sailing in the boats upon the pond. . . . The hotel stands on a sort of headland and the thick shade of trees give it a very pretty effect. Our sail was an extremely pleasant one, we had a song, and enjoyed ourselves considerably."[30] Another describes the visit by the class of 1829 that, one August evening, walked over to the hotel and sampled Mr. Wyeth's "most superb supper" served with claret, champagne, and Madeira.[31]

By 1816 Jacob Wyeth had earned enough money from the hotel venture to build a grand new home for his family, which now included four children, all sons. The house was located on the promontory, just a few yards from the hotel (see figure 2.10).

Jacob Wyeth was enormously successful at turning other people's enjoyment of Fresh Pond into a profit for himself. In

2.12 The Fresh Pond Hotel was moved in 1892 to its current location at 234 Lakeview Avenue, where it became an apartment building. Jill Sinclair, 2004.

the early 1820s he retired from active business with a sizeable fortune, and he lived in the house he had built for himself and his family until his death in 1857 at the age of ninety-two.

His son, Nathaniel, subsequently ran the hotel, followed by his nephew, Jonas, who, to keep up with the fashions of the day, remodeled the building in the Greek Revival style, adding gables around 1838. Jonas also proved successful at turning the delights of the pond into a "satisfactory fortune"[32] for himself. Retiring from running the hotel around 1840, he bought forty acres of farmland that ran between the pond and Mount Auburn Street. The homestead he built there still stands, although much extended, and later became well known as the home of Harvard president Charles W. Eliot.

With Jonas's retirement, the hotel passed out of the hands of the Wyeth family. By about 1840 it was owned and run by Lyman Willard, who worked hard to add to the appeal, and the fame, of the hotel. He produced commemorative china decorated with images of the hotel as a way of attracting more customers (see figure 2.13). In addition, he introduced "refreshment facilities,"[33] presumably located outside, which were to become a major feature of the hotel in its later years.

Willard left before the end of the 1840s and, perhaps inspired by his success, built himself a new four-story hotel to run at 38 Brattle Street, in the center of town. At Fresh Pond, the hotel passed through other hands in the third quarter of the century,[34] but it seems to have remained well known and popular.

Mount Auburn Cemetery

The hotel business benefited greatly from the founding in 1831 of Mount Auburn Cemetery just a few hundred yards south of Fresh Pond. Planned specifically to attract visitors, it was America's first designed landscape of any size to be open to the public, and its first "rural" style cemetery. Its picturesque design was to inspire the public parks movement in the second half of the nineteenth century.

Encouraged by guidebooks, visitors rapidly found their way to the new cemetery. From the high ground, there was an attractive view of the pond: "On the north, at a very small distance, Fresh Pond appears, a handsome sheet of water, finely diversified by its woody and irregular shores. Country seats and cottages, in various directions, and especially those on the elevated land at Watertown, add much to the picturesque effect of the scene."[35]

2.13 Lithograph of the Fresh Pond Hotel c. 1845, issued by its then owner Lyman Willard, advertising the many attractions of the hotel at that time. The image includes, from left to right, the boathouses with sailboats and rowboats for rent, the long stairway leading up to the hotel in its idyllic setting among the trees, games being played on the lawn, the Jacob Wyeth family house, plantings of fruit and ornamental trees, stabling for horses (from where sleigh rides were offered in the winter months), and, on the far right of the image, a cage where ducks were kept and then released for sport.
Cambridge Historical Society Collection, Cambridge Historical Commission.

2.15 A stereograph showing the pleasing view of Fresh Pond from the Mount Auburn Tower, c. 1870s. The hotel and Jacob Wyeth House are visible on the wooded promontory to the right, and the ice houses to the left, with Fresh Pond Farm just discernable through the trees on the far bank.
Image Courtesy Mount Auburn Cemetery Archives.

2.14 A detail from an engraving made in 1847 by James Smillie of the view from the top of Mount Auburn Hill. The cemetery had been founded just south of Fresh Pond in the previous decade and purposely incorporated the surrounding "borrowed landscape" into its scenery. Through the trees, to the right of the new Bigelow Chapel, can be glimpsed the Fresh Pond Hotel and Jacob Wyeth House. To the left of the chapel is the first known image of the icehouses on the western shores of Fresh Pond. The boathouse and other outbuildings of Fresh Pond Farm are just visible on the far shore.
Image Courtesy Mount Auburn Cemetery Archives.

It was only a short carriage drive or walk from the cemetery to Fresh Pond, and many guide books recommended seeing both attractions on the same day.

Harvard Students at the Pond

By the end of the seventeenth century, Fresh Pond had become a regular haunt for undergraduates from the new university, escaping their studies for a few hours. There are stories of two Harvard students, William Maxwell and John Eyre, drowning while skating there one Sunday in 1696. Harvard president Increase Mather had to reassure their parents that their deaths did not contravene puritan ethics about enjoyable activity on the day of rest: "Although death found them using recreations . . . they were lawful recreations."[36]

In the first half of the nineteenth century, with no boats yet available for hire on the Charles River, Fresh Pond was also the obvious choice for anyone wishing to row or sail. Students frequently came to rent the hotel's boats, although one student apparently stood out for actually having his own boat there:

> I never heard of any boat as being owned by a student, except a ducking-float on Fresh Pond, claimed as the property of a member of '39, afterwards Chief Justice of the State of New Jersey. It was currently reported that he had been cited before the Faculty for owning it, and that, on his pleading that it was in no way a malum prohibitum, he had been told that no student was allowed to keep a domestic animal except by permission of the Faculty, and that a boat was a domestic animal within the meaning of the statute.[37]

FRESH POND.

2.16 Sailboats and rowboats on the water at Fresh Pond, with a glimpse of the hotel among the trees on the promontory in the background. This 1835 drawing (which is the first known illustration of Fresh Pond) accompanied an article describing how young men from the university visited the pond for fishing, for sport, and to dine at the hotel. It listed the kind of fish that could be caught, and it recommended the hotel for the other recreation it provided and for the plentiful summer fruits that grew there.
The American Magazine of Useful and Entertaining Knowledge 2 (December 1835): 155.

Well into the nineteenth century, Harvard students continued to assemble at the pond and continued to record their happy memories of the place. A classmate of William H. F. "Rooney" Lee (the son of Robert E. Lee), for instance, remembered a freshman society meal in the 1850s with obvious affection, writing that "we had a fine repast at the Fresh Pond Hotel. The champagne sparkled, roast ducks spluttered, and we ate. At a late hour in the morning all returned home, some drunk, some sober, some middling."[38]

They also continued to make use of the outdoor attractions, perhaps further encouraged by the refreshment facilities that Willard had installed. Skating remained particularly popular, with hundreds of people enjoying the ice each winter weekend. One former student wrote a jocular reminiscence about life at Harvard in the late 1850s that included a tale of students skating near the hotel and falling through the ice. It begins with a party of friends heading for Fresh Pond "to enjoy the first skating of the season, and peradventure a flirtation with some fair-ankled beauty of breezy Boston. The pond has long been famous for this double diversion, which is well suited to the temperament of our New Englanders."[39] (The writer frequently used the phrase "breezy Boston" to imply high society or the delights of the big city. Cambridge's erudite, urbane reputation seems to have come later.) A famous story is told of future president Theodore Roosevelt skating for hours on the pond while an undergraduate in the late 1870s, in weather so cold that his companion was astonished at his hardiness and the strength of his will.

Other recreation was popular too. One student remembered that, even after Fresh Pond began to supply the city's drinking water, he and his classmates would avail themselves of the opportunities there for swimming and if, "as an old friend of mine said, he 'detected a slight scholastic flavor in his water, we were doubtless responsible for it.'"[40]

Although the introduction of recreational facilities at Harvard somewhat reduced Fresh Pond's appeal to the student body, into the twentieth century it still had its uses. In the years leading up to the Great War, for instance, Fresh Pond gained a reputation as a nighttime "lovers' lane": poet E. E. Cummings was among the many Harvard students who would take girlfriends there for moonlight drives.[41]

An Inspiration to Artists

Fresh Pond was held in strong affection by many of those who lived nearby, and it served as a muse for a number of local writers and artists. One teacher in 1850 wrote a celebratory poem about the potential of the eighty or so young schoolboys who were part of a sleigh party to the Fresh Pond Hotel that January. His pupils included a grandson of President Quincy, as well as boys from other well-known local families: a Lyman, a Lowell, an Appleton, a Storer, and a Codman.

> These children, that seem of no note in your eyes, -
> So little in knowledge—so little in size, -
> What may they not be? and what may they not do?
> The first in the nation were once such as you, . . .
> All of merit, though various, in school's early days,
> And none without promise for Life's opening ways.[42]

The poet James Russell Lowell visited frequently, and in his twenties he referred affectionately to boating in "those dear coves at Fresh Pond."[43] Fellow poet Henry Wadsworth Longfellow and his family, living on nearby Brattle Street, would visit often, just to walk or ride, or sometimes to row on the lake. A story about Longfellow's oldest son, Charles, tells of his shooting his thumb off in an accident at Fresh Pond when he was a boy and then walking home to Brattle Street for some medical attention.

On many mornings while he lived in Cambridge and worked as an illustrator in Boston, the painter Winslow Homer would walk two miles to fish at the pond before breakfast,

Fresh Pond, Cambridge.

2.17 An 1874 book featured pen and pencil drawings of America's most picturesque scenery. Fresh Pond was included as a "lovely expanse of water" and depicted by an image that was a fashionable combination of the wild and the beautiful. It featured five modishly dressed members of the upper classes in a rowboat.
William Cullen Bryant, *Picturesque America*, centennial edition, vol. 2 (Secaucus, N.J.: Lyle Stuart, 1974).

and he found inspiration for his work in the surrounding scenery. Noted ornithologist William Brewster was to write at length about his schooldays in the 1860s, spent catching birds around Fresh Pond, often in the company of Daniel Chester French, subsequently one of the country's finest sculptors. He documented the range of birds to be found in the swampy land and orchards to the east of Fresh Pond, including redwings, Wilson's snipe, warblers, vireos, sparrows, and fly-catchers. He also wrote about taking his boat onto the water every October to shoot ducks, sometimes as many as forty in one morning.[44]

Working Class Use

It was not just the wealthy and well-to-do students who were attracted by the hotel and the various recreations available at Fresh Pond. These are the best-documented visitors. But there are glimpses of a rather different use, increasing during the century, by members of the working classes.

A novel written in 1839 is set partly at Fresh Pond and provides a vivid account of the activities engendered by the outdoor facilities of the hotel.[45] It is a completely different impression of the pond from the genteel, picturesque image described earlier. A novel, of course, is not a reliable source of factual information (indeed the book is set in 1688, long before the hotel was built, and breezily maintains that the story is located in the grounds of a fictitious hotel that previously stood on almost the same site). But its descriptions, although no doubt exaggerated for narrative impact, are to some extent supported by other reports from later in the century. It refers explicitly to Fresh Pond in the 1830s, describing how "Cambridge students were seduced away from their books to enjoy the glories of nature, and the abominations of milk-punch, amidst the water-lilies and the fruit trees, and the thousand beautiful et-ceteras of that romantic region." Turning to the supposed 1680s, but perhaps still based on contemporaneous events, the novel describes the grove around the hotel on the day of a fair. It was teeming with groups of sailors, mechanics, publicans, and other working people. There was a "rude piazza" in the shade of the large trees, with settles and benches placed underneath. People "of various character" sat there to smoke and gossip. Elsewhere tents and booths sold assorted goods, including liquor of all kinds. It was evident that many people were already drunk, although the scene was set in the morning. There was loud talking and laughing, singing and some drunken quarreling and fights. Swings were provided for both men and women to use, as well as two nine-pin alleys, and planks were laid out for couples to dance, stamping their feet on the boards in time to music from a fiddler, while crowds of onlookers cheered them on.

While this account may be partly fictitious, it is certain that guilds of workers made frequent use of the outdoor facilities for recreational gatherings. Cambridge printers, for instance, had a picnic every summer at Fresh Pond Grove. The program for 1868 shows that the day started at 10.30 am with sports such as the 100-yard foot race, high leaps and long leaps, and a mile walk.[46] There were also more amusing competitions such the donkey race, walking backward fifty yards, a potato race, and a "wheelbarrow race, blindfold—fifty yards." With an intermission for refreshments, the day continued with various boat races in the afternoon, dancing in the pavilion, and,

finally, the distribution of prizes. As well as workers' guilds, sporting clubs such as the Myopia Base Ball Club in the 1870s also made much use of the facilities at the hotel.[47]

By the 1870s the hotel had certainly developed a reputation for the large, drunken gatherings described in Rufus Dawes's novel forty years earlier. There are official accounts of ten thousand people picnicking on the grove on a single day.[48] Lyman Willard's outdoor refreshment facilities had become "three or four lager beer saloons" with a "place for dancing." According to one account, the grounds of the hotel were "the scene of debaucheries such as never should be permitted on Cambridge soil." Once they had finished drinking, the picnickers would go out onto the lake in dozens of boats "and do very dirty and filthy things right on our pond—Cambridge people. They ought to be ashamed of themselves."[49] This is typical of the disapproving accounts given by members of the upper and middle classes at this time about the widespread habit of the working classes to drink freely when not at work. Until about the 1830s, drinking rum and beer had been a normal, expected part of a laborer's working day. But with the gradual arrival of industrialization, which produced tighter discipline and shorter working days, drinking was increasingly prohibited at work. This gave rise to illicit kitchen-based liquor sellers, providing alcohol for workers during their increased leisure time, and then to licensed saloons and other drinking establishments run by the working classes for the working classes.[50] Fresh Pond must have been one of the many places where such activities took place, much to the annoyance of the growing temperance movement.

2.18 Scores of people were accommodated at a time on the large pleasure boat, the *White Swan,* a side-wheel steamer that sailed on Fresh Pond probably in the late 1860s. This image shows the steamboat later, after 1873, when a top deck had been added, and it plied between Waltham and Auburndale bridge on the Charles River, carrying parties of picnickers. The Jackson Homestead, Newton, Massachusetts.

The Sisters of St. Joseph

Much of the literature on Fresh Pond tells the tale of local prohibition "bringing an end to the gala affairs"[51] at the hotel in 1886. With the sale of alcohol suddenly banned, so the story goes, the building overnight went from money-making drinking den to secluded convent.[52] The neat symbolism of the story is almost certainly apocryphal. Yet the arrival of the Sisters of St. Joseph does mark the closing stages of an era in the story of Fresh Pond.

The grandeur of the hotel had gradually slipped away. Writing in 1942, one local citizen remembers his childhood when "we boys . . . knew the place only in its disreputable senility."[53] By 1881 the hotel had been acquired by the Warren Institution for Savings, a Boston financial company, no doubt foreclosing on the mortgage held by the previous owner. In 1884 it was on the market. Whatever the reason for the hotel's financial problems and sale, it was not the introduction of prohibition. The "no license" provision was not introduced into Cambridge until May 1887, after a surprise vote in its favor by Cambridge citizens in December 1886.[54]

The Sisters of St. Joseph bought the hotel from the Warren Institution for Savings on January 24, 1885. It cost $22,500. Included in the sale were seven buildings apparently all in need of repair. As well as the hotel, these were two private homes, an open pavilion, a boathouse, an icehouse, and a stable. There were also "12 acres of pleasure grounds formerly known as Fresh Pond Grove and reputed to be one of the most beautiful and picturesque spots in New England."[55]

The sisters were soon busy remodeling the buildings. The hotel became a school for the Catholic secondary education of girls, and was named Mount St. Joseph Academy. The students' schedule was a mix of study (including history, geography, writing and mathematics), worship and outdoor recreation. They had to be up in time for mass at 6.30 am, followed by morning prayers in the chapel. After breakfast, there would be an hour of exercise outside ("running, jumping and playing lively games") before a morning of classes. A meal was followed by more time outdoors, afternoon recitations, luncheon, another obligatory hour in the open air, further classes, and a 5.30 pm supper. More outdoor recreation preceded night prayers and an 8 pm bedtime. There can hardly have been a greater contrast in the use of the buildings and grounds than between the "debauchery" for which the increasingly disreputable hotel became famous, and the strict discipline and asceticism of the academy.

Clearly the girls did not always respond well to this strict schedule. One sister recorded a certain frustration at the academic dedication of her pupils: "Real mental effort, any attempt at reflection is apt to prove very trying, very distasteful to them: thinking, setting their minds to work is a thing which the minds of most growing girls have an instinctive aversion to." The nuns themselves also found the new location difficult on occasions. The rooms in the Jacob Wyeth House were large and cold in winter. Water stored in pitchers would be frozen by morning. As Sister M. Magdalena recalled, "The endeavor was heroic, and every resource was strained to meet the demands of the undertaking. So great was the poverty and hardship of the sisters that through the years the expression 'Fresh Pond Days' has come to mean deprivation and sacrifice."[56]

2.19 Mount St. Joseph Academy opened in the former Fresh Pond Hotel, on September 7, 1885, as a boarding school for young ladies, with four teachers, two classrooms, and eleven pupils. The Jacob Wyeth House (to its right) was turned into a convent with its own chapel. A novitiate was established in what the sisters called the "brick yard house." Even the pavilion among the pines was put to use, being festooned with flowers and evergreens to form the setting for the annual commencement ceremony. The new road and fencing in the foreground is the work of the city's water board, whose activities were to lead to the sisters' enforced departure after just six years at Fresh Pond. Image c. 1888–1892.
The Wyeth Family Collection, Cambridge Historical Commission.

Time seems to have mellowed people's memories. On the twenty-fifth anniversary of the founding of the academy, one of its first graduates wrote fondly of her time at Fresh Pond:

Those among us who had the good fortune to attend the academy while it was situated there can never forget the beauty and loveliness of the spot—nature had endowed it bounteously. As you entered the ground a row of stately pines greeted you, and following this path on the right was the convent, and farther on the Academy. . . . Following the winding path still farther on to the right we arrived at the grove in which were many species of trees, shrubs, ferns and wild flowers. Here too was the pavilion where we held our graduation exercises. . . . The academy was an old wooden building and had on the south east side two long verandahs overlooking a little body of water called Fresh Pond.[57]

3   Industry at the Pond

The sparkling surface of our beautiful ponds, restored by the kindly hand of nature as often as it is removed, has yielded, and will continue to yield, . . . a perpetual reward to the industry bestowed upon them."

The Hon. Edward Everett, 1856

During the period from around 1830 to 1880 New England was transformed by the impact of the Industrial Revolution. Originally, many Americans in colonial and early national times had been involved in agriculture or commerce. In New England the land was generally poor and its farmers struggled to compete with the more fertile lands being settled to the west. And so it was New Englanders, always keen to find other ways to make a living, who took advantage of the new technologies emerging from Europe and led the way in industrialization in the United States.

Great New England inventors like Eli Whitney, Elias Howe, John Deere, and Samuel Morse revolutionized processes for harvesting, production, manufacturing, transport, and communications. Entrepreneurial members of the new business class made their fortunes through establishing power-driven machinery to produce goods and exploiting the region's natural resources on an increasingly large scale. Massive textile mills and factories were established in towns such as Lowell and Lawrence, powered by the water from New England's plentiful supply of streams and rivers. Traditional small-scale artisanal systems were soon ousted by the new industries, and there arose for the first time a working class, comprising of wage earners toiling in often poor conditions and with little hope of advancement.

Steam power was to become the defining technology of the nineteenth century, leading to the arrival of the railroad in Massachusetts in the late 1820s and early 1830s and the gradual replacement of sailing ships by the steamship. Such innovations significantly reduced the cost of transporting both harvested and manufactured goods.

This new business activity meant an increasing shift of people and power into urban areas. Many former agricultural workers moved from the countryside into the towns and cities to find jobs. Large-scale immigration also provided more workers and additional consumers for the goods being produced. From about 1840, repeated crop failures and political unrest led thousands of Irish men and women to emigrate to the Commonwealth. Between 1846 and 1855, almost 130,000 passengers arrived directly from Ireland, and many others came by way of Canada. By 1855, almost 30 percent of the population of Boston and 22 percent of Cambridge had been born in Ireland. Many French Canadian workers also arrived after the Civil War, beginning around 1870. By 1890 they numbered about 165,000 in Massachusetts.[1]

Frederick Tudor, the Ice King

The ice industry was one of the more unusual businesses that thrived in Massachusetts during the onset of the Industrial Revolution. Ice had long been collected from New England's frozen winter lakes for the preservation of perishable foodstuffs. Country houses and hotels near a water supply, such as those at Fresh Pond, would frequently have an underground vault where the ice could be kept until it was needed. A few enterprising businessmen had even thought to sell ice to those who did not have ready access to a supply. By the turn of the nineteenth century there was a small domestic market, with farmers earning extra money by cutting ice from Fresh Pond for sale in Boston. By its very nature, however, it was a small, localized, and unremarkable business.

It took the entrepreneurial skills and extraordinary resilience of one man to turn this trade into a global, multimillion-dollar industry. The man was Frederic Tudor. He was born in 1783, the son of William Tudor, attorney and politician, who had briefly owned Fresh Pond Farm. Eschewing college in favor of early attempts to make his name and fortune, Frederic hatched a scheme with his older brother in 1805 to sell ice to the tropics. Aged just twenty-two, he was so confident that his venture would be vastly profitable that he insisted their plans be kept secret, for fear that other traders would immediately join in. In fact, when news did leak out, his idea was met not with the admiration and jealousy he had expected, but with derision and mockery. The idea of transporting ice thousands of miles on board ship, with no means of keeping it cold, and expecting it still to exist on arrival, was seen as utterly impractical and absurd. One local newspaper carried a very brief piece as Tudor's first shipment set sail: " No joke. A vessel with a cargo of Ice has cleared out from this port for Martinique. We hope this will not prove to be a slippery speculation."[2]

Tudor's thinking was clear. He was going to trade in one of the great resources available in New England. There may not have been rich, fertile soil or plentiful supplies of minerals, but there was an abundant supply of pure ice that, he reasoned, would be of great value to those living in hot countries. He foresaw the ice being used to make cold drinks and ice cream, to preserve dairy and meat products, and generally to provide cooling relief. It was a vision to which he clung doggedly.

For a long time, however, it appeared that his detractors would be proved right. Although he quickly demonstrated that it was possible to transport ice great distances, many ship owners were reluctant to take it as a cargo. Once a shipment arrived in the tropics, the locals were frequently baffled by the product he was offering and, in any event, had no means of preventing it from quickly melting. He was frequently left with a supply with no demand and nowhere to store it. When he did manage to create a demand, he would run out of ice and have no means of quickly obtaining more. Incompetent employees, trade embargoes, and an importunate family all added to his problems. He was frequently hiding from his many creditors and was more than once imprisoned for debt. He endured unseasonably warm winters that left him with no supplies and shipwrecks that destroyed what he had managed to harvest. His health deteriorated and he suffered a mental breakdown. Later, when it looked as if he was finally succeeding, a foolish financial speculation left him bankrupt.

Most people would have accepted that it was after all a "slippery speculation" and abandoned the business. But Frederic Tudor remained certain that he could make his fortune from selling ice to those in tropical climates, and he was eventually to be proved right. He persisted in creating markets for ice and in finding ever more efficient ways of cutting, storing,

3.1 This 1857 sketch by Dr. R. U. Piper shows Frederic Tudor in his early seventies, enjoying the garden he spent almost forty years creating at his treasured country estate in Nahant. He lived there contentedly with his wife and family until his death in 1864. A similar interest in cultivation was displayed in the way he managed his estate on the shores of Fresh Pond.
Nahant Historical Society.

and shipping it. The ice industry became enormously profitable, for Tudor and for the competitors whom he had rightly predicted would appear once it was established that money could be made. Ice was shipped from many New England ponds to warm places all over the world, including the Caribbean, India, Singapore, South America, parts of Europe, and even Australia. Demand from the domestic market became even more significant than the foreign trade, with ice regarded as a "common necessity of life"[3] by most Americans.

Fresh Pond's Nathaniel Wyeth

Fresh Pond took center stage in the natural ice industry. Although his first supply in 1806 was probably from Rockwood Pond on the family farm north of Boston, Tudor quickly saw the benefits of using the pure waters of Fresh Pond. Under the state's Great Pond rights, the ice that formed there was effectively freely available to anyone who had access to the shoreline and the ability to harvest it. As early as 1807, he "almost certainly"[4] made use of Fresh Pond to supply the ice for three shipments to Havana, where he had constructed an icehouse to receive and store the cargo on arrival. As funds and trade embargoes allowed, Tudor continued to cut supplies from Fresh Pond for his struggling business. By the early 1820s he had eventually built up enough trade (in Cuba and the southern United States) to feel that the business was beginning to succeed. Harvesting the ice, however, was a slow, laborious process using hand-held tools. This aspect of the business was about to be revolutionized, and by someone inextricably linked to Fresh Pond.

3.2 Nathaniel Jarvis Wyeth, hotel manager, inventor, ice trader, and explorer, aged about thirty, 1832. Oregon Historical Society, image number OrHi 305.

NATHANIEL J. WYETH
OREGON PIONEER OF 1832

Nathaniel Jarvis Wyeth was the youngest son of Jacob, the founder of the Fresh Pond Hotel. He was born at the hotel in 1802. Unlike his father, he chose not to go to college and instead helped run the hotel from an early age. By some accounts, however, he did not relish managing the family business,[5] and he wanted to establish his independence by gaining his income from elsewhere. Married at the age of twenty-two to his cousin, Elizabeth Jarvis Stone, he built a new home on the family estate and planted fruit trees that became a feature of the hotel's grounds (writing to his wife that "perhaps they will not grow for our use but some one will get the benefit and it will be pleasant to leave even such a memorial of our having once existed"[6]).

Wyeth had been involved in collecting ice from Fresh Pond for the hotel's own use since he was a boy and, by the 1820s, was one of the people supplying Tudor's business. In 1825 he invented a horse-drawn plow that transformed the way ice was harvested, supplying larger and more regularly shaped blocks at a much quicker rate than the old pickaxes and chisels. He continued throughout his life to design and refine ways of harvesting ice, inventing other tools and increasingly mechanized ways of moving it from the pond into the icehouses, where it was stored, and from there to the ships for its transport abroad. It was Wyeth who realized that icehouses above ground would be more effective that the traditional underground vault. Built of double layers of timber, with an insulating material such as sawdust packed in between, the vast houses could preserve ice supplies for a year or longer until they were needed for shipping.[7]

Tudor was struck by the ingenuity and enthusiasm of the young Wyeth. He recognized that his own ability to ship and sell ice, combined with Wyeth's aptitude for improving the way it was harvested and stored, could be a very profitable combination. He promptly offered Wyeth five hundred dollars a year to manage the cutting, storing, and loading of his supplies, and in November 1826 Wyeth, keen to make money outside the hotel business, readily accepted.

Other traders had noticed that Tudor's seemingly absurd business was beginning to make sense, and they themselves started to harvest and sell ice to those in tropical climates. By 1827 several rivals owned or leased sections of the Fresh Pond shoreline, which guaranteed them access to the ice as it formed. But Tudor, working closely now with Wyeth, was still

SCRAPING

GROOVING.

PLANING AND RIBBING.

SAWING, CALKING AND BREAKING OFF.

3.3 The process for cutting ice devised largely by Nathaniel Wyeth, illustrated at Fresh Pond. After any loose snow was scraped away, a horse-drawn device cut long grooves in the ice, to mark out the blocks. Then the plow, with its sharp teeth, cut through the ice to create a checkerboard of cubes. Porous ice on the surface was planed off, and then the blocks were further sawn as necessary and maneuvered into clear water before being hoisted into the icehouses for storage. These 1875 drawings include one of the clearest views of the vast icehouses on the western shores of Fresh Pond. *Scribners' Monthly*, August 1875. Courtesy of Cornell University Library, Making of America Digital Collection.

very much the major player. Over the next few years, the two of them worked furiously in good cold winters and, perhaps even more so, in mild damp ones, when their main source at Fresh Pond barely froze and the poor slushy ice had to be supplemented from more northerly sources.

Wyeth, however, began to see that he would never make a fortune from being Tudor's employee. By the start of the 1830s, he had decided that major profits were to be made from a very different business some three thousand miles away, in the Oregon country. While he was not quite as inexperienced as some sources claim,[8] it was still an extraordinary decision by a young man, not yet thirty years old, to plan an overland expedition across the continent to set up trading posts in an unknown and undeveloped region. This was a time when the memory of Lewis and Clark's epic expedition was still inspiring Americans to make the pioneering move westward. The frontier was seen as wild and raw ("a howling wilderness" in a much-used phrase), where those brave enough to travel could readily find adventure, and make fortunes. In contrast, Fresh Pond, the only place Wyeth really knew, must have seemed small, overly familiar and unrewarding to someone with such imagination and energy. Wyeth also saw the trip as a chance to spend time away from his young wife, who seems to have become an alcoholic.[9] Various people tried to dissuade him, including Tudor, who wished his right-hand man in the ice business to stay at Fresh Pond, but Wyeth was determined to go.

With his group of twenty-three men, Wyeth set off in March 1832, on what turned out to be a disastrous expedition. The cruel reality of the journey westward was in considerable contrast to what the men had imagined, and some quickly dropped out, while others became too sick to travel. John B. Wyeth, a seventeen-year-old second cousin, returned early to Cambridge and published an account of the trip, which contrasted the seemingly exhaustive planning with the realities of the journey. In particular, and with hindsight, young John was critical of his cousin's desire to abandon the familiar beauty and considerable advantages of life at Fresh Pond for the West's unproven promises.[10]

Nathaniel Wyeth was not deterred by such criticism. Indeed, he subsequently led a second trip in September 1834. Again the journey was long and treacherous. Seventeen men were to die from disease, drowning or in battles with Native Americans. None of his plans for obtaining or trading goods worked and he found it impossible to compete with the Hudson's Bay Company, already firmly established in the area. Within twelve months he had decided to return home, and he finally reached Cambridge in September 1836, tired, sick, and dispirited.

Quickly persuaded back into the ice business by a salary much higher than Tudor had previously paid him, he found Fresh Pond busy with rivals aggressively cutting ice. Leonard Stone, one of the other traders, was blatantly using a device similar to Wyeth's horse-drawn plow, which he had patented back in 1829. Having passed the patent to Tudor before leaving for Oregon, Wyeth needed Tudor's involvement to be able to sue and, for whatever reason, his employer would not help. When he unexpectedly received some cash from the sale of his Idaho trading post to the Hudson's Bay Company, Wyeth decided to stop working for Tudor and instead concentrate on expanding his own ice business. Like his former employer, he continued to grow crops on his land at Fresh Pond, and he would pack apples and other produce among his ice cargoes to sell as an extra source of income. Such was his ingenuity throughout his life that Wyeth's obituary was to note that all ice tools and machines of any merit (in what was, by his death in 1856, a vast and profitable industry) "look to Fresh Pond as the place of their origin."[11]

Rights to the Ice

By the late 1830s, ice harvesting at Fresh Pond was a major business. Tudor, reinvigorated by his recent marriage to a very young bride, had started shipping ice from the pond to India, where the sweltering British seized upon it with delight. This new source of income was to save him from the bankruptcy caused by an unwise speculation in coffee, which left him with debts of over $200,000.

In 1836 one observer recorded how "cubes of ice from Fresh Pond incessantly, from before daylight to after sunset, pass in six-horse teams without an interval of half an hour"[12] on their journey from the icehouses to the ships at Charlestown. Around the same time, Tudor noted in his diary that he had counted as many as 127 men, 105 horses and one bull working on the pond, about half of them in his employ.[13]

Facing considerable competition at Fresh Pond, Tudor decided to take some dramatic action to ensure his continued access to the ice and conveniently to interfere with the supplies of some of his most serious rivals. In April 1838, he paid sixteen thousand dollars to W. Foster to become the owner of Fresh Pond Farm. His diary records that the property consisted of:

about 120 acres of land—with country seat—farm house & barns—two Ice Houses at the most valuable boundary on Fresh Pond which it any where possesses. On these lands (which are now leased to Stearns one of the three principals of the opposition) are situated several of the Ice Houses of these people. The situation is their citadel from whence they have annoyed my business beyond longer bearing. I purchased this estate at a high price: but independently of its value and the power it gives me of the Pond, it is a beautiful situation as a country seat. It has been so considered and justly although it has not the advantage of extensive views. It is somewhat remarkable that the estate once belonged to my father temporarily.[14]

Although he bought the estate primarily for the access it gave him to the ice, Tudor was also committed to continuing its use as a farm. He installed John Barker as his manager to turn a profit from the crops that they grew on the arable part of the estate. There are references in his books of account to apple and pear orchards, and picking cranberries, plus the cutting and storing of "English hay" (deliberately planted cool-season grasses), and the harvesting of wood cut from the side of the pond. In 1859, for instance, the farm under Barker's management made a profit of $1423.89.[15] Around the time of Tudor's ownership, a grand avenue of elms was planted, leading up to the house, suggesting that he also valued its history as a country seat. Some of the trees remained in 1920 (see figure 6.14) and at least one source thought that remnants of the elm avenue were still present in the 1970s.[16]

In 1838 Tudor also purchased a small lot with an existing icehouse on Cambridge Nook, on the other side of Alewife

3.4 The 1841 "ice rights" map, drawn by George A. Parker, which showed how Fresh Pond was to be apportioned for ice harvesting between the various owners of its shoreline. Frederic Tudor, the new owner of Fresh Pond Farm, was allocated the largest share (over forty-eight acres). Nathaniel Wyeth had access to almost forty-four acres, some of it still owned by his father. Nine other traders shared the remaining ninety acres between them.

With permission of the Harvard Map Collection, Harvard College Library.

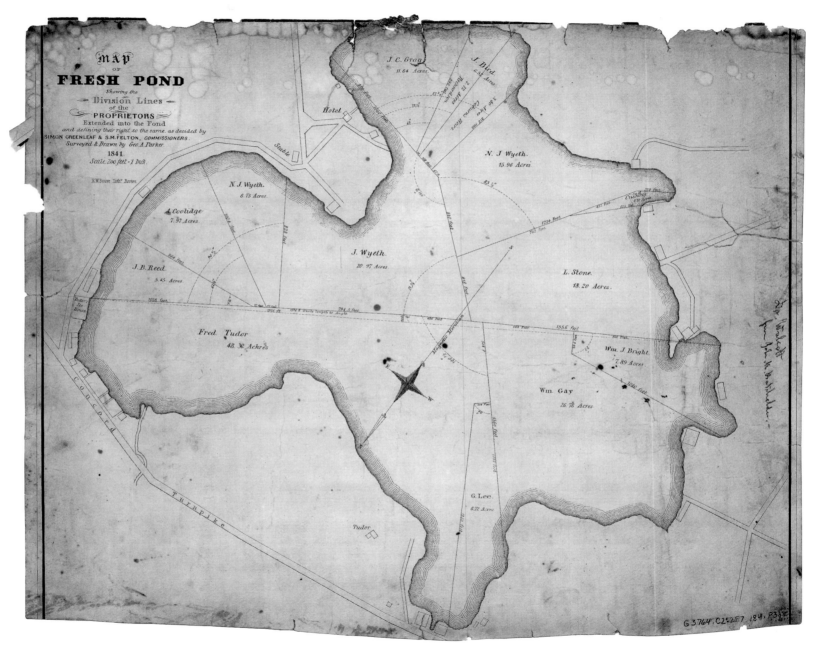

Brook. These purchases, and the continuing success of the ice business, set off a flurry of building around the shores of the pond. That same year, Tudor built two large houses, able between them to store almost four thousand tons of ice.[17] Between 1838 and 1842, he added some eighteen new houses in total, to supplement those he had acquired from his rivals on purchasing the farm.

In 1840 one of the harvesters erected a large new icehouse on the shores of Fresh Pond. His rivals took it to mean that he intended dramatically to increase the amount of ice he cut, indeed to harvest from portions of the pond that they considered their own. Recognizing that it was unclear how the valuable harvest should be apportioned among the increasing number of traders, Wyeth suggested they appoint an arbiter to produce a definitive ruling on the matter. A committee under Simon Greenleaf, a Harvard law professor, duly recommended that each trader's rights to the ice should depend on the amount of shoreline he owned.

The impact on land prices around the Fresh Pond shoreline was dramatic: Tudor, for instance, reported that he had paid $130 an acre when he acquired Fresh Pond Farm in 1838. Ten years later he turned down an offer of $2000 an acre for part of his land.[18]

The Greenleaf method was to become widely used as the increasingly profitable industry spread to other parts of New England and made questions of ice ownership the subject of angry, sometimes violent, debate. In fact, subsequent legal opinions suggested that this apportionment would not have been legally enforceable.[19] Under common law, the Commonwealth still held Fresh Pond in trust for its citizens and so no one could claim exclusive rights to the water or the ice.

Greenleaf's approach, however, was seen to be equitable and was respected by the traders. The smaller proprietors were duly bought out by other ice merchants, principal among them Jacob Hittinger and Addison Gage. Hittinger was a Watertown farmer. He was one of the major lobbyists for the creation of the new town of Belmont and a member of its first board of selectmen when it took over the north and west shores of Fresh Pond on its incorporation in 1859. Addison Gage was a liverystable keeper who was to become "the leading retail ice dealer of Boston."[20]

Together they formed the firm of Gage, Hittinger & Co. in 1842. Their earliest transaction was the first attempt to sell Fresh Pond ice in England. Following the approach often used by Tudor, Hittinger traveled with the cargo and set up a fancy dinner in London, where he arranged for a selection of iced drinks to be produced with a flourish. Hittinger later recalled the unexpected results:

> The hour arrived. . . . Now, thought I, I am all right. At a given signal the well-trained waiters appeared, laden with the different drinks. The effect was gorgeous, and I expected an ovation that no Yankee had ever had. But, alas! the first sounds that broke the silence were: "I say—aw, waitaw, a little 'ot wataw, if you please; I prefer it 'alf and 'alf." I made a dead rush for the door, next day settled my bills in London, took . . . the steamer for Boston, and counted up a clear loss of $1,200.00.[21]

Despite this setback, Gage and Hittinger went on to great success, trading at Fresh Pond and owning major ice establishments elsewhere.

Changing the Shoreline

In an effort to produce reliable crops of ice early in the season, and to ensure ice even when the weather was too mild to freeze the whole pond, traders would create shallow coves by filling in areas of the shore with gravel. Tudor in particular resculpted much of the shoreline around Cambridge Nook, forming a shallow basin immediately between his two main icehouses.

Even more dramatically, Tudor created an entirely artificial, large, shallow lake on his property, just north of Concord Avenue.[22] It was known as the Glacialis and was about seven acres in size and no more than six feet deep. Originally stiffly rectangular, the action of the water and of muskrats gradually softened the edges. The lake was fed by an artificial outlet constructed from Fresh Pond, and any overflow was directed into Alewife Brook.

3.5 A drawing showing the gated cove constructed by Frederic Tudor between two of his large icehouses on the north shore. Its still, shallow water would have frozen earlier than the main pond. By 1888, the date of this sketch, the business had been acquired from Tudor's heirs by the Boston Ice Company. Cambridge Water Board minutes, 1888.

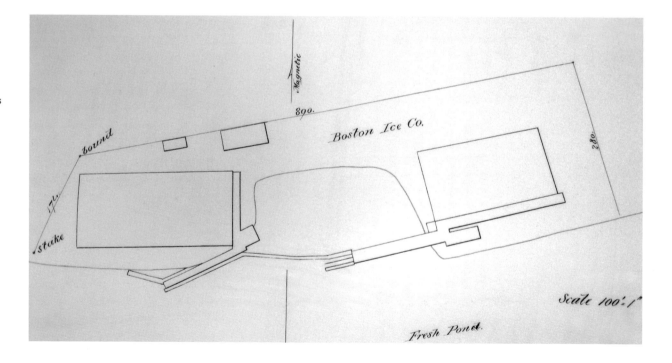

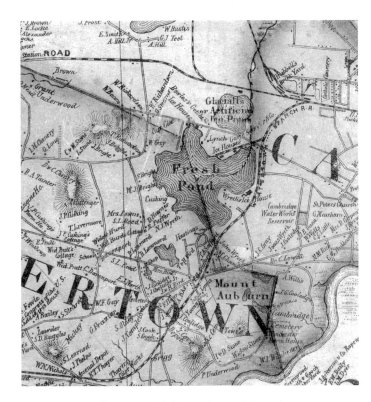

3.6 The H. F. Walling map of Middlesex County, Massachusetts, 1856 (detail) shows Tudor's shallow Glacialis, constructed to the north of Concord Avenue, in a failed effort to create reliably early ice. The marshy ground had too many underground springs to allow the ice to freeze sufficiently, and the artificial pond became instead a location for swimming and skating.
With permission of the Harvard Map Collection, Harvard College Library.

The Coming of the Railroad

Nathaniel Wyeth was always looking for new ways to increase his efficiency and profitability. He realized that one of the slowest and least effective parts of the process was moving supplies from the Fresh Pond icehouses to the wharves at Charlestown for shipping. This was originally done by manually loading the ice onto horse-drawn carts, which then trundled over rough, rutted roads to the ships to be unloaded by hand. The ice frequently got broken en route and sometimes the heavy carts became stuck in the muddy roads.

Wyeth saw the potential of the new railroads dramatically to improve the way the ice was transported. The Charlestown Branch Railroad had been built in 1837 to link the Boston & Lowell Railroad (completed two years earlier) in East Cambridge to the docks in Charlestown. Wyeth duly campaigned with other traders (although not Tudor, who seemed uninterested in the idea) to have this branch extended to Fresh Pond. It seems that that the ice business was still seen by many as something of a joke. Certainly the traders' propaganda stressed that they were involved in a serious business and deserved access to the railroad as much as the granite or coal industry did.[23]

They were soon successful. The traders gained permission for the extension and found the necessary financial backing. In 1841 the Charlestown Branch laid a track from the Boston & Lowell junction in East Cambridge through Somerville and around the north side of Avon Hill to Fresh Pond. In December of that year, the first trainload of ice was duly transported from Fresh Pond on the new railroad to the ships at

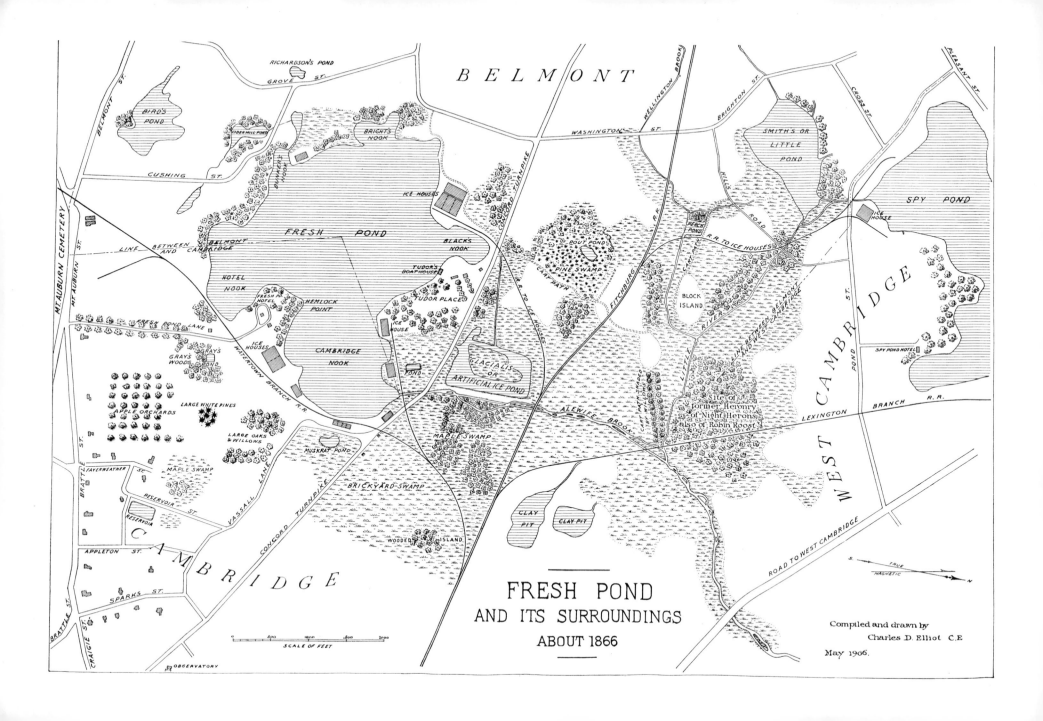

FRESH POND
AND ITS SURROUNDINGS
ABOUT 1866

Compiled and drawn by
Charles D. Elliot C.E
May 1906.

B E L M O N T

W E S T C A M B R I D G E

C A M B R I D G E

RICHARDSON'S POND

GROVE   ST.

BIRD'S POND

CIDER MILL POND

BRIGHT'S NOOK

ICE HOUSES

BELMONT   ST.

CUSHING   ST.

SMITH'S OR LITTLE POND

SPY POND

WASHINGTON   ST.

WELLINGTON BROOK

BRIGHTON ST.

CROSS ST.

PLEASANT ST.

HILLS   ROAD

FRESH   POND

BLACKS NOOK

PERCH POND

POUT POND

PINE SWAMP

BLOCK ISLAND

ICE HOUSE

LINE BETWEEN BELMONT AND CAMBRIDGE

BELMONT

HOTEL NOOK

FRESH PD. HOTEL

HEMLOCK POINT

TUDOR'S BOAT HOUSE

TUDOR PLACE

ICE HOUSE

R.R. TO ICE HOUSES

CLAY BATH

R.R. TO ICE HOUSES

FITCHBURG

LITTLE RIVER

LINE BETWEEN BELMONT AND WEST CAMBRIDGE

SPY POND HOTEL

MT. AUBURN CEMETERY

MT. AUBURN ST.

LINE BETWEEN AND CAMBRIDGE

FRESH POND LANE

ICE HOUSES

GRAY'S WOODS

GRAY'S

WATERTOWN BRANCH R.R.

CAMBRIDGE NOOK

POND

GLACIALIS OR ARTIFICIAL ICE POND

Site of former Heronry of Night Herons; also of Robin Roost

LEXINGTON BRANCH   R.R.

APPLE ORCHARDS

LARGE WHITE PINES

LARGE OAKS & WILLOWS

MUSKRAT POND

MAPLE SWAMP

ALEWIFE BROOK

CART WAY FLOODED

BRATTLE ST.

FAYERWEATHER ST.

RESERVOIR ST.

RESERVOIR

VASSALL LANE

CONCORD TURNPIKE

BRICKYARD SWAMP

CLAY PIT

CLAY PIT

ROAD TO WEST CAMBRIDGE

APPLETON ST.

WOODED ISLAND

SPARKS ST.

CRAIGIE ST.

OBSERVATORY

0   500   1000   1500   2000
SCALE OF FEET

S
TRUE
MAGNETIC
N

3.7 A reconstructed map, drawn in 1906, of Fresh Pond, c. 1866, showing the Fitchburg Railroad, with its spurs to the Tudor icehouses and to those of Gage and Hittinger at Black's Nook; and the Watertown Branch added in 1847 that took passengers to the Fresh Pond Hotel and Mount Auburn Cemetery.
William Brewster, *The Birds of the Cambridge Region of Massachusetts* (Cambridge Mass.: Nuttall Ornithological Club, 1906).

Charlestown. It was part of the remaining ten thousand tons of ice harvested the previous season, still safely stored in the icehouses around the shore.[24] Wyeth, as might have been predicted, had designed specially insulated freight cars for the ice to make the journey.

A year later, the Fitchburg Railroad began service between Boston and Waltham on a parallel track. This opened up the possibility of harvesting ice from previously inaccessible sources. Author and naturalist Henry David Thoreau was to write angrily about the arrival in the winter of 1846 of Tudor's men at Walden Pond, now within easy reach of the railroad. Seeing the vast, mechanized trade as essentially being in conflict with nature, Thoreau's writings describe how Tudor "took off the only coat, ay, the skin itself, of Walden Pond in the midst of a hard winter." His men were hauling away on sleds "all the terra firma there was." With some satisfaction Thoreau reported that, for whatever reason, most of the ten thousand tons harvested were never used. They were left on Walden's shores gradually to melt over the following summer, and "Thus the pond recovered the greater part."[25]

Many of the early railroads, including the Charlestown Branch, were designed for the transport of freight. But once they started running, there was such strong demand that provision was introduced for a passenger service as well. This was probably hastened by the economic depression of 1837-1842, which made such local additional sources of revenue attractive to the railroad owners. Stations opened across the network and the new passenger business grew rapidly.[26] In January 1842, the Charlestown Branch began a passenger service between Cambridge and Charlestown with a coach attached to a

3.8 The Fresh Pond Railroad station was built in 1876–1877 at the end of Lexington Avenue, replacing previous stops on Concord Avenue and Fresh Pond Lane. It was demolished in 1925. Image c. 1920s.
H. B. Crouch Collection, Cambridge Historical Commission.

train of ice cars. The Fitchburg Railroad carried both freight and passengers from 1843. In 1846 it absorbed the parallel Charlestown Branch and the following year opened a new line, known as the Watertown Branch, which ran along the east shore of Fresh Pond to Mount Auburn. Suburban service continued until 1938 and was a major factor in affording public access to the pond and the cemetery.

The Rise of the Brick Industry

The railroad's arrival also greatly stimulated the local brick industry. For a long time, clay had been dug out from the Great Swamp on a small scale to produce building materials. But once the railroad made transportation easier, there was something of a "clay rush."[27] Again it was Nathaniel Wyeth who was at the heart of this. In 1844 he leased some of his land to local traders Peter Hubbell and Almon Abbott to produce bricks. Their financial success led to the spawning of a major industry. A complex of clay pits, drying kilns, brickyards, and tramways was soon established to the northeast of the pond.

Wyeth had a particular interest in gaining access to a large local supply of bricks. He had realized that sparks from the new trains created a risk of fire for the timber icehouses (indeed many were to burn down over the years). So he decided to create the first brick-built storage for his supplies. Not a man to miss an opportunity to increase his chance for profits, he installed a truly monumental new icehouse at Fresh Pond, on the other side of the promontory from the hotel (see figure 3.6). A local newspaper reported its size and design with some awe:

> An immense ice house has been erected at Fresh Pond . . . of most extraordinary dimensions, nearly as large as the store-houses erected by Joseph, in Egypt, for grain. The main building is composed of a triple wall, 40 feet high, 178 feet wide, and 199 feet long—enclosing more than 3/4ths of an acre of land, and capable of containing upwards of 39,000 tons of ice.—The walls are of brick, and measure 4 ft. from the outside of the outer wall, to the inside of the inner one. About 1,500,000 bricks, and 800,000 feet of boards and other lumber, have been used in its construction.

3.9 This photograph of the brickyards northeast of Fresh Pond was taken in 1890 or 1891. The view is looking northeast from behind the present Fresh Pond Shopping Center. The frozen pond was one of the largest clay pits in the Great Swamp (now the site of Danehy Park). Across the middle of the image runs the Fitchburg Railroad main line, with its half-timbered railway signal tower, to the right of which is the start of the Watertown Branch that took passengers to Fresh Pond and Mount Auburn. In the foreground are the tracks of the tramway that carried clay from the pits to the kilns. The large building in the center may have been a dormitory for brickyard workers; it was demolished before 1900.

Photograph by Henry L. Rand—Number 5191—from the Southwest Harbor Public Library Photographic Collection.

3.10 This modern (1977) map shows the various "urban fringe" activities located around Fresh Pond by the 1880s, including the extensive brick industry to the northeast.
Survey of Architectural History in Cambridge, Report Five: Northwest Cambridge.

Almshouse
City Poor Farm

Tanneries

Horse Car Barns

Harvard Botanical Garden

Glacial

Harvard Observatory

Slaughter house

Pumping station

City gravel pit

Reservoir

Fresh Pond

Convent

Marble works

Horse car barns

0   600   1200
scale in feet

Brickyards
Ice House
Cemeteries
Nurseries
Streets in 1886

The article goes on to praise the architecture of the building, with "pilasters, entablatures, covings, and other projections" to provide some visual relief on what would otherwise have been vast blank walls. It also describes a large adjoining tool house where all the necessary apparatus was stored, sharpened, and repaired by teams of workmen, using horsepower to grind the tools. Two other buildings were added. One was used to transport the ice straight to the railroad cars if it was not to be stored. The other was to store Wyeth's specially designed cars when they were not in use. The article concludes approvingly with details of the speed with which ice could now be loaded and unloaded: "Arrangements have been made by which 7 cars can be laden with 28 tons of ice in 4 1/2 minutes, and unladen in one minute and a half!"[28]

Tudor subsequently also built a large brick icehouse, on the north shore of the lake, using bricks supplied from the thriving local industry by the same Peter Hubbell.[29]

The Private Water Industry

In the middle of the nineteenth century the ice trade was to give rise to the most enduring industry at Fresh Pond: the water supply business.

Like many communities, Cambridge had made use of natural wells and springs to supply water for both residential and business use. For many years this had been sufficient. But with Cambridge increasing in size, plus a growing demand for pure drinking water, private companies started to see an opportunity to make money from a more organized water supply. The first such attempt in Cambridge was by the Cambridgeport

Aqueduct Company, which in 1837 secured a charter to supply water (probably for firefighting purposes) from Prospect Hill via a cistern near today's Kendall Square. Then in 1852 three local businessmen saw the potential of Fresh Pond, already famous for the purity of its ice. Estes Howe, Gardiner Hubbard, and Moses Rice duly formed the Cambridge Water Works, a private company, and gained a charter to supply drinking water from Fresh Pond for the newly incorporated city. The outlay on infrastructure was substantial, at $215,000.[30]

The ice traders were not happy with this new development. While they enjoyed the rights conferred by the colonial ordinance freely to take supplies from the pond, they resisted the idea of sharing the resources with other businesses. Twice, Wyeth and others unsuccessfully sought legal injunctions to stop the building of the water works, and the pumping of water to the new reservoir. In response the legislature passed an act giving the new company the necessary powers to obtain the water from the pond. The company also ensured it had legal access by obtaining about 20,000 feet of shoreline from Josiah Coolidge. The new company, no doubt troubled by the threat to its business of the continued legal challenges, issued a plea to the ice merchants. It asked them to accept that, despite a large ice harvest and the commencement of pumping, "the water in the Pond has not for many years been as high as at present, nor has the ice been thicker. We therefore hope our neighbors will make no further expense and trouble in this matter, being satisfied by our experience that there is an ample supply."[31]

The ice merchants may then have pressed for financial compensation from the state for the potential loss of resources.

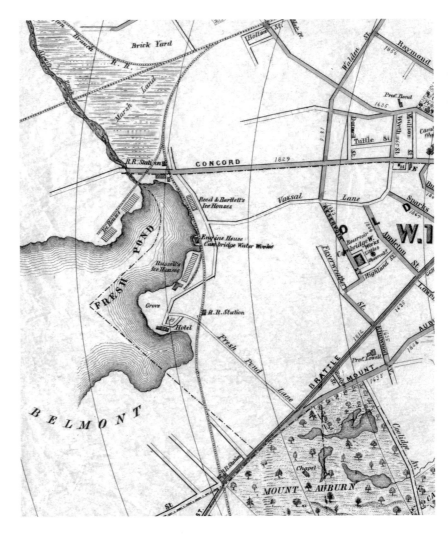

3.11 The 1865 J. G. Chase map of the city of Cambridge (detail) shows the private Cambridge Water Works' engine house, with its steam-powered pumps, built in 1856 on the eastern shores of Fresh Pond, and the distributing reservoir uphill of the pond on what became Reservoir Street. With permission of the Harvard Map Collection, Harvard College Library.

Certainly a legal opinion was sought in 1858 about how far the abutters had rights to the water and ice in the pond. Again the relevance of Great Pond rights was confirmed: all citizens had the right to make use of the water, but none were guaranteed the right to make a profit from it, and so no damages would be due to the ice traders.[32] After that, although occasional legal wrangles appear to have continued,[33] the two businesses coexisted at the pond for several decades. The Water Works company eventually bought out the small Aqueduct business and became the main supplier for all of Cambridge.

Workers and Workers' Housing

The ice and brick industries required large numbers of manual workers. Many were immigrants, often Irish and, later, French-Canadian, who found employment in the brick industry during the summer and the ice trade during the winter months. The great-great-grandparents of U.S. Speaker of the House of Representatives Thomas P. ("Tip") O'Neill were among those Irish immigrants who settled in North Cambridge to labor in the local industries.

At first many of the Irish workers were forced to live in little more than tents, cabins, and other temporary shelters to the northeast of the pond. Then the brickyard owners and ice traders began to provide boarding houses, often adapted from old colonial farmsteads. Even Fresh Pond Farm, once a country seat, was converted by Frederic Tudor to provide housing for his employees. Other boarding houses began to be built around the pond specifically to cater for the growing number of workmen.[34]

In the 1840s and 1850s unproductive brickyard lots to the north and east of the pond were subdivided for small laborers' houses, to be located behind the larger homes of the brickyard owners. Pressure for land in the area continued and, in 1855, a Trotting Park on today's Rindge Avenue, which had become the principal venue in the Boston area for organized trotting horse races, was subdivided into 275 lots. Originally aimed at more middle class families, the lots were later sold mainly to laborers. The adjoining hotel, the Trotting Park House, became a boarding house for brickyard workers. Arriving after the Civil

3.12 Mrs. Malloy's boarding house, built for Tudor's ice men at 515 Concord Avenue around 1859. The property was demolished in 1985. Image c. 1977.
Richard Cheek photograph, Cambridge Historical Commission.

War, French-Canadians often displaced the Irish from their jobs in the brickyards, and took over the workers cottages and tenements that the Irish had begun to leave.

There was a similar trend in the housing development to the south of Fresh Pond. In 1847 two large plots of land were acquired and subdivided into suburban neighborhoods. Strawberry Hill was designed by Alexander Wadsworth, with standard house lots, except for a new road which curved around a small park and offered fine views of Fresh Pond. The other subdivision, designed by John Low, was named Auburn. It took a similar approach, with a circular drive called Woodland Street (later Woodlawn Avenue). Aimed at middle-class Boston families, the areas proved too far from churches and schools for the intended buyers. A few small workers' houses began to be built while larger lots remained vacant. Some lots were sold to the ice traders and railroad owners for industrial use. Gradually, as the original protective deed restrictions were relaxed, the lots were further subdivided and more modest laborers' homes were added into the 1870s. Here lived mainly African-Americans and Italian immigrants, working at Mount Auburn cemetery or Fresh Pond.

Local ornithologist William Brewster described the way the area to the east of Fresh Pond was rapidly developed. During his schooldays in the 1860s and 1870s "there was not then a building of any kind. Most of the land was occupied by broad, smooth mowing lands; bubbly and, in places, boggy pastures; and fine old apple orchards, many acres in extent. There were also one or two bushy swamps, several groves of large oaks, a conspicuous cluster of tall white pines, a few isolated shell-bark hickories of the finest proportions, and a number of scraggy wild apple trees." (See figure 3.7.) In contrast, by the turn of the century the whole area south of Concord Avenue, around Vassal Lane and Reservoir Street, was "thickly settled."[35]

3.13 and **3.14** Two typical styles of workers' housing erected in the 1840s and 1850s to the northeast of Fresh Pond (left, 119 Harvey Street; right, 205 Rindge Avenue). Both images c. 1977.
Both: Richard Cheek photographs, Cambridge Historical Commission.

An Unsuitable Barracks

Rail, brick, and water: all these followed on from the ice industry. So too did a small role for Fresh Pond in the Civil War. The account of the soldiers' time at the pond gives an insight into why it was more suited to industry and recreation than residential dwellings.

In the early days of the war, the volunteers who had joined the Massachusetts First Regiment of Infantry needed local quarters before they were called to the fighting. For a few days they were located in Boston's Faneuil Hall, but it proved too small for the thousand or so men who made up the Regiment.[36] So the state authorities acquired the Reed and Bartlett icehouse on the eastern shores of Fresh Pond (see figure 3.11), and partially fitted it out for the soldiers' use. On June 1st, 1861, the Regiment marched to Cambridge and took occupation.[37]

A contemporary newspaper report gives some details of the way the icehouse had been adapted:

> The house is of wood . . . and comprises six compartments, each of which is sixty feet deep and thirty feet wide. These have been fitted up as well as the circumstances would admit of, three tiers of bunks being erected on each side, and it is supposed that 180 men can be stowed away in each. The building is very dark, each compartment being lighted only by the door and a window, but it is supposed to be dry, not having contained any ice for two years, and provision has been made for good ventilation.[38]

At first the soldiers were happy enough with their new barracks, christening it "Camp Ellsworth" in commemoration

3.15 Private Allen Kingsbury, member of the regiment briefly quartered at Fresh Pond during the Civil War, c. 1861.
Allen Alonzo Kingsbury, *Hero of Medfield* (Boston: J. M. Hewes, 1862). Courtesy of the Medfield Historical Society.

of the famous Colonel Elmer Ellsworth who had been shot while taking down a confederate flag in Virginia a few days before. Being right on the shores of the pond, the location offered "unlimited advantages for bathing."[39] Hot water was available from the Cambridge Water Works, and there was easy access to the camp by both the railroad and the horse cars on Mount Auburn Street. The regimental officers took up residence in a dwelling-house about 100 feet from the icehouse, while work began to construct a building to serve as a kitchen. The soldiers drilled for hours at a time on the shoreline, at one point doing some considerable damage to fencing while "charging at double quick in line of battle."[40]

Soon, however, it became apparent that, even in June, packing a thousand men into a large icehouse was not going to be conducive to their health: the journalistic optimism about the level of ventilation quickly proved mistaken. Within a few days of arrival, Private Allen Kingsbury, a twenty-year-old farmer from Medfield, was writing home: "It is an awful place here, fresh pond, on one side and a bog hole on the other, and is damp and foggy all night. If we stay here a week longer we shall all be sick with the cholera, for aught I know."[41] Many of the soldiers rapidly succumbed to colds and other respiratory infections, caused apparently by the damp air. A lieutenant heard of the complaints and inspected the quarters. He decided that the icehouse would not after all serve as a barracks and made arrangements to find more suitable accommodation.[42] As a result, on June 13th, the Regiment left for new quarters at Camp Cameron, a mile away in North Cambridge, located on either side of what is today Cameron Avenue.[43]

The soldiers may have only been on the shore of Fresh Pond for a little under two weeks, but their link with the area endured. Celebrating their return to Boston three years later, a local newspaper referred explicitly to that early "camp near Fresh Pond" and the soldiers' wish to be home: "After three years of trials and hardships marching many hundred miles enduring storms and privations of all kinds and going through many hard fought battles, always in the advance, and sent to positions of the most exposure and danger, is it to be wondered at, that what few there are left of them, are anxiously waiting for the day of their redemption, when they can tread once more upon free soil."[44]

Shifting Reactions to Industry at the Pond

Attitudes toward industry's impact at Fresh Pond changed as the nineteenth century progressed. In the middle of the century, there was a genuine civic pride in the way that local New England resources were being used to make money. The ice industry could be seen as a celebration of nature's endless power and of America's ability to use nature for the benefit of others. In 1856 one newspaper reported a lengthy speech in this vein by politician, pastor, diplomat and professor the Hon. Edward Everett. In his speech, he expressed his delight that the money ("gold") spent by Frederic Tudor on his palatial estate in Nahant was derived:

> from the ice of our own Fresh Pond. It is all Middlesex gold, every penny of it. The sparkling surface of our beautiful ponds, restored by the kindly hand of nature as often as it is removed, has yielded, and will continue to yield, . . . a perpetual reward to the industry bestowed upon them. The sallow genius of the mine creates but once; when rifled by man the glittering prize is gone forever. Not so with our pure crystal lakes. . . . This is a branch of Middlesex industry that we have a right to be proud of. . . . I look upon Mr. Tudor . . . as a great public benefactor.

Everett told how he was thanked by the president of the Indian Board of Control for the benefits Americans had brought to his country through the shipment of ice, which supplied not only comfort in the heat but life-saving cold for those suffering from fever. His effusive praise concludes with an almost Christ-like analogy: "I must say I almost envied Mr. Tudor the honest satisfaction . . . that he had been able to stretch out an arm of benevolence from the other side of the globe, by which he was every year raising up his fellow-men from the verge of the grave."[45]

Although not quite as fulsome as Everett, other writers also saw the attractions of the ice industry as it stamped its mark on the landscape at Fresh Pond. Well into the second half of the nineteenth century, most people accepted, even enjoyed, the intermingling of industry and recreation in the same landscape. There was nothing of our modern sensibility that sees industry as essentially ugly and destructive, and that demands it be confined to areas already "spoiled" by similar development. Indeed for people in the middle of the nineteenth century, the icehouses and the winter harvesting became significant tourist attractions in their own right. (And at the peak of the ice industry, there were some fifty large icehouses dominating Fresh Pond's shoreline.[46]) One English writer who visited Fresh Pond during her travels in 1849 and 1850 is typical in her attitude to what she saw. She admired the bucolic scenery, and (without any surprise) noted the way society was keen to celebrate the industry and its production techniques, most of them designed by local man Nathaniel Wyeth. She wrote, "The water is like liquid diamonds, so transparent and sparklingly pure. The scenery around is worthy of being mirrored in it. I am told, in the winter it is one of the gayest scenes in the world. During the time of the ice-cutting, innumerable sleighs assemble on the spot, and the beau monde of Boston are all to be met there."[47]

Toward the end of the nineteenth century, however, attitudes began to change. Some came to share Thoreau's views that the beauty and purity of nature were being sullied by an unjustifiable drive for profit. George Perkins Marsh's landmark book *Man and Nature*, published in 1864, attempted to demonstrate that increasing commercial activity was damaging the environment, bringing changes in vegetation, climate, soil and wildlife habitats. He argued for a more thoughtful approach to the harnessing of natural resources, one that recognized how humanity and the natural world were essentially all part of one organic system.[48]

Such thinking came to change people's attitude to the developments at Fresh Pond. One of the Cabot brothers remembered his youth there, when he had hunted birds, and when the marshes to the north of the pond were still a wilderness and the Concord Turnpike was "a lonely road . . . causewayed above the bog." Returning in 1870, he recoiled from what he saw as a "dreary waste" with "brickfields, shanties, and ice ponds, with a line of ice houses blocking the sun."[49]

Similarly, Mrs. Joseph Lyman, who had spent many happy hours of her childhood playing at Fresh Pond Farm in the early 1800s (described in the previous chapter), revisited the estate in 1865, when it was being used as a boarding house for Tudor's icemen. While much of the scenery remained the same, she was horrified by the way industry had encroached on what she remembered as a genteel country seat: "The visit was on a lovely Autumn day. The trees were just changing color. The grass was still green and fresh. The pond was as blue as ever and as beautiful, and the natural repose of the place was over all. . . . [But at the house m]any changes had taken place. . . . Desolation reigned around."[50]

ICE-CUTTING AT FRESH POND, CAMBRIDGE, MASS.

3.16 A view of the ice cutting process and the large icehouses on the western shores of Fresh Pond, 1853. Once cut, the blocks of ice were hauled up ramps into the houses by a mechanized pulley system and then traveled down a chute to be stored in neat stacks. The drama of the harvesting process became a popular winter spectacle. Author's collection.

4   Social Reform and the City

Nature has done much to furnish Cambridge with a large storage basin, very convenient, and with attractive surroundings, combining the useful and beautiful in an unusual degree.

Cambridge Water Board, describing its reservoir and planned water park at Fresh Pond, 1884

In the second half of the nineteenth century, the Industrial Revolution was radically affecting people's working and living conditions. American cities were growing and changing rapidly as labor shifted from the country to the industrial centers, and with the arrival of many immigrant workers. This shift "forced all residents to confront new, even alien, work and interpersonal relationships, to confront the sights and sounds of an accelerating urban economy as well as the remarkable cultural diversity of the urban population."[1] Trade and industry had once been celebrated as evidence of the power of human endeavor to conquer and harness nature. After the Civil War, its reputation changed. Now industry's poor working conditions, polluting emissions, and accompanying cramped housing were increasingly blamed for the spread of disease and for social disorder among the working classes.

Social reformers, who included politicians, religious leaders, and physicians, sought to introduce measures that would protect public health and improve public morals. Although the attitudes and approaches of the reformers may seem paternalistic or elitist to modern sensibilities, they were often driven by a genuine desire to realize their vision of what America could become. They foresaw a "new and civilized . . . urban environment"[2] with a reliable supply of clean water, proper sewage disposal, and family-oriented housing. They believed that, by providing such facilities, they could reduce levels of disease and help the poor to acquire the habits and behavior of the educated classes.

In many places, it had at first been private enterprise that led to clean water being piped to residents. But gradually cities wanted to be in control of both the supply and its purity. In New York and then Boston in the 1840s, new water supply systems had been designed and installed at public expense. By the early 1850s, around a dozen U.S. cities had followed their example. This increasingly interventionist role for government led to arguments about the relative merits of the private and public sector in supplying services for the community: some argued that free enterprise and the market would always provide the most efficient solution, and they resisted the use of wealthy taxpayers' money to provide a service to the poor. Fears also arose about the growing power of municipal government. But the social reformers' arguments held sway: it was essential to supply basic services to everyone, not just those who could afford to pay, if the health and moral well-being of society were to improve.[3]

As well as water, reformers also stressed the value of easy access for all to outdoor space that encouraged family-oriented activity. Nature was seen as providing a much-needed moral compass in an industrializing world. It encouraged the natural, good human impulses that had been tainted by exposure to the corrupting forces of city life. Even contemplating

4.1 Between 1866 and 1870, the largest public works project in the city of Boston's history produced the Chestnut Hill reservoir in Brighton. Laid out around its edges was the first large-scale rural park in the city and a circular carriage drive, which became immensely popular, featured in guidebooks and pictured on postcards. Chestnut Hill was to serve as an explicit inspiration for the water board's work at Fresh Pond. Image c. 1878.
Edwin M. Bacon, *Boston Illustrated* (Boston: Houghton, Mifflin and Co., 1886). Courtesy of Jeff Kelley of kellscraft.com.

the water in a fountain or pond would help improve morals through exposure to one of the essential elements of nature. Thus a major part of the social reform movement focused on the provision of naturalistic parkland within the city. With the success of Central Park in New York (created in the 1850s, inspired in part by European public parks), demand for similar open spaces grew in cities such as Philadelphia, Baltimore, and Boston. By 1874, a doctor in Philadelphia was crediting a striking drop in the death rate in that city to the creation of Fairmount Park. Its reservoir supplied copious, cheap water, while its surrounding parkland gave "even the very poorest citizens [the opportunity] for the enjoyment of pure air. . . . The extent to which this is valued by the citizens may be inferred from the fact that the park was visited in 1874 by 11,000,000 persons."[4] In the late 1860s the city of Boston oversaw the construction of the reservoir and parkland at Chestnut Hill, and then in 1878 commissioned Frederick Law Olmsted to design the first park in what was to become known as Boston's Emerald Necklace. The city of Cambridge was rather slower in recognizing the need for an urban park system, but by the early 1890s concern was growing about the damage being done to the population's health and well-being by the way Cambridge was swiftly becoming a modern city: "Probably Cambridge . . . with its limited area and rapidly increasing population, is one of the most marked examples in the Commonwealth of a sudden transition from semi-rural to urban conditions."[5]

Fresh Pond was perhaps an obvious target for social reform. It was the site of Cambridge's main water supply, although under private ownership clean water was available only to those who could afford the necessary fees. There were

4.2 This photograph from c. 1884–1888 captures a moment in the dramatic physical transition of Fresh Pond, with the past and future landscape both evident. Fresh Pond's nineteenth-century history is still visible, with the hotel building in the center of the image and much of its thickly wooded grove untouched. But vividly slashed across the foreground of the photograph, and along the edge of the grove, is the city's new dyke and carriage road under construction; the overhanging trees to the far left show where the bank has not yet been cleared to make way for the road.
Frederick Law Olmsted Jr., "The Relation of Reservoirs to Parks," *American Park and Outdoor Art Association, 1899* (Boston: Rockwell & Churchill Press, 1899).

4.3 An 1899 photograph shows the easternmost entrance from Concord Avenue to Fresh Pond. Taken after the engineering work was complete, it captures the main objectives that the city was striving to achieve: the sleek new reservoir with its straightened edges and protective fence; one of the new gatehouses, installed to manage the water supply; the wide, inviting carriage road, built on the new dyke, and offering uplifting views of the water to the visitor; the new tree and shrub planting; and the city sign erected over the entrance to "Fresh Pond Park," promoting the use of the roadway as a Pleasure Drive.
Courtesy of the National Park Service, Frederick Law Olmsted National Historic Site.

increasing concerns about the levels of pollution that might be seeping into the water from the surrounding industries. Indeed, with the many trades around its shores, Fresh Pond had become what one writer has described as Boston's "urban fringe." There were the icehouses, the large brick industry with its clay pits and brick kilns, and the piggeries and slaughterhouses (with their associated trades of tanneries and glue factories). Added to these were the railroad, the myriad workers' housing, and the cemeteries (some of them rather less picturesque than Mount Auburn). (See figure 3.10.) West Cambridge was becoming the location for any "necessary but unpleasant" urban activity.[6]

Thus, inspired by the successes of other cities,[7] the Cambridge Water Board saw the opportunity at Fresh Pond to improve the health of local citizens by creating a safe public water supply, and the chance to tackle the rowdy behavior of the thousands of picnickers on the grove (so frowned on by members of the upper and middle classes), by redefining the landscape as a new public park designed for family-oriented recreation.

Civic Pride and Civic Expansion

In 1865 the city acquired the private Cambridge Water Works company franchise and property, at a cost of $291,000. The purchase, approved in a vote by residents, included the engine house at Fresh Pond, the distribution system, the reservoir on Reservoir Street, and about 200 acres of land around Fresh Pond.

4.4 The impressive new pumping station built by the city of Cambridge in 1872. The building later housed an iconic Leavitt steam pumping engine, while the grounds were laid out by the renowned Olmsted landscape architecture firm. It was demolished when the land was sold in the 1950s and the plot became the Chevrolet car showroom at what is now 275 Fresh Pond Parkway.
Cambridge Tribune, Harvard Bridge Souvenir, 1890, Cambridge Historical Commission.

Some Cambridge inhabitants had been anxious about the city taking over the business. As Chester Ward Kingsley, the president of the water board,[8] recalled: "There was a difference of opinion among some of our best citizens as to whether it was best to buy, or not . . . an enterprise which private enterprise had failed to make profitable, and that it would be likely to become a financial burden, if the city took it."[9] Because of the risk of financial loss, the city decided to keep separate accounts for the water supply business, "to determine which class of our citizens was right."[10]

Over the next decade or so, the water board invested in improving and upgrading the infrastructure it had acquired. The work reflected the civic pride that the city took in creating a publicly owned supply system for its citizens. The water board's annual reports detail with some satisfaction how new mains, pipes, and pumps were installed, the old reservoir was almost completely rebuilt, and a second one was added on Reservoir Street, to increase storage capacity. Floodgates were installed on Alewife Brook around 1870 to prevent brackish water running back into the pond at high tide, and a few years later the board filled in the brook as far as Concord Avenue. In 1872 a new pumping station was built on the other side of the railroad tracks from the original engine house. In common with other public buildings at this time,[11] the classical design of the new station reflected the municipality's wish to create handsome monuments to its endeavors. A later commentator noted the "splendid engines for the water works" and the "palace" that had been built over them, "the wonder and admiration of visitors, interested in waterworks, from all parts of the country."[12]

4.5 A large, geyser-like fountain marked the entry of the Stony Brook supply pipe into Fresh Pond. The feature was designed both to aerate the supply as it entered the reservoir and to provide inspiring water views to the visitor. Image c. 1888–1892. *1906 Cambridge Blue Book,* Cambridge Historical Commission.

As well as improving the infrastructure, the water board was also aware of the need to increase the quantity of water it was supplying for the fast-growing city. Fearful that Fresh Pond might prove too small, the board began to hunt for supplementary supplies and, for a while, even considered abandoning the pond altogether.

As an initial step, in 1875 the water board put in a conduit between Fresh Pond, at Black's Nook, and three neighboring bodies of water: Little Pond and Wellington Brook, both in Belmont, and Spy Pond in Arlington (see figure 4.14). Mayor Isaac Bradford objected, believing that, if only the board could be more frugal with existing supplies, the city would not be "forced to introduce into Fresh Pond water of a doubtful quality."[13] On quality, he was proved right: within three years the conduit was largely abandoned.

On the wider issue, though, the water board seems to have won the argument. By 1884 the city was successfully petitioning the Commonwealth for permission to obtain a significant new supply of water from Stony Brook, on the borders of Waltham and Weston. This was achieved by building a dam and aqueduct to divert water from there into Fresh Pond. The additional supply was operational by 1888.

In 1892 Payson Hill in Belmont was chosen as the site of a new larger storage reservoir, to replace the two constructed on Reservoir Street. Payson Hill was part of the old Bellmont estate, which had quickly been sold off after John Perkins Cushing's death by his sons. The new storage reservoir came on line in 1897, as did the second new source of supply, the 600-acre Hobbs Brook reservoir, which stretched over parts of Lexington, Lincoln, and Waltham.

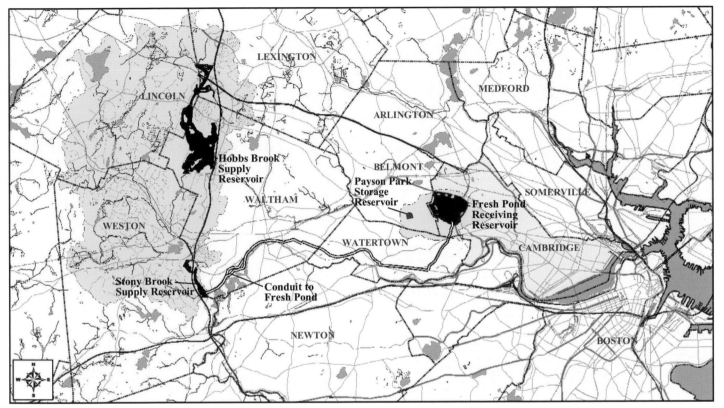

4.6 Today's water supply system for Cambridge was essentially in place by 1897. As shown in this 2008 map, the primary sources for water are the two supply reservoirs, Hobbs Brook and Stony Brook, located outside of the city. From there the water travels via a seven-mile conduit to Fresh Pond, which acts as the receiving reservoir. It is then pumped to the Payson Park storage reservoir in Belmont, from where it is gravity fed to Cambridge residents and businesses via about 190 miles of water mains. Although the board's work in the 1890s has proved farsighted, at the time these extensions to the system were controversial. The city of Cambridge had acquired hundreds of acres of land situated in adjoining towns and was subject to criticism for the apparently inconsiderate way it chose to manage them. There was also much coverage in contemporary newspapers about the unsanitary conditions engendered by the camps of immigrant workers employed to build the new reservoirs and dams.
City of Cambridge Water Department, titles added by author.

Battles over Water Quality

Contemporary records show that, in the 1870s, there was little scientific agreement about the causes of any pollution to the pond's water, or about the best means of protection. Despite this, there were undoubtedly strong feelings about the purity of the newly acquired supply. As one eminent concerned citizen was to remark, "our water supply should be, 'like Caesar's wife,' above suspicion."[14]

Cambridge and its citizens angrily pointed fingers at those who were believed to be polluting the water. The alleged culprits, fortuitously for the self-righteous citizens of Cambridge, always seemed to be across the town borders in Arlington and, especially, Belmont.

Concerns exploded over the construction in 1878 of the Niles Brothers' slaughter-house in Belmont, just to the north of the pond. As one Cambridge man explained, "Alarm, widespread and reasonably entertained, was specially excited when we learnt that the town authorities of Belmont, notwithstanding the solemn protest of the official guardians of our water supply, had deliberately authorized the erection of a slaughterhouse so near Fresh pond as to cast its pollutions into the water we were to drink."[15]

Over 2,500 Cambridge citizens put together the biggest petition ever presented to the city, pressing for action. Other probable sources of pollution were quickly identified, including the Richardson Pond and piggery, the icehouses, backflow from Alewife Brook (even though its natural link to the pond had been severed in 1875), the artificial link that Frederic Tudor had constructed to provide water to his Glacialis, and sewage from workers' houses "of an inferior class" in Belmont's Strawberry Hill.[16]

A report commissioned in 1879 concluded that the city needed to acquire a strip of land around the Fresh Pond shoreline up to fifty rods (about 825 feet) wide, to remove buildings from around the shore, and to annex the parts of the neighboring towns of Belmont and Arlington that abutted the pond.

The owners of the land in question fiercely resisted annexation because becoming citizens of Cambridge would mean paying significantly higher tax rates. The hearing of Cambridge's petitions led to venomous, bitter exchanges between the towns' representatives. As well as the specifics of probable polluters, Cambridge complained about the generally destructive nature of Belmont people: "If Fresh Pond should be abandoned as a means of water supply, notwithstanding the beauty of the pond, the inhabitants of Belmont, with a spirit akin to that with which the Vandals and Goths desecrated Rome, would seize on the pond at once and pollute its waters to the last extremity."[17]

This is typical of the tone of the exchanges. Belmont residents were portrayed as disreputable scoundrels who responded to polite requests with "contemptuous treatment." They continued to allow swimming and boating from the Belmont shore, even though it meant from time to time dead bodies had to be pulled out of the water. Cambridge saw itself as an innocent victim suffering the "bitter experience of the indifference and negligence of an adjoining town."[18]

Belmont's representatives were equally vituperative in response. Cambridge citizens were dissembling and hypocritical, busy pointing out failings elsewhere when terrible things were

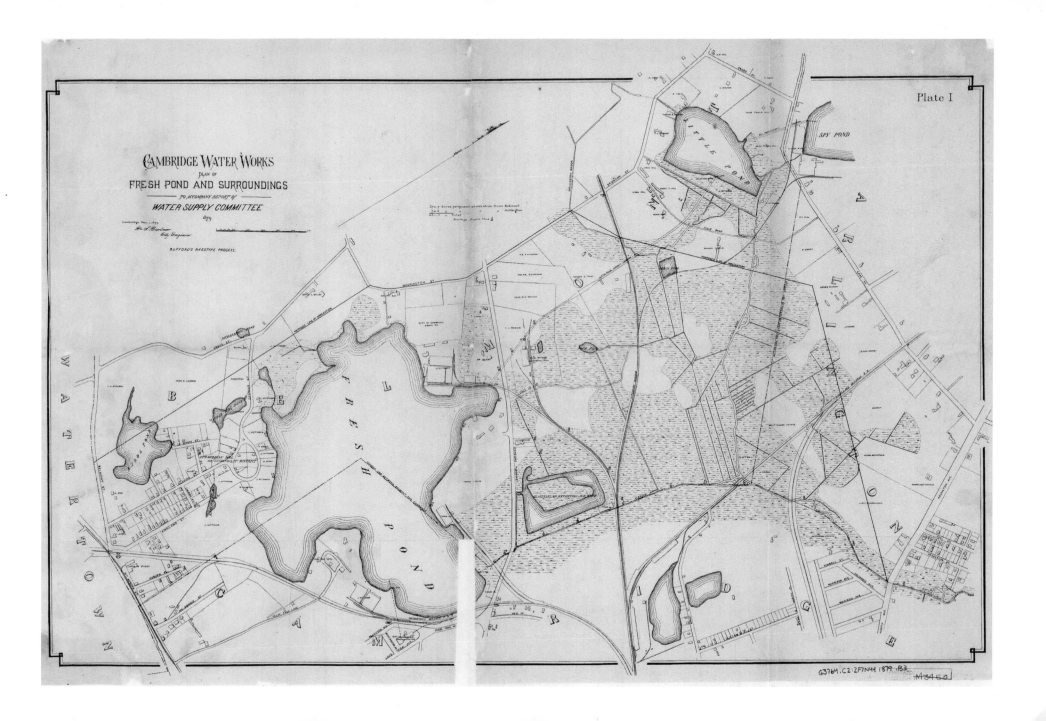

Plate I

CAMBRIDGE WATER WORKS
PLAN OF
FRESH POND AND SURROUNDINGS
TO ACCOMPANY REPORT OF
WATER SUPPLY COMMITTEE
1879

4.8 The plan by William S. Barbour of the land at Fresh Pond authorized by the legislature to be taken by the city of Cambridge to protect its water supply, March 16, 1888. This detailed plan, preserved in the State Archives, shows buildings, structures, roads, trees, and land ownership at a pivotal moment in the pond's history. The dark line traces the shoreline as it was in 1841, at the time of the Parker "ice rights" map: the actions of the ice traders and the water board had since contrived to produce a smaller and much more regularly edged pond. Courtesy Massachusetts Archives.

allowed in their own city. There were colorful descriptions of the amount of sewerage and slops that went straight from the hotel into the pond. The hotel grounds allegedly included "a privy with three holes . . . a urinal . . . six water closets . . . a long board tank where ten men can stand at a time and discharge the lager beer that they have drunk" and all these "lead directly into the pond." Other Belmont representatives complained that hundreds of French Canadians, employed in the brick industry (and who, it was claimed, "are not the cleanest people in the world") were allowed to swim in the pond from the Cambridge shore. One Belmont resident even carefully explained his calculation that 18,000 gallons of human and horse urine were added to the pond during a single ice-cutting season, as well as countless loads of horse manure.[19]

After years of such mutual invective, Cambridge finally got the upper hand. Armed with its 1879 report, and able to demonstrate that it had taken some steps to put its own house in order (for instance by placing the Fresh Pond Hotel under the supervision of the state board of health, and employing boys on sleds to gather up the manure from the ice industry's horses), Cambridge managed to persuade the legislature of its case for annexation. Some 570 acres of Belmont and 70 acres of Arlington were duly transferred to the city of Cambridge.

Clearing the Shoreline

Throughout the 1880s, after the annexation of the shoreline, the water board's annual reports continued to report problems with pollution. Black's Nook was several times described as "foul." As late as 1890 the report included a plea to the city council to act, to abate the "stench" and effluvia emanating from the Niles Brothers' slaughterhouse. And so the board pressed for the right to own the abutting land, as the only way it could fully control what was happening at the pond.

Its first step was to act on an earlier authorization by the legislature, to acquire a strip of land five rods (just over eighty-two feet) wide around the pond.[20] In 1886 the board duly bought ten narrow plots at cost of almost $65,000 and took three others by eminent domain. It now owned nine-tenths of the land immediately abutting the pond, and it embarked on building a dyke and roadway around the shore to make a proper boundary and to put a barrier between any buildings and the water supply.

In 1888, after further pressure from the city, the state legislature passed an act that was to have a profound effect on the appearance, management, and use of Fresh Pond. Designed to allow the city to "better guard and protect" its water supply, the act gave the city of Cambridge the right to take all the remaining land and buildings around the reservoir, either through an agreed purchase or, if necessary, by the power of eminent domain.[21]

The resulting activity was dramatic. The act led to remarkable change at Fresh Pond, much of it accomplished during an extraordinary period of sustained civic activity over just five years or so. By 1890 the city owned all of the land around the pond, and within another two years it had virtually cleared the shoreline of buildings.

The two ice companies were the first to go. The Fresh Pond Ice Company, formed in 1882 as an outgrowth of Jacob Hittinger's business by his sons, had successfully developed the

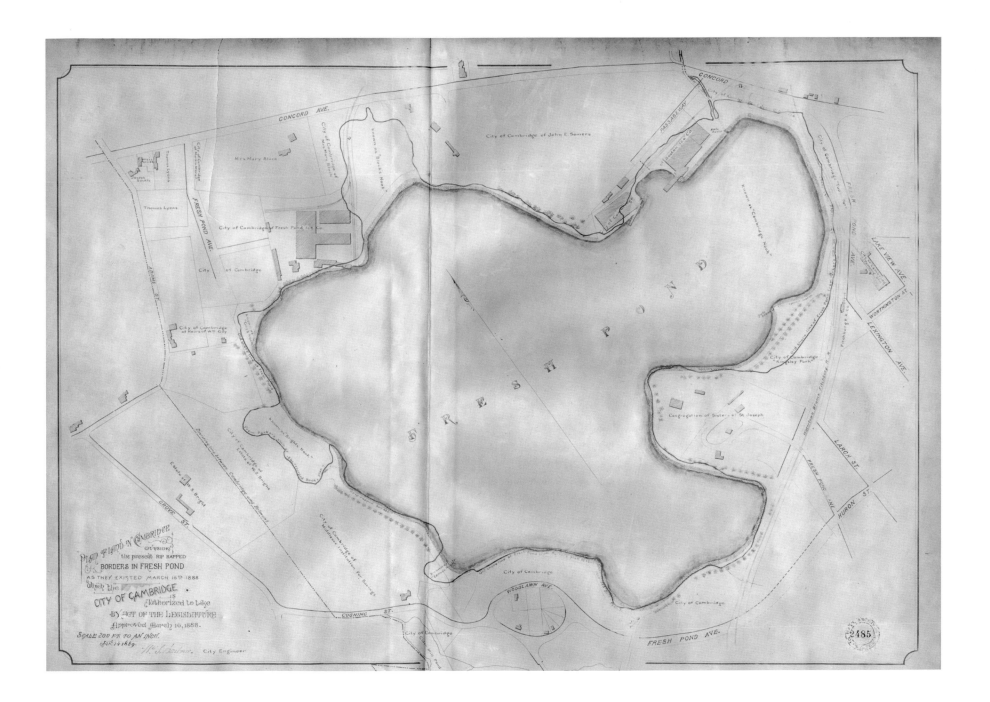

CONCORD AV.

CONCORD AVE.

City of Cambridge of John E. Somers

PASSAGEWAY

Boston Ice Co.

City of Cambridge of Mrs Mary Black

Mrs Mary Black

Known as Black's Neck

Known as Cambridge Neck

FRESH POND AVE.

LAKE VIEW AVE.

City of Cambridge of Fresh Pond Ice Co.

WORTHINGTON ST.

City of Cambridge

LEXINGTON AVE.

F R E S H   P O N D

City of Cambridge of Heirs of Wm Gay

City of Cambridge Kingsley Park

Congregation of Sisters of St. Joseph

ADAMS ST.

Known as Bright's Neck

LARCH ST.

City of Cambridge of Estate of J.S. Bright

Estate of Mrs S. Bright

HURON ST.

GROVE ST.

City of Cambridge of Cambridge Installation for Sewage

City of Cambridge

WOODLAWN AVE.

CUSHING ST.

City of Cambridge

City of Cambridge

FRESH POND AVE.

Plan of Land in Cambridge
OUTSIDE
the present RIP RAPPED
BORDERS IN FRESH POND
AS THEY EXISTED MARCH 16th 1888
Which the
CITY OF CAMBRIDGE
IS
Authorized to take
BY ACT OF THE LEGISLATURE
Approved March 16, 1888.
SCALE 200 FT. TO AN INCH.
Feb. 14 1889.

City Engineer

2485

4.9 The Fresh Pond Ice Company continued to rely on its original name long after the enforced move of its supply to Brookline, New Hampshire. It was emblazoned on its fleet of 53 insulated ice cars, which were in use until the 1930s.
Boston & Maine R.R. Mechanical Dep't, Boston, *Drawings Showing Position of Lettering and Numbers on B.&M.R.R. Freight Equipment* (April 1907). Courtesy of Brian Bollinger, of Bollinger Edgerly Scale Trains.

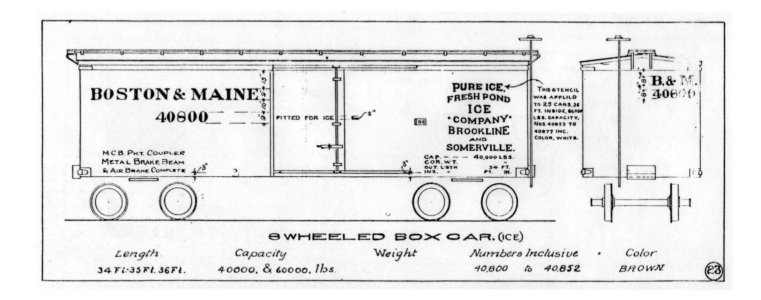

local ice trade after the foreign market fell away. The company tried to negotiate with the city to be allowed to continue harvesting ice indefinitely from Fresh Pond after its land was acquired. There was a proposal that the icehouses could be moved back from the shore with a canal linking them to the water; the city would then take just the hundred-foot strip adjoining the pond. Unfortunately the 1888 act did not allow for such partial acquisition of land, and the city was not minded to press for more legislation. Instead it briefly considered taking over what was clearly a thriving business itself, so that it would supply both water and ice to its citizens. Attorneys for the Fresh Pond Ice Company indignantly petitioned the mayor

for the company to be allowed to continue to run the business itself, if the alternative was the city simply taking it over.[22] In the end, the city withdrew its plans and the company agreed to surrender its icehouses in 1891 and to look for a new location, as its business was "too large and too profitable to be given up."[23]

The other ice business still trading at Fresh Pond was the Boston Ice Company, operating from Frederic Tudor's old icehouses on Fresh Pond Farm. Tudor's widow Euphemia (probably against Tudor's wishes) had taken over the ice business on his death in 1864, and continued trading at Fresh Pond and elsewhere. After her death, her son decided that there was more money to be made selling and leasing the company's property than from continuing in the ice business. So on July 1, 1886, fellow ice trader Spencer Child paid a total of $1,625 for the last Tudor ice from two vaults at Fresh Pond. In January 1887 the Tudor Company's ice account closed forever.[24]

The land and equipment at Fresh Pond were bought by Hittinger's former partner, Addison Gage, in the mid-1880s. Unable to agree on a price with Gage's new business, the city took the land and buildings of his Boston Ice Company by eminent domain in 1888. An acceptable price was finally agreed to in 1892. By July of that year all the buildings of the two ice companies had been sold, presumably for the raw materials, and were being demolished.[25]

The Boston Ice Company had bought only the icehouses from Tudor's estate. Fresh Pond Farm itself, with its ancillary buildings and surrounding farmland, had been sold to Dr. John E. Somers in 1885. Somers was a Canadian, a graduate of St. Francis Xavier University, who had qualified in the United States as a medical doctor and become a prominent local citizen. He had apparently intended to bequeath his newly purchased estate to the Holy Ghost Hospital for Incurables,[26] and he certainly resisted its acquisition by the water board. The city and Dr. Somers finally settled in 1893, the last of the claims arising from the 1888 act to be resolved. Perhaps seeking to justify the delay, the city rather self-righteously reported that they had paid Somers $9,800 less than the commissioners' award.[27]

It was common at this time for unwanted houses to be sold and moved intact to other nearby lots. The practice made good economic sense, as labor was relatively cheap and house materials expensive: in Cambridge as many as sixty each year

4.10 The brick house built in 1859 by Frederic Tudor on Fresh Pond Farm for John Barker, his farm manager, was the only building of substance retained by the water board, which carried out repairs and then used it as a home for its employees. It remained on the reservation until it was finally demolished in 1971 (the time of this photograph), a lingering vestige of the ice industry.
Arthur Krim photograph, Cambridge Historical Commission.

were duly bought, jacked up from their foundations, and pulled by horses or oxen to vacant lots elsewhere.[28] According to the superintendent's report, the "old Somers' house" (presumably Fresh Pond Farm itself) was sold and relocated, although there are no definite records of where it went. Certainly one house that had been owned by the Tudor Ice Company was moved to the Belmont side of Blanchard Road in 1893, and it remained there for eighty years.[29]

Although ice traders were fair game, there seems to have been some reluctance to evict the Sisters of St. Joseph, only recently arrived at the former Fresh Pond Hotel. A local newspaper felt the need to urge the board to acquire the property, however "excellent" the school, as the need to safeguard the water from "inevitable contamination" by sewage was of "much greater importance."[30] In fact the city had, just a few days previously, taken the former hotel and its grounds by eminent domain. The following year, the city settled with the sisters on what it saw as "an amicable basis."[31] The sisters voted to accept $40,750 from the city for their land and buildings (almost twice what they had paid for the estate five years previously).

June 1891 saw the last commencement at the former hotel. The building was acquired by ex-alderman Parry, moved to Lake View Avenue, and converted to apartments, where it remains today (see figure 2.12). By October that year the sisters,

their pupils, and the novices had all left Fresh Pond. It is difficult to tell what the sisters thought of their enforced move: their annals just record in a matter-of-fact way that, on June 8, 1889, the city took possession of the estate. It appears as a single-line entry among notes about day-to-day matters of examinations, retreats, rehearsals, and visitors.[32] Any regret at being forced to leave their "Fresh Pond days" behind them was probably tempered by the knowledge that their new building in Brighton was to be "one of the finest of its kind in the city . . . built after the most modern and approved styles of architecture."[33]

In 1888 the city took by eminent domain the Gay family estate from the heirs of William and Rosella Gay, whose family had in 1826 acquired two farmhouses built in the 1660s by John Holden on the west shores of the pond. The buildings were probably razed.

The Bright family had owned land at Fresh Pond since the Revolutionary War. Their property abutted a cove that was known for a long time as Bright's Nook (now Little Fresh Pond). Joseph Bright, a veteran of the Continental Army, had built a homestead there around 1781. His son Josiah had farmed the land and harvested ice in a small way from Fresh Pond around the turn of the nineteenth century. The city acquired the Cambridge portion of the Bright estate in 1889 and, in the following year, bought the remainder, some thirteen acres of land just over the new Belmont town line. Within another year, Cambridge had obtained legislative permission to annex this piece of land as well.

With all this acquisition, the city solicitor was "constantly engaged"[34] in litigation from the various land takings. Undeterred, the city continued to acquire land into the 1890s. In 1892 it took part of Strawberry Hill (the site of the "inferior" workers' houses), auctioned off the houses for relocation elsewhere, and made plans to build a public road outside the reservoir grounds. Local residents were apparently "up in arms" about the house auction, as it necessitated the removal of several "handsome shade trees" to allow the houses to be moved.[35] In 1897 the board acquired the Fitchburg railroad as it passed through the reservation for $9,200, so that it now owned "every foot of land" in the area.[36]

The Loss of Great Pond Rights

In the short third section of the 1888 act, the Commonwealth relinquished all rights and controls over Fresh Pond, and gave the city "power to prevent all persons and animals from entering in, upon or over the land and waters."[37] Thus were the Great Pond rights surrendered.

The city did not enforce all of its new-found rights at Fresh Pond immediately, and it encountered problems when it tried to do so. Fowling apparently had largely ceased before the city took control of the shore, simply because the waterfowl had deserted the area. Any gunners who did appear after the city acquired the land, hoping for some sport, were dissuaded by policemen patrolling the shoreline. As a result, the birds quickly reestablished themselves at Fresh Pond. They were helped by increasing supplies of fish, from a ban on fishing, and by the new fountain, which kept a small area of open water even in the winter.[38] Once the number of birds had grown substantially, fishing was reintroduced. It was allowed between 4 am and

4.12 The city met opposition to its 1889 ban on skating, as this photograph from January 1892 makes clear. The fence circling the reservoir had been installed in 1888 as soon as the Commonwealth surrendered its Great Pond rights, but it clearly did not always deter people from the pond. It was probably intended more to protect carriages from the water. Within six months of this photograph being taken, all the Fresh Pond Ice Company icehouses, visible in the background, had been demolished.
Photograph by Henry L. Rand—Number 5382—from the Southwest Harbor Public Library Photographic Collection.

8 am, the hours chosen by the city to encourage early rising,[39] perhaps out of some paternalistic sense that exercise at daybreak would bolster its citizens' moral fiber. But by 1898 the birds had become so numerous that the policemen themselves were firing blanks in an attempt to scare them away.

Swimming and boating appear to have been banned during the bitter fights with Belmont over annexation in the late 1870s. In 1889 the city made an abortive attempt to ban skating on the pond. It had for so long been a favorite pastime of Harvard students that the undergraduate newspaper encouraged readers to lobby against the decision:

> The city of Cambridge, for some incomprehensible reason, has forbidden any one to skate on Fresh Pond this year. At first it was thought that this action was taken for the sake of preventing persons from venturing on the ice before it was strong enough to bear. But now that the ice is four or six inches thick, this excuse for forbidding skating is no longer plausible. . . . Now, there is a double incentive for daring boys to skate on the Pond in defiance of the policeman who patrols the shore. . . . Besides, many men wait till evening, when they can enjoy the fine ice on Fresh Pond uninterrupted rather than struggle over the rough ice on the Glacialis in the afternoon. If the policeman was paid to warn men away from the thin ice he would be doing a much more useful work, and the splendid ice on Fresh Pond could be enjoyed by every one. The regulation that forbids the enjoyment of perfectly safe ice seems to us more than nonsensical—it is unjust and outrageous—and we hope some appeal will be made to the mayor to abolish it.[40]

Such complaints seem to have been effective, as an image shows people freely skating on the pond three years later. It was not until 1899 that the water board was finally able to report that skating had been permanently forbidden on Fresh Pond.

Public Works

The water in Fresh Pond was not at this time filtered or treated to improve its purity: cleaning was effected simply by storing the water for some time in the reservoir, so that any unwanted particles gradually sank to the bottom. This approach required a number of activities to ensure the water was pure enough for drinking, and the water board energetically embarked on all of them.[41] First it was necessary to ensure that the water entering the reservoir was as unpolluted as possible: hence the board's concern to remove any buildings and prevent any activities that might allow pollution into Fresh Pond's watershed.

The water needed to be made consistently deep, because troublesome vegetative growths could thrive in shallow coves and contaminate the supply. This was a major risk in a natural lake such as Fresh Pond, with its reedy coves and gently sloping banks. The coves known as Eames' Nook and Gay's Nook (both named after former ice traders), to the west of the pond, were therefore filled in to grade. The artificial cove that Frederic Tudor had created between his two icehouses to the northeast of the reservoir was similarly filled in. Fortuitously for the board, when the Boston Ice Company buildings were torn down, the bricks, although sold, were never collected, and so the board was able to dump them into Tudor's cove as fill. Conversely, Boathouse Nook to the south was dug out to increase its depth by some three feet, old boathouses were removed, and willow trees on the shore's edge were cut down.

Black's Nook had been so "foul" a water source for so long that the board took particular action to try to stem its polluting effects on the reservoir. Since 1876 attempts had been made to clean it out. When it became clear that this would not succeed, the board installed a dam to close the nook off from the main water supply, with a sluiceway and gates to allow ice trader Mrs. Mary Black to continue to float ice from the main pond into her icehouse.

In 1886, the board bought Mary Black's icehouse and two acres of land and embarked enthusiastically on filling the nook to grade. By 1889 filling was well underway. Within three years it appeared the work was going to be successful and the superintendent reported that he did not expect to have to refer to Black's Nook again "as being in existence."[42] But two years later the board was adding some 700 cubic yards of fill daily and it seemed to be making little difference. One summer evening a large section of the imported fill suddenly sank about seventeen feet and, a hundred feet away, the muddy bottom of the swampy ground of the nook bulged up some thirty-five feet into the air.[43] Surprised and alarmed, the board arranged for soundings to be taken, to try to work out how deep the mud was, and to ascertain its quality.[44] It seems that the soundings did not help: the following year, 1895, the board admitted defeat and abandoned attempts to fill Black's Nook.

Elsewhere, however, the board's work on the shoreline did have the necessary effect. The final step was to add some protection, to ensure that the newly formed steep banks of raw earth could withstand the eroding action of the water.

4.13 The naturally occurring coves to the west of the pond known as Bright's Nook (in the foreground) and Eames' Nook (behind), photographed around the time of the commencement of the water board's improvement work, c. 1884. The large stones of the new riprap edging are just visible on the sloping bank. To prevent vegetative growths that could contaminate the water, Eames' Nook was completely filled in, while a gravel dyke was installed to separate the larger Bright's Nook from the main body of water. It was renamed the Lily Pond (now Little Fresh Pond).
Cambridge Water Department Collection, Cambridge Historical Commission.

4.14 A sketch of Mary Black's property at Black's Nook, 1886. She had been running an ice company on the shores of the nook since the death of her husband, William. The icehouse and surrounding land were bought by the city in 1886, to allow work to begin on the carriage drive. The city subsequently also acquired her dwelling house and grounds; the house was moved to a now unknown destination. To the right of the sketch is the conduit that brought water of "doubtful quality" from adjacent ponds into the reservoir. Minutes of the City of Cambridge Water Board, 1886.

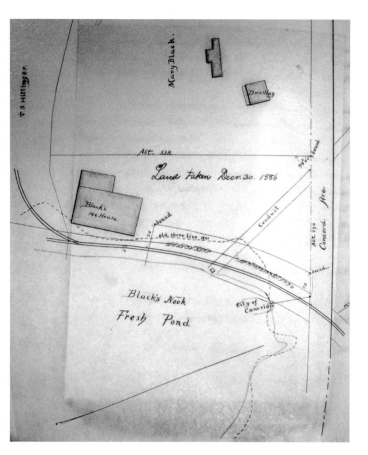

This was done by creating a uniformly sloping border of heavy stones all around the edge (commonly known as *riprap*). Work on this started as early as 1878. Now, as the water board completed its major program of work, the entire shoreline was to be protected by riprap. This task in itself changed the shape, as well as the appearance, of the reservoir: it was easier to build the new stone banks on straight stretches of shoreline, or regular curves, rather than on the naturally undulating shape of the water's edge. And so much of the Fresh Pond shoreline acquired a simpler, more geometric outline as a result of the riprap process. The board was pleased with the result, describing the new lines of the shore as "true and uniform."[45]

The board also decided to tackle the marshy ground that surrounded much of Fresh Pond, so that "instead of the stagnant, slimy water . . . in close proximity to our reservoir, we shall have a clean green field."[46] The annual reports of the late 1880s and early 1890s are full of descriptions of the hundreds of acres of land that were cleared of trees, filled, graded, and then covered with lawn, to create "neat," "clean," "attractive" areas: these three adjectives occur again and again in the water board's descriptions of the work it was undertaking.

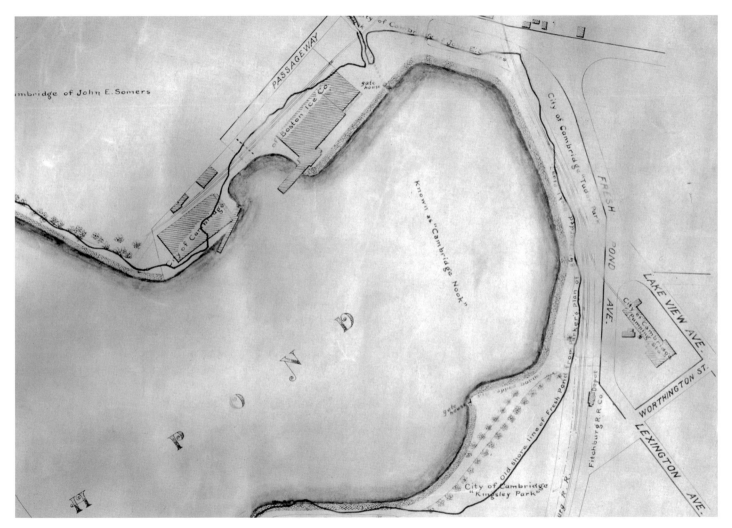

4.15 The 1888 Barbour plan reveals an abundance of detail about the landscape at that time. Here a detail from the eastern side of the pond shows the thick, pale gray line that marks the newly riprapped edges of the reservoir, and the solid black line of the more irregular shoreline as it existed in 1841. At the top of the image it is clear that the icehouses built by Frederic Tudor (and subsequently acquired by the Boston Ice Company) were constructed largely on land filled in by the Ice King. The gated cove he created between the icehouses is still visible. Further right, between the railroad tracks and Fresh Pond Avenue is Tudor Park, with the "palace" of a pumping station just the other side of the road. Tudor Park was created in the late 1870s on a narrow strip of land donated for the purpose by Tudor's heirs. It was graded with material dredged from the pond, covered with loam and lawn, and planted with sixty-six Scotch elm and maple trees. The water board expressed the hope that it would become a place where Cambridge citizens would bring visitors and show off the source of their water supply with some pride. Further south is another plot of land, labeled Kingsley Park, also developed as public parkland by the board (now the site of the treatment plant and parking lot).
Courtesy Massachusetts Archives.

4.16 An 1899 view from the new drive around the pond, looking over the recently filled part of Black's Nook, toward the former Fresh Pond Farm, showing the bare slopes where some of the hill has been removed to provide fill for the reservoir.
Courtesy of the National Park Service, Frederick Law Olmsted National Historic Site.

4.17 A postcard showing some of the five-acre park created by the water board on land acquired in 1884 from Joseph Hittinger. The board removed Nathaniel Wyeth's vast brick icehouse, which had been on the site, and in 1887 replaced it with lawn and a double row of trees, marking out where the carriage drive would soon run. (It is clear from figure 4.15 that almost all of the land visible in this image was created by the ice traders filling in part of the pond.) The area was named Kingsley Park, after Chester Ward Kingsley, the first president of the Cambridge Water Board. Although an 1894 map suggests that virtually all the landscape around Fresh Pond became known as Kingsley Park, the name seems quickly to have been used principally to mean the promontory. Image after 1888.
Postcard Collection, Cambridge Historical Commission.

The sheer amount of gravel required as fill also affected the landscape at Fresh Pond. Some of it came from digging out shallow places in the reservoir and then using the gravel to build up banks elsewhere. But the majority came from cutting away the hills and ridges that surrounded the pond. The unwooded hills to the south and west of the reservoir were the main source, but some significant cutting of ridges and high ground was done throughout the reservation, including the former Fresh Pond Farm and the wooded slopes on the grove where the hotel had stood (see figure 1.6). All this was necessary to produce enough "clean gravel and stone, so as to make it a clean and proper reservoir."[47]

The Pleasure Drive

Originally seen as a barrier against pollution entering the water, a dyke and roadway had been planned around the shores of the reservoir since the 1870s. But the annexation and acquisition of the abutting land, and the major engineering works described above, lessened the need for the road for water quality purposes. Instead, the water board came to see it as a pleasure drive, intended for public recreation. Construction started in the mid-1880s. A twenty-foot-wide stretch of driveway was built from Boathouse Nook, near the Stony Brook supply pipe, around most of the south and west shores, to Black's Nook.

In 1888 the driveway was extended to the north and east. Another new driveway entrance was created from Concord Avenue (see figure 4.3). As the water board proudly reported, "When our roadway is completed all around the pond, which must come soon, the nearly three mile drive around our Fresh

4.18 Fountain Terrace, a new carriage drive entrance, was created over the Stony Brook supply pipe, allowing carriages to come in to the park from the south and gain an immediate view of the fountain. The bridge seen in this 1901 photograph was added when Huron Avenue was extended.
Courtesy of the National Park Service, Frederick Law Olmsted National Historic Site.

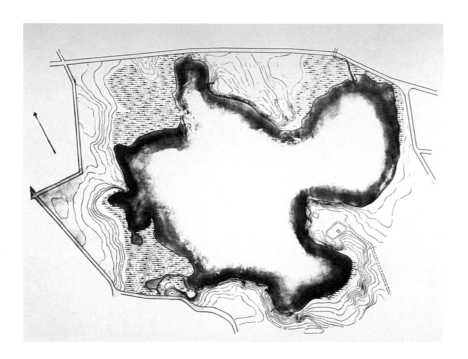

4.19 and **4.20** These two undated sketches illustrate the impact on Fresh Pond of the water board's work to protect its water supply. The shoreline before the engineering work (left) is undulating and marshy, with a number of natural coves. Afterward (below), the coves have been filled or separated from the reservoir, the shoreline is more regular, and some of the banks to the north, east and south have been excavated for fill. Around the edges of the water runs the new carriage road.
Frederick Law Olmsted Jr., "The Relation of Reservoirs to Parks," paper 32 in *American Park and Outdoor Art Association, 1899* (Boston: Rockwell & Churchill Press, 1899).

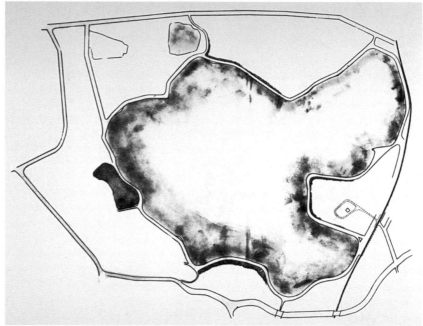

Pond reservoir will be one of the pleasantest to be found in the vicinity of Boston."[48] By the following year the board noted that, although it was not yet complete, the driveway was being increasingly used by carriages. It took four more years to finish, with sections added at the edge of the two former ice company properties and further work on the driveway through the grove. The water board also invested in new bridges and roads leading to Fresh Pond, to encourage visitors to come, and to provide easy access when they did so.[49] It is perhaps ironic that, even as the city was for the first time preventing public access to the water for recreation, it was trying so hard and investing so much money in attracting people into a new park around the shores. The board continued to report with pleasure that it was creating "one of the most attractive drives and walks in Boston."[50]

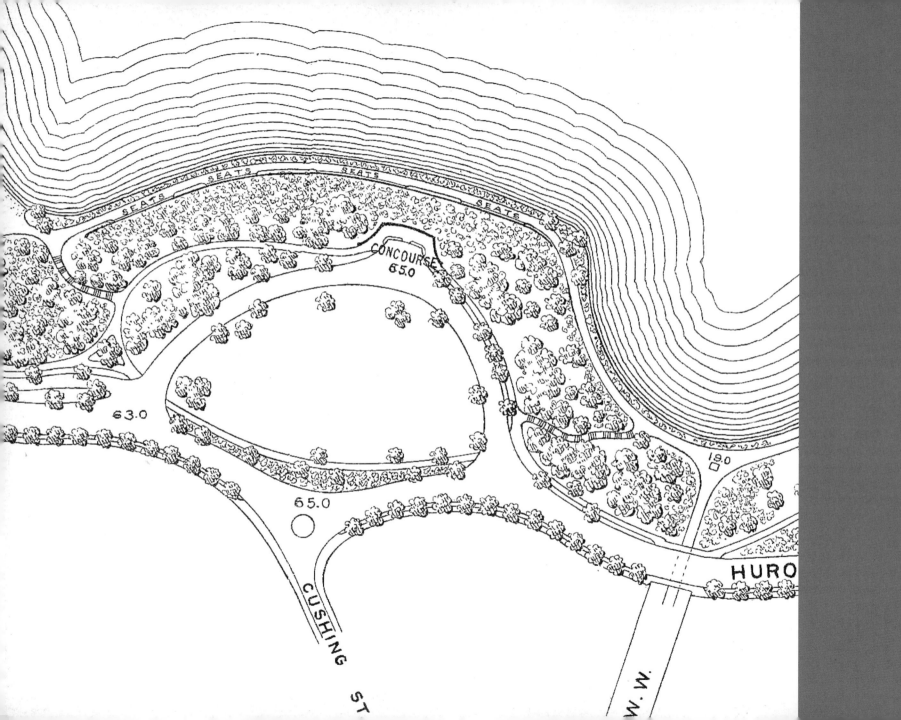

SEATS

SEATS

SEATS

SEATS

CONCOURSE
65.0

63.0

65.0

19.0

CUSHING ST

HURO

N. W.

5 Professional Design

This modern crowding into cities results in a counter invasion of the country; and it is just here that the special modern need of an art and profession of landscape gardening is first felt. How can we add roads . . . to natural landscape, without destroying the very thing in search of which we left the city? . . . How shall the public park, to which many hundreds or thousands will resort at one time, be so made and preserved as to be to all city dwellers a revelation of nature's beauty and peace?

Charles Eliot, 1889

In the nineteenth century, the traditional three professions (divinity, medicine, and the law) were joined by an increasing number of other specialized occupations that gradually established their own professional standing. Architects, civil engineers, and landscape designers all emerged as members of distinct professions and sought to define themselves as trusted experts in relation to the planning and construction of parks, roads, recreational facilities, and other parts of the built environment. To enhance their professional status, such occupations introduced vocational training and qualifications to impart and assess understanding of the necessary specialist knowledge, as well as a professional association or body to regulate, protect, and promote their area of work. There was soon a clear division of labor, with an increasing demarcation between members of the emerging professions and the unqualified amateur.

The Olmsted Firm

The instigator of landscape architecture as a profession was Frederick Law Olmsted. Active from the 1850s until around 1895, he remains the most famous and influential landscape architect that America has produced. New York's Central Park and Prospect Park, and Boston's Emerald Necklace, stand as testament to his enduring vision. Although now mainly regarded as the creator of the country's first and most beautiful pastoral parks, Olmsted's work was driven as much by social and political goals as aesthetic ones. He believed in the restorative powers of natural scenery, and he saw his work creating public parks as an essential part of the social reform movement, whose advocates believed that the "physical spaces humans occupy influence their patterns of behavior."[1] Memorably he described what he saw as a duty to help those who apparently could not help themselves: "The poor and the wicked need more than to be let alone."[2]

Olmsted strove to establish landscape design as a prestigious profession that worked with nature to produce fine art. His landscapes were seemingly untouched by human hands, while in fact being tightly managed to retain their naturalistic feel. His vision was of nature and humanity working in harmony, with human interventions ensuring a greater level of beauty, usefulness, and sustainability than nature could achieve on her own.[3] He was so successful at turning challenging urban sites into pastoral landscapes that often they were subsequently viewed as pieces of nature preserved, rather than brilliantly constructed systems. His life was to end sadly, with prolonged dementia, but not before he had identified and trained individuals who would carry on his landscape architecture business.

Charles Eliot, an apprentice and later a partner in Olmsted's firm, shared his view of the civilizing effects of landscape on the working classes, believing that exposure to nature had an impact "something like a moral revolution."[4] This view was based on seeing how public squares in Europe apparently fostered health and virtue among those who used them. Echoing the sentiments of many social reformers, he pressed for the creation of public parks, not on aesthetic grounds, but because they were "as necessary for the preservation of the civilization of cities as are sewers or street lights."[5] A Cambridge native and son of the president of Harvard, Eliot was a landscape designer, regional planner, historian, writer, critic, early environmentalist, and strikingly successful advocate of landscape conservation. He achieved an extraordinary amount in ten short years, before his death from meningitis at the age of thirty-seven. As well as running his own successful design practice in Boston, he was instrumental in persuading the legislature to set up two organizations to acquire and save open land in metropolitan Boston and to make it accessible to the public. The first was the Trustees of Public Reservations (the organization later dropped the word *Public* from its name), which could hold, protect, and preserve special places on behalf of the public. Incorporated in 1891, just fifteen months after Eliot first proposed the idea, it worked by encouraging donations of land, and it directly inspired the creation of the National Trust in England two years later. The second was the Metropolitan Park Commission, a new part of the state government that was to create a regional network of public open

5.1 Charles Eliot, aged about thirty-two, c. 1892. One of the first landscape architects from New England, Eliot prepared carefully for his chosen career with postgraduate study at Harvard's Bussey Institute, a professional apprenticeship under Frederick Law Olmsted, and a period of extensive travel and study through the United States and Europe to further his understanding of the natural and designed landscape. Courtesy DCR Archives.

spaces to promote the health and happiness of the inhabitants of metropolitan Boston. Having done so much to safeguard important landscapes for the public, Eliot was persuaded in 1893 to rejoin the Olmsted firm as a partner.

After Eliot's premature death in 1897, the firm was headed by Olmsted's stepson, John Charles Olmsted, who was senior partner until his death in 1920. With a flair for business management, he turned what became Olmsted Brothers into the biggest landscape architecture practice in the world. He continued his stepfather's quest to establish landscape design as a prestigious profession, and to distinguish the skills and experience necessary for its practice. He was a founder member and the first president of the American Society of Landscape Architects (ASLA).[6]

John's half-brother was originally called Henry Perkins, but his father renamed him Frederick Law Olmsted Jr., a sign of his impassioned wish that he should carry on the family name and fully establish the status of the new profession. After his father's retirement, he became a partner in the firm and, at John's death, senior partner. Like John, he was a founding member of ASLA, and he served twice as its president. He was also instrumental in establishing the first landscape architecture university course, at Harvard, where he taught, and he served on the McMillan Commission that was appointed to reinterpret the central core of Washington, D.C.[7]

By the time the brothers were running the Olmsted firm, there was a clear division between designers (who publicly portrayed themselves as artists, or guardians of aesthetics) and engineers, who established their role as practical scientists. Such distinctions lay both professions open to accusations of, on the one hand, being involved merely in surface decorations, and, on the other, of being uncultured and uninterested in art or aesthetics.

Opinions of Fresh Pond Park

In 1894 the Cambridge Water Board commissioned Olmsted, Olmsted and Eliot, landscape architects, to work at Fresh Pond reservation. The board believed that it had already carried out all the major engineering work necessary to turn the landscape into a public park. It now sought professional design advice on ways of beautifying the borders around the reservoir.

Charles Eliot was the partner first in charge of the project. Cambridge municipal clients were generally wary of the public parks movement: they resisted investing in parks that might prove of more benefit to Boston residents, and in particular they feared metropolitan cooperation that could lead to the city being subsumed into Boston, as had happened to the formerly independent towns of Roxbury, Dorchester, Brighton, and Charlestown. But with his family background, local roots, and network of influential supporters, Eliot proved uniquely able to secure the trust of these Cambridge clients, and he brought several of them to the Olmsted firm when he joined as partner. He already knew Fresh Pond from his work for the Cambridge and Metropolitan Park Commissions. Under the guidance of Eliot and journalist Sylvester Baxter, the latter commission began in 1893 to establish a regional system of open public spaces or reservations around metropolitan Boston. A contemporary newspaper reported that one of the new Metropolitan Park Commissioners had visited Cambridge and

5.2 The shoreline to the northeast of the pond, looking toward the pumping station. This 1899 photograph shows the completed pleasure drive, a fence along its outer edge, the post-and-rail guard fence protecting the water, and the large stones of the riprapped banks. Charles Eliot criticized what he saw as the essentially urban nature of the new park, with the "incongruously stiff lines" of the engineer's work on the shores, and the road that seemed to be "obtruded" as if it were the whole purpose of the park.
Courtesy of the National Park Service, Frederick Law Olmsted National Historic Site.

said "no-one could have done better in laying out the Fresh Pond drives and Kingsley Park than the water board has."[8]

Eliot clearly did not agree with this assessment of the board's parkmaking. When providing proposals to the Cambridge Park Commission for locating public parks in the city, he wrote a separate letter about Fresh Pond, which can be read as an implicit plea to the commission to take over the management of this landscape ("the largest open space Cambridge can ever hope to possess"). He pressed for the repair of what he saw as its newly disfiguring features (see figure 5.2). Eliot felt strongly about the need to restore the "natural scenery" at Fresh Pond because he saw it as a "singularly unified, and therefore a singularly pleasing landscape."[9] Whatever the politics of the matter, the commission did not take on Fresh Pond, but it did formally record a wish that the water board should seize "the opportunity [that] is given to them to make it the gem of the entire park system."[10]

Frederick Law Olmsted Jr. also described the firm's initial reaction to the landscape at Fresh Pond.[11] While recognizing that much of the engineering work carried out by the board had been essential, he was critical of its aesthetic impact. The criticism was part of a wider argument that taxpayers' money would be better spent if city reservoirs were also professionally planned from the outset as public water parks. Olmsted argued that it was unreasonable to expect hydraulic engineers to tackle the challenges involved in creating a successful park; their expertise lay elsewhere, and they needed the help and advice of the newly emerging profession of landscape architects.

Both Eliot and Olmsted Jr. used the term *natural* to describe the scenery at Fresh Pond before the board's engineering works. By this time, the word had begun to take on some of the rhetorical complexities that it embodies today. Nature was imbued with such a range of meanings (from an absolute moral standard, synonymous with reality and goodness, to a corrupting, brutal wilderness), that the word *natural* was used to seize the moral high ground in support of a number of often conflicting arguments. Eliot thus criticized a newspaper writer who complained that the Metropolitan Park Commission was "defeating nature": he firmly pointed out that the truly natural state of the landscape was primitive forest, which no one was arguing should be restored; the land had been modified many times by many owners and the commission was simply adapting it for current use.[12] So Eliot and Olmsted Jr. used the word *natural* deliberately and carefully about Fresh Pond, to emphasize the social reformers' argument that parks were a refuge from the city and so needed to avoid the stiff, hard lines that characterized industrial or urban settings. The word also implied that landscape architects had the insight and training to balance aesthetics with practicality, whereas the engineers at Fresh Pond had produced something useful but not beautiful.

Feeling strongly that Fresh Pond needed much more of a comprehensive program of work than the water board envisaged, Eliot asked for approval of certain conditions before accepting the commission. These included agreement that the purpose of the work was to create "an agreeable landscape" for the "pleasure of visitors" with the water as the main feature, but with the option to add other means of recreation, including more roads and walks. Eliot also sought agreement to the relocation of the carriageway in a number of places, by bringing it up onto some of the bluffs above the water, by buying

5.3 and 5.4 The "original" pathway (above) along the north shore of Fresh Pond, at the foot of a hill covered with beech and birch trees; and (below) the wooded shores of the grove. Both images appeared in an article by Frederick Law Olmsted Jr. that used Fresh Pond as an example of a reservoir where the parkmaking had initially been part of the engineering work. These undated photographs suggested that Fresh Pond was an untouched pastoral landscape before the board's intervention, while the accompanying descriptions refer to the "natural" or "original" condition of the shoreline, its hills covered with native trees and the only sign of human presence "a charming narrow path or cartway." There were just fleeting acknowledgments of the previous industrial and recreational use of the land: the shoreline in one spot had been widened by the "gradual deposit of sawdust" from an icehouse; the grove was once a favorite picnic place for Harvard students.
Frederick Law Olmsted Jr., "The Relation of Reservoirs to Parks," paper 32 in *American Park and Outdoor Art Association, 1899* (Boston: Rockwell & Churchill Press, 1899).

5.5 and **5.6** Two 1899 photographs of the pond, after the board's engineering works were complete. Above is the new sharp turn at Wyeth Point, where part of the hillside on the grove was cut away to allow construction of the road along the shoreline, leaving a steep, raw bank. Below, an established oak tree near Black's Nook had been left perched and dying on an artificial mound, once the gravel bank behind was excavated, to provide fill for boggy areas elsewhere in the park. Olmsted Jr. described the impact of the work as "artificial," "unhappy," "inharmonious," even "painful." Frederick Law Olmsted Jr., "The Relation of Reservoirs to Parks," paper 32 in *American Park and Outdoor Art Association, 1899* (Boston: Rockwell & Churchill Press, 1899).

more land, or by extending the shoreline into the water. Finally he looked for assurance that various activities carried out by the board could be unpicked, especially some of the grading and the straightening of the shoreline.[13]

The water board was told the contents of Eliot's letter and subsequently visited the pond with him. Clearly the firm must then have received some sort of assurance about extending the scope of its work at Fresh Pond, as within a few months Olmsted, Olmsted and Eliot had embarked on what was to be a lengthy working relationship with the Cambridge Water Board. By January 1895, there was a formal contract in place for the firm to provide "designs and plans for the improvement of the land upon the borders of Fresh Pond and for professional advice in connection therewith."[14]

Design Vision for the Landscape

In 1897, the firm produced a plan for the whole reservation. The carriage road was to be substantially relocated, remaining close to the shoreline only in the narrow northeastern strip adjacent to Tudor Park. From there, going northward, it rose up the hill to the north of the pond, where Fresh Pond Farm had once stood. Here a refectory or lunching place would offer views through trees of the water below. The road then briefly returned to the water's edge before swinging across the meadowland to the west of the pond and climbing to the top of the

5.7 The General Plan for Fresh Pond Park, 1897, which proposed some significant changes to the landscape installed by the water board. Doubtless inspired largely by the thinking of Charles Eliot, it was submitted shortly after his death and so bore the new name of the firm, F.L. & J.C. Olmsted. It was a comprehensive program of work with the aim of providing access to natural scenery, including views over the reservoir, by bicycle, on foot, and in carriages.
With permission of the Harvard Map Collection, Harvard College Library.

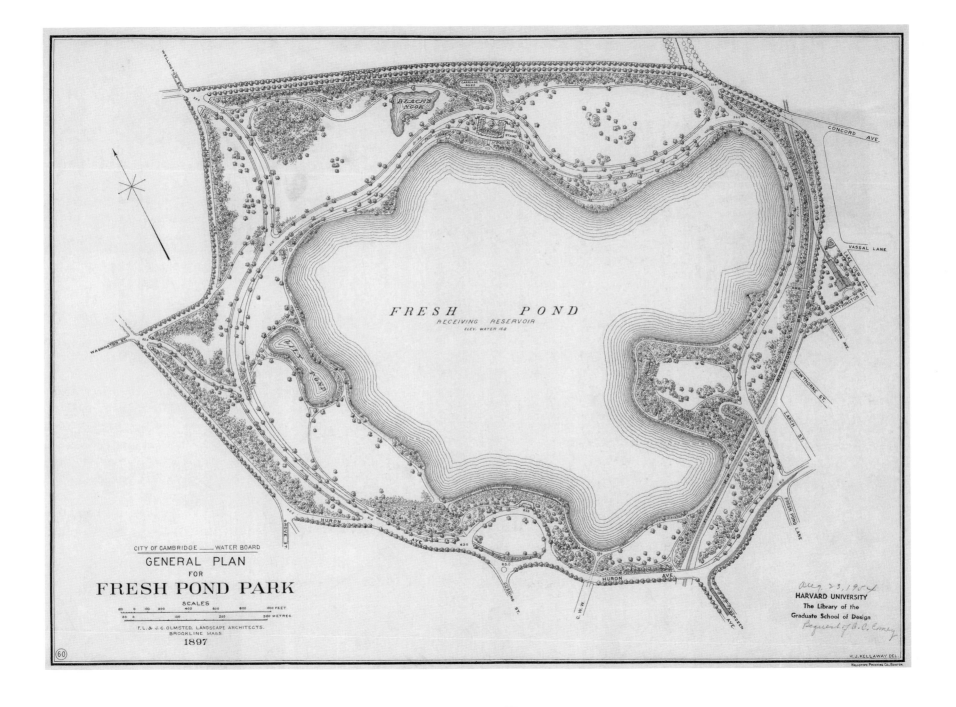

CITY OF CAMBRIDGE — WATER BOARD

GENERAL PLAN
FOR
FRESH POND PARK

FRESH   POND
RECEIVING RESERVOIR
ELEV. WATER 18.8

SCALES

F. L. & J. C. OLMSTED, LANDSCAPE ARCHITECTS.
BROOKLINE MASS.
1897

high bluff to the south. Here a gathering space or concourse was to provide dramatic views down onto the water. The slope would be planted with just low shrubs and vines, with perhaps a few small trees at the foot of the bluff, to preserve the commanding views. The road remained elevated as it passed across the grove and eventually rejoined the shoreline near Tudor Park. The firm believed that the drive would be made more interesting by these changes of level and by the mix of water views and woodland groves. The changes also meant that many views of the water would not be marred by the sight of the road trundling monotonously around its edge.

As well as the new carriage road, the plan produced by the Olmsted firm proposed a circular path for people on foot. This would more or less follow the water's edge, but it would be considerably narrower than the existing driveway, with its route softened by sloping ground and planting. At some spots there would be a few yards of turf and shrubs between the path and water's edge; at others the path would be right on the shoreline. Near Tudor Park and on part of the northern shore, it would run alongside the carriage road; elsewhere it would be separate and provide opportunities for quiet contemplation of the scenery without the distracting noise of passing carriages. Between the footpath and the road was to be a separate bicycle path.

The plan also proposed introducing a more varied shoreline, by breaking up the overly straight edges, replacing the riprap with more natural beaches, and introducing a mixture of plant material along the water's edge.[15] This would include overhanging shrubs, trailing vines, and a few trees, whose reflections in the water would add to the beauty of the landscape. Charles Eliot had even considered urging the retention

5.8 The area to the west of the pumping station, 1899, where the Olmsted firm's plan called for the road to be retained and widened (by filling somewhat into the reservoir) so that it would be broad enough to allow for the removal of the guard fence without any danger of carriages slipping into the water. The riprap was to be replaced by a sandy or gravel beach.
Courtesy of the National Park Service, Frederick Law Olmsted National Historic Site.

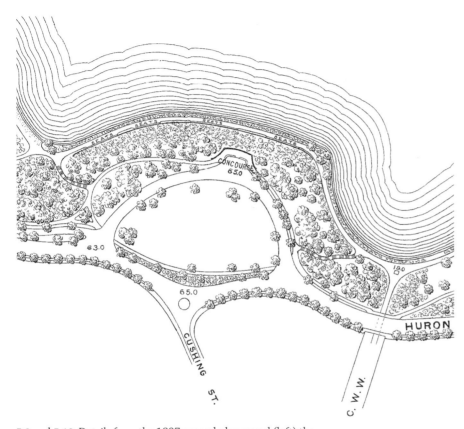

5.9 and **5.10** Details from the 1897 general plan reveal (left) the sweeping new carriage road proposed for the bluffs to the south (now Glacken Field) and, along the shoreline below, a footpath with seats to allow for contemplation of the water. Kingsley Park (right) was to be reserved very largely for those on foot, with a series of meandering pathways, including one around the shoreline, a pergola, a large shelter, and two look-out points.
With permission of the Harvard Map Collection, Harvard College Library.

5.11 and **5.12** These undated elevations show the area west of the reservoir, around the Lily Pond (now Little Fresh Pond). Above is the landscape after the water board's work, the dotted line showing where the hill had been excavated. All such raw banks, where gravel had been removed for fill, would be covered with loam and planted with shrubbery and vines. Below is a study of how part of the same area would look after planting. Note the intention to move the carriage road from the edge of the reservoir to the top of the hill.
Frederick Law Olmsted Jr., "The Relation of Reservoirs to Parks," paper 32 in *American Park and Outdoor Art Association, 1899* (Boston: Rockwell & Churchill Press, 1899).

or re-creation of some of the nooks filled in by the board,[16] but apparently this idea had been discounted by the time the general plan was produced.

Extensive planting was proposed: even an initial plant list, produced probably in 1895, suggested that over 108,000 plants would be needed at Fresh Pond, most of them native, including forest trees such as liriodendrons (tulip trees), large shrubs like the staghorn sumac, and fast-growing material, such as willows, that could withstand the wet ground while more choice specimens established themselves.

Reality on the Ground

The vision of the Olmsted firm was never to be fully realized. There was a fundamental disagreement between the board and the firm over the role of the landscape architects. This is apparent from the early correspondence quoted above, and it rumbles on throughout the relationship without ever really being addressed or resolved. Following the approach of the firm's founder, Olmsted, Olmsted and Eliot believed that they had authority to create a working landscape system, complete with carefully designed parkland, drainage systems, circulation paths, and even public transportation routes. The board, however, clearly commissioned them for some surface aesthetics: the firm was to "fine tune" the grading and produce decorative planting plans.

Evidence of this disparity appears from time to time. For instance, the Olmsted firm was aware that the polluted water from Richardson's Pond to the west and Cider Mill Pond to the south still flowed into Fresh Pond. Members of the firm wrote several letters proposing solutions, including rerouting the water to Alewife Brook or creating holding lagoons. After several noncommittal replies, a member of the water board finally wrote back in exasperation that the firm had no "province" in the matter. It was not responsible for drainage and should just get on with the landscape: "You were employed to lay out the ground for Park purposes or to beautify the property."[17]

Similarly, early on in their thinking, the firm wrote with two initial proposals for the board's consideration. One outlined the major work necessary to relocate the carriage drive along the bluffs to the south. The other was a proposal for a plant nursery, to produce the substantial amount of material that would be necessary, and an initial planting list. The board discussed the letter and agreed to the nursery and the purchase of the suggested plants, but it made no obvious comment on the more substantial proposals for the carriage road.[18]

It is also clear that the board's attention simply was elsewhere. Busy with the plans to create new supply and storage reservoirs at Hobbs Brook and Payson Park, the board minutes of the time are full of discussions of land acquisitions, pipe laying, and major contractual issues. Occasional mentions of the work of the Olmsted firm appear, but only in passing, and letters are usually just noted and filed, or passed to someone to take action, with no decision or input from the board.

Only one member of the board seems to have spent any significant time on the Olmsted firm's work, and he became its only real advocate. Stillman Kelley had joined the water board in 1894 and was soon appointed to head the committee on improvements around Fresh Pond. In that capacity he met and corresponded frequently with Charles Eliot and other

members of the Olmsted firm. It was Kelley who lobbied for sufficient funds to be made available for the firm's proposals and to whom the board usually remitted any decisions. In his absence (and he was away from work because of stress for a long time around 1897), little was achieved. John Charles Olmsted acknowledged his role with some gratitude: "We have very much appreciated your invaluable services in securing the appropriations for the improvements of the borders of Fresh Pond and fully believe that practically nothing would have been accomplished if you had not taken the personal interest in the matter that you have."[19] Kelley was to retire from the board in 1903. Although he lobbied the mayor and some aldermen to take an interest in the park after he had gone, responsibility for the improvements at Fresh Pond passed to the Committee on Reservoirs and Pumping, whose name suggests that its main role and interests fell elsewhere.

5.13 Kingsley Park in 1897, at the time of the production of the Olmsted firm's general plan. The water board published this photograph in celebration of its new storage reservoir at Payson Park, which came on line that year: its new gatehouse is just visible to the right. *City of Cambridge Water Board Annual Report,* 1897.

As well as a lack of commitment from most of the board, members of the Olmsted firm also grappled with the political realities of working for a part of city government. First, as so often with such jobs, there was not enough funding available for the work. The water board had borrowed some two million dollars over the past few years, so the need to repay that debt meant there was little spare money. In addition, board members were committed to using only surplus water receipts on their plans to improve the borders, which limited the amount they could spend. Even then, they needed formal appropriations from the city council, who could always choose to use the surplus receipts for other work. The city council was itself short of money, and tax rates had already been raised to fund the work of the new Cambridge park department. As a result, in some years there were simply no appropriations at all for the work and the landscape architects had to sit on their hands and wait.

Even when a few thousand dollars was made available, the Olmsted firm was always trying to keep down costs, so that as much as possible could be achieved. Many of the grading plans were amended to reduce the amount of extra fill or loam required. The grading and walks around Black's Nook, for instance, were originally designed partly to preserve "the large elms on the hill." Later the Olmsted firm suggested reducing the levels and sacrificing at least one elm, simply to save the cost of fill.[20] Large parts of the plans were never implemented, such as the refectory where Fresh Pond Farm had once stood, or the concourse on the bluffs to the south. Those elements that were attempted were sometimes left rough and unfinished, with poor quality materials used. This paucity of com-

mitment and funding led Stillman Kelley sometimes to feel that his attempts were all but hopeless: "I am so discouraged on this Park matter that I have hardly any courage to drive around it, but possibly it may come out all right in the future so I will hang on."[21]

There were other political issues as well. The mayor sometimes intervened, pressing for changes he believed would be popular. At one point, Mayor Sortwell wanted the banks on the grove graded and indicated that he would in return "favor granting the Board sufficient appropriation" to complete the roadway.[22] When this did not happen, he raised technical accounting objections that for a while halted all work at Fresh Pond. Water board members themselves were not above making design suggestions that varied dramatically from the Olmsted firm's plan. Early on, they proposed some new ponds in the meadow complete "with a nice large fountain."[23] Later John Charles Olmsted made a plea that a new appropriation should not be "frittered away in executing the ideas and whims of various Commissioners and others as to attractive and popular features."[24]

The board was also clearly alive to popular opinion, at least as reported in the local newspapers. For example, the Olmsted firm proposed border mounds or ridges around the edge of the park to create a sense of seclusion and to block noise from the roads. It was to be an essentially separate refuge from its surroundings, a work of art to be admired and enjoyed for its own sake. But the newspapers complained that border mounds would also close off the views into the park that were currently enjoyed by surrounding residents. The board promptly indicated that the mounds should be reduced or abandoned.

5.14 A 1901 view of the Stony Brook fountain. The notice proclaims, "No scorching allowed on this driveway." (Scorching was a term used at that time to mean bicycling at high speed.) The popularity of such activity probably prevented the implementation of the landscape architects' plans for a more meandering carriage road.
Courtesy of the National Park Service, Frederick Law Olmsted National Historic Site.

5.15 An 1899 view of one of the raw gravel banks on the grove. The substantial cutting done by the board to create the roadway had left steep slopes and had apparently so dried the soil that many of the hemlocks had died. As a result of public pressure, work started in 1904 to regrade the raw slopes and cover them with loam.
Courtesy of the National Park Service, Frederick Law Olmsted National Historic Site.

At this time, speedways for carriages and bicycles were popular: the Olmsted firm designed a mile-long driver's speedway on the Boston side of the Charles River Basin, which opened in 1899 and was in active use for over fifty years.[25] The long, flat, clear drive at Fresh Pond was apparently ideally suited for such racing: as early as 1895, the water board had been trying to discourage "fast bicycling" around the driveway.[26] Although not a fan of racing, the board seems to have appropriated the public interest in speedways in support of its wish not to unpick all the work it had done creating the driveway: it reported to the Olmsted firm that there was a "strong opinion in the Board and among the public in favor of retaining the road all around the margin."[27] This meant that almost none of the plans to relocate the carriage drive were ever implemented.

As a result of public opinion, the work schedule was altered as well: the board had originally wanted the grading and planting to progress systematically from area to area, finishing the plans for the west portion before starting elsewhere. But eventually, under pressure from the mayor and facing something of a "public clamor,"[28] it decided to undertake some major work at Kingsley Park.

The Olmsted firm was not fully in control in other ways as well. It was not in any sense what we today would call a "design and build" company. Just as they were deliberately separating themselves from the distinct business of engineering, so Charles Eliot and the Olmsted brothers were trying to establish their position as trained professional designers, rather than artisans or gardeners. So, while members of the Olmsted firm often oversaw the installation of their plans, they did not generally provide or employ the labor. At Fresh Pond, the work was carried out by staff employed by the water board, under the direction of the superintendent. Frequently when a member of the firm visited Fresh Pond, he found that the plans were not being carried out correctly or at all. On one occasion the foreman was busy trying to reroute a major pathway because some pine trees had been incorrectly planted where the plans showed the path should be.[29]

Finally, the terrain itself proved a major challenge to the implementation of the Olmsted firm's plans. The combination of artificially sloped banks and low-lying marshland meant that much of the ground was either too dry (and steep) or too wet for plants to thrive. Throughout the fifteen years of the Olmsted firm's involvement at Fresh Pond, its correspondence is full of references to the difficulties this caused: the firm tried substantial regrading, land drains, catch basins, and planting trees on two-foot mounds. It lobbied for Alewife Brook to be cleared out so that the area south of Concord Avenue could drain into it. It even persuaded the water board to put a drain "surreptitiously" into Fresh Pond to take the storm water from the south and west.[30] But much of the ground remained wet, and many of the plantings struggled to establish themselves. The plants were also affected by the understandable reluctance of the board to fertilize the ground so close to the water supply.

What Was Achieved

Much of the time and money expended at Fresh Pond went for further grading work. Starting near the Lily Pond, the firm supervised work to change levels, add loam, and plant. It worked all along the northern border, adjacent to Concord Avenue, to

5.16 A 1904 image of the marshes just north of Fresh Pond, looking toward Watertown, showing the sort of boggy conditions faced by the board and the Olmsted firm.
Courtesy DCR Archives.

5.17 Work along Cushing Street, 1895, south of the pond, where the Olmsted firm's plan called for changes in level up to sixteen feet. Courtesy of the National Park Service, Frederick Law Olmsted National Historic Site.

the west and east of Black's Nook, through the entire western and southern borders, including the high bluffs at the south of the park (site of the proposed concourse), to the Fountain Terrace entrance, round to the railroad, and up to Kingsley Park. This grading was not simply refining the work previously carried out by the board. The Olmsted papers refer to changing levels in places by thirty feet (for instance, when reducing a knoll at the sharp corner in Huron Avenue).

Where the water board was not prepared to see major grading work, the landscape architects did what they could to soften the steep inclines and artificial banks. Raw slopes were covered with loam and planted with trailing vines and shrubs. Trees and bushes were added to banks that had previously just been turfed (and which had attracted Frederick Law Olmsted Jr.'s comment that "to find a more obviously artificial or inharmonious bank would require some search"[31]). The firm thought that the effect was much better, but that only regrading would make such a slope completely natural in appearance.

As part of the regrading, some of the proposed new paths and drives were laid out, at least to subgrade. It is not certain exactly how far this work extended, although figures 5.19 and 6.14 give some sense, and there are descriptions of the reworking of the entrance road at the far northwest corner[32] and of new driveways and paths to the west,[33] although even by 1904 they were still unfinished and rough.

As well as grading much of the reservation, the firm also produced extensive planting plans for almost the entire area, which were largely implemented.[34] Along the Concord Avenue boundary, there was a temporary screen of maples, sycamores, willows, and lindens, with more permanent plantings including

5.18 An artificial bank near the Huron Avenue entrance, showing how the landscape architects planted trees and shrubs through the turf to give a more harmonious appearance, 1899.
Courtesy of the National Park Service, Frederick Law Olmsted National Historic Site.

5.19 A 1947 aerial photograph of the northwest corner of the reservation, after much of the area had been covered by the municipal golf course, shows traces of the distinctive curves of the Olmsted firm's paths and driveways installed some fifty years earlier.
Eastern Aerial Surveys, Boston, Mass., Cambridge Historical Commission.

5.20 The slopes either side of the Fountain Terrace entrance were planted in spring 1901 with pines at the top and deciduous shrubs lower down, through grass.
Courtesy of the National Park Service, Frederick Law Olmsted National Historic Site.

plane trees, a range of oak species, walnuts, chestnuts, Kentucky coffee trees, and ash. Near the site of the proposed refectory the firm established a clump of beech trees and a selection of other plantings. Less successful was the planting of the low area in the northeast corner, which was too wet for trees to establish. Even some planted on mounds did not thrive.

A border grew "luxuriantly"[35] to the north of Black's Nook, and many shrubs were planted between the nook and the pond. Trees, shrubs, and plants (including hemlocks, birch, and oaks) were establishing in the northwest corner, along the new entrance roadway and in all the borders to the west of the reservation, giving what the water board described as "gratifying" results.[36] Along Huron Avenue were pines, elms, large honey locust trees, and some shrubs. At the base of the bluffs to the south, the extensive shrub planting included summersweet, ornamental pears, and viburnum. The pine plantations to the southeast thrived and needed thinning to reduce the risk of fire.

One hundred years later, an inventory identified a number of trees that still survived from the work of the Olmsted firm, including an area at the far northwest that the consultants called Olmsted Grove for the wealth of trees they believed originated from this time. They included beech, red oak, hackberry, tupelo, river birch, white birch, black birch, red maple, hop hornbeam, Kentucky coffee trees, and shagbark hickory.[37]

Perhaps the most enduring work that the Olmsted firm did for the water board was in Kingsley Park, carried out toward the end of its time at Fresh Pond. A plan to replant part of the grove with surplus stock thinned from the pine plantation plus some hemlocks, although only partly implemented in 1901, led a member of the firm to note that "the general appearance of Kingsley Park is greatly improved by the planting."[38]

The following fall heard the "clamor" for further improvements at Kingsley Park, and the board duly sought funds from the city council to do more work. It was 1904 before there was a suitable appropriation. The money was used to implement a grading plan approved by the board, which included making the slopes to the shore more gradual. It allowed them to soften the dangerous sharp bend in the road, known as Wyeth Point, that had been the cause of some accidents, as speeding carriage drivers could not see what was approaching from the other direction until too late. More trees and shrubs were planted, and some other trees were removed to open up the views. As ever, changes were made to the plans to keep costs down: the proposed bicycle path was omitted, while the footpaths, reduced to a width of just eight feet, were (in John Charles Olmsted's view) too narrow for a public park. Two look-out points were installed, to provide views of the water (although stones used for the parapets were less large and rugged than the Olmsted plans had specified).

Later the superintendent managed to obtain some funds for a drinking fountain that was installed on the left of the drive, just after the railroad bridge, and a "sanitary" among some bushes to the right. The Olmsted firm duly designed and commissioned the sanitary building that, with its concrete walls and red tile roof, was described by the board as "quite an ornamental structure."[39]

The final activity of the Olmsted firm on Kingsley Park was also its last intervention at Fresh Pond. It was the one place

5.21 A postcard of picnickers at the grove, c. 1908; the Olmsted firm's lookouts shown here were later replaced by the similar but rather larger structures that survive today.
Postcard Collection, Cambridge Historical Commission.

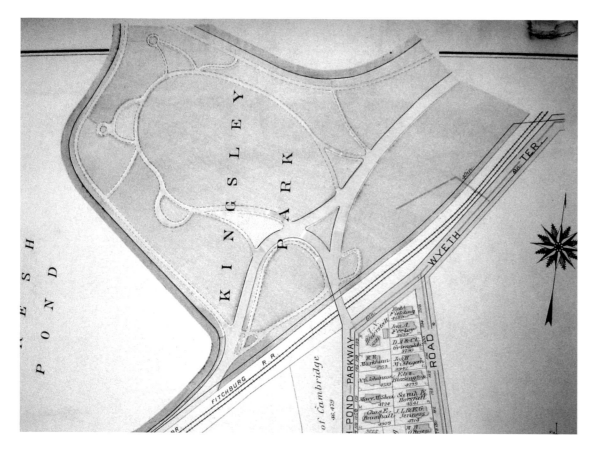

5.22 This 1916 map shows how far the landscape architects' plans for Kingsley Park were implemented, with the new carriage road away from the water's edge, footpaths along the shoreline and through the grove, and the two look-outs providing views of the water.
G.W. Bromley & Co.'s *Atlas of the City of Cambridge* (1916).

where, finally, it achieved Charles Eliot's wish to relocate the carriage road away from the water's edge. In 1908 a new road was built according to the firm's plans that passed through the eastern side of the grove. From the entrance, carriages could then drive in either direction, turning left toward the fountain or right toward Tudor Park. The original carriageway along the shore was turned into a walkway, and the greater part of the grove became a place for enjoyment on foot.

The Parkway

The Olmsted firm was also commissioned by the Metropolitan Park Commission to design Fresh Pond Parkway, to the southeast of the pond. Influenced by the thinking of Olmsted Sr., Charles Eliot saw parkways as a way of linking larger areas of parkland together to produce a whole metropolitan park system. The parkways were to be wide, tree-lined streets, designed solely or principally for pleasure traffic (rather than commercial vehicles), thus giving people an agreeable way of traveling between the large reservations. In this case, Eliot proposed a parkway in 1893 to provide a broad connection between the reservations along the Charles River and the large new park around Fresh Pond, using the colonial Fresh Pond Lane as the basis for the new road. To Eliot, there was a strong natural link between the two reservations, as both secured the edges of rivers and ponds as public parks, and so provided a particular sense of space and openness, and were a source of the special pleasure that people derived from the contemplation of water. Others were inspired by Eliot's vision for the parkways: the president of the Cambridge Parks Commission imagined a time when "the entrances to Cambridge will, at last, be beautiful. The city that holds within itself treasures with which few can be compared will have border lands worthy of its riches." He described the parkways and drives that, at their end, would "reach our beautiful pond . . . which Mr. Olmsted has been free to call one of the finest natural features about Boston."[40]

After Eliot's death, the Olmsted brothers were duly commissioned by the Metropolitan Park Commission to design the parkway linking the Charles River with Fresh Pond. Instead of Eliot's proposed route, they chose to lay out a gently curving road that ran from Mount Auburn Street through the Larches estate as far as Huron Avenue. The parkway opened in October 1900. It was extended by one block in 1916, to cross the Watertown Branch railroad into Kingsley Park (see figure 5.22).[41]

The Impact of the Olmsted Firm's Work

By the time the work at Fresh Pond came to an end, the Olmsted firm had achieved much of what the water board had hoped: the grounds were substantially regraded, and most of the reservation had been planted. In many ways, the borders had indeed been beautified. There is some evidence that the reservation was used as a public park and the carriageway as a pleasure drive. Students from Radcliffe College, for instance, organized an annual freshman-senior "Tally Ho" to Fresh Pond, followed by a picnic on the grounds, around the turn of the twentieth century.[42] A number of postcards exist from the same period that depict the scenery, walks, and roads in a positive, attractive light.

5.23 A 1909 photograph of Fresh Pond Parkway, which had opened in 1900, near the junction with Huron Avenue. Courtesy DCR Archives.

Two writers offered views on the landscape in the early years of the twentieth century, when most of the Olmsted firm's work was already in place. Neither is complimentary about what he saw. The American novelist Henry James returned to the United States in 1904, having spent most of his adult life in Europe. He published a memoir that compared his youthful memories of the country with the reality of what he found on return. America had changed beyond recognition. When he was growing up, "the claims for regional distinctiveness, small town aloofness and pastoral space could still count for something." By the start of the twentieth century, the age of "industrial capitalism" was well established.[43]

James was particularly struck by the changes he saw at Fresh Pond, which had been a favorite haunt of his youth: he had spent many hours walking along the shore, in intimate discussions of art and literature with friends. He remembered it fondly as almost a secret world, free from authority or adult responsibilities. On return, he explained how he traveled:

> for the pleasure of memory, to Fresh Pond, dear to the muses of youth, the Sunday afternoons of spring, and had to accept there his clearest vision perhaps of the new differences and indifferences. The little nestling lake of other days had ceased to nestle; there was practically no Fresh Pond any more, and I seemed somehow to see why the muses had fled even as from the place at large. . . . There had come, thereabouts too, the large extension of the "Park System," the admirable commissioners' roads that reach across the ruder countryside like the arms of carnivorous giants stretching over a tea-table of blackberries and buns. . . . The desecrated, the destroyed resort had favoured, save on rare

feast days, the single stroll, or at the worst the double, dedicated to shared literary secrets; which was why I almost angrily missed, among the ruins, what I had mainly gone back to recover—some echo of the dreams of youth, the titles of tales, the communities of friendship.[44]

The description has some of the romanticism of Frederick Law Olmsted Jr.'s article in ascribing to Fresh Pond an idyllic, pastoral past somewhat at odds with its vast ice industry and popular hotel (James's reference to "rare feast days" may be an oblique admission of the existence of the thousands of carousing picnickers). He also apportions blame in slightly the wrong direction, citing the Metropolitan Park Commission as builders of the road. But his piece does give a vivid sense that people felt nature somehow had been displaced at Fresh Pond by expansive views and wide public roads, just as modern industrialized life had forever replaced the small-town, more agrarian communities of previous years.

Writing two years after Henry James, local resident and ornithologist William Brewster also offered a sharp critique of the appearance of Fresh Pond. "Time was—and that not so very long ago—when Fresh Pond had perfectly natural shores, well wooded in places and indented by no less than five large reedy coves, or 'nooks' as we used to call them." Even if slightly disfigured by the icehouses, it was still "remarkably pretty." He claimed that the work to turn Fresh Pond into a public park unfortunately "was entrusted to persons who possessed neither sound judgment nor good taste . . . as the results abundantly show." The landscape had been utterly spoiled by removing the hills and ridges that surrounded the water, filling in three of

5.24 and **5.25** Two views of the carriage drive around the pond, n.d. (c. 1900–1920). The photograph above shows the view of the water from one of the entrances to the park; right is a family enjoying a carriage ride on the driveway relocated by the Olmsted firm, at the southeastern edge of Kingsley Park.
Library of Congress, Prints and Photographs Division, Detroit Publishing Company Collection.

the coves, and obliterating the original shoreline. All this was, he felt, "needless vandalism." There was also the "grave blunder" of putting the carriage road along the shoreline, rather than laying it out to meander through the hills and just appear now and again at the water's edge. Such a design would have been more pleasant and certainly less obtrusive, as "any competent landscape architect" could have advised.[45]

This is so similar in its criticisms to the Frederick Law Olmsted Jr. article quoted above that it may well have been inspired by it. Indeed the paragraph may have been intended to support the case for more fundamental change at the pond. But, published just three years before the firm's work ceased there, it now reads almost as a statement of the ultimate failure of the landscape architects to convince the city to address the main design issues that they had identified.

It is not clear exactly when and why the Olmsted firm's plans stopped being implemented. The last significant Olmsted papers from this time are a copy of a plan of the refectory grounds, on the site of the old Fresh Pond Farm. The board apparently encouraged the production of the plan but then took no action. Finally there is a brief note of a visit by Frederick Law Olmsted Jr., checking the recent plantings on Kingsley Park.[46] There does not seem to be a record of a formal decision by the board to stop the work. There is certainly no correspondence in the Olmsted archives marking the end of the relationship. But with much of the planting done, the constant lack of sufficient appropriations from the city council, the absence of an advocate to replace Stillman Kelley, and the criticism of some of the results, maybe the enthusiasm for the

Olmsted firm's work had run its course. It just petered out in early 1909.

In any event, the world for which the board and the Olmsted firm were designing was coming to an end. In the first decade of the twentieth century, carriages were rapidly being replaced by automobiles. In 1901 the board pressed the city council to ban their increasing use of the carriageway at Fresh Pond: the horses were "taking fright" at the sight of them, and "the pleasure of a few should not be allowed to imperil the safety of the vast majority of visitors who do not, or cannot, ride motor vehicles."[47] The board was attempting to resist the inevitable: the Model T Ford went into mass production in 1908 and, just two years later, wear on the driveways from motor vehicles was "very great."[48]

The arrival of the automobile did not simply mean the end of the use of the driveway for the purpose for which it had been constructed. The landscape was now being experienced at a faster speed, through a car window, rather than the leisurely stroll or carriage drive for which it was so carefully planned. Its perceived aesthetic and moral value decreased in line with the length of time it was viewed. Car ownership also meant greater individual mobility. People could travel further and gain access to the countryside at state and even national parks: pastoral-style parks within the city like Fresh Pond were no longer the principal refuge from the stress of urban life. Perhaps this realization was another reason that the Olmsted firm's work at Fresh Pond was never completed. It is certainly striking how quickly the focus on the landscape at Fresh Pond principally as parkland was to disappear.

5.26 The water board may have tried to counter criticisms of its work through the choice of images it used of Fresh Pond in the early years of the twentieth century. Instead of trumpeting the wonder of its engineering works and its carriageway, the board began to focus on the aesthetic qualities of the scenery at Fresh Pond. Its 1904 annual report, for instance, contains this full-page image of a family posing in a wooded grove at the pond, which is labeled "truly-rural."
City of Cambridge Water Board Annual Report, 1904.

6 Municipal Expansion

This Board has always felt that the Fresh Pond reservation is primarily a part of the water system, rather than a park system.

Cambridge Water Board Annual Report, 1921/22

It is no longer possible to reserve whole watersheds simply for the production of drinking water—there are too many competing demands on the land near urban areas. Today land must serve multiple purposes.

Council on Environmental Quality

The first half of the twentieth century saw a colossal growth in the scope and scale of the activities of government, at both the national and the local level. The reasons for this are complex. The growing concentration of people in urban areas led to more demand for municipal services, while increased migration meant that the support, care, and protection traditionally supplied by the extended family now needed to be provided from elsewhere. In addition, a greater uncertainty about employment led to more demand for relief and a greater acceptance of government intervention in individuals' lives.

This shift was reinforced by global events, especially the two World Wars and the Great Depression of the thirties; the depression in particular led to massive federal intervention through national relief, recovery, and reform programs (such as Roosevelt's "New Deal"), perhaps most famously the Works Progress Administration, introduced to provide work for the unemployed. Locally too, government continued to grow, with new state and municipal agencies being created to provide for the young, poor, elderly, and infirm. There were complaints from some quarters about the growing reach of government, but its size and power were ever increasing.

The trend was reflected in the public supply of water. Its arrival in rapidly expanding towns and cities across America led to significantly increased demand. Sanitation and indoor plumbing, which addressed major health concerns, quickly became considered necessities in all new buildings. Original supply systems soon became too small. Massachusetts, for instance, was faced with expanding urban areas and increasing demand for water throughout the eastern part of the state. In response its General Court introduced a Metropolitan Water District to organize new supplies of water for many of the municipalities in the industrialized east of Massachusetts. The water was obtained from the center of the state, with the Nashua River dammed in 1906 to create the Wachusett reservoir, then the largest reservoir in the world. Supported by the state legislature, the Metropolitan Water Board was to continue to favor taking vast supplies from the largely unpolluted center and west of Massachusetts. In 1939, its successor, the Metropolitan District Commission, completed work on the colossal Quabbin reservoir in western Massachusetts.

The city of Cambridge was also continuing to expand. In 1880, at the time of the annexation of land from Belmont and Arlington, it had had 52,700 residents. By 1910, it had 104,800. Thus the population had doubled in thirty years. The demand for water had risen even more dramatically, increasing from a daily requirement of 2.4 million gallons to 10.5 million in the same period.[1] The water board became concerned

6.1 Located on the eastern shores of Fresh Pond, the filtration plant and its ancillary buildings were a sign of the evolving nature of the water board's stewardship of the city's water supply. No longer was the pond to be protected from possible pollution by cleared land and dykes; science would instead remove all traces of impurity. Once the new filtration plant was operational in 1923, the board believed that its technology would counteract any risk of pollution seeping into the water from a change in use of the surrounding land. This building was thus the first of many intrusions into the park in the second quarter of the twentieth century, arguably destroying the "singularly unified" nature of the landscape perceived by designer Charles Eliot in the 1890s. Image 1946. City of Cambridge Annual Documents, 1946, Cambridge Historical Commission.

that, if such growth were to continue, all the work it had done at Stony Brook, Hobbs Brook, and Payson Park would prove insufficient. It was also aware of continuing concerns about the possible pollution of the water. There had been an outbreak of typhoid at Payson Park during its construction in 1896, and the board had had to issue reassuring statements to the public about the safety of the water supply. The water was still cleaned simply through its storage at Fresh Pond and Payson Park and, while the science was imperfectly understood at this time, it was known that diseases such as typhoid could be spread by infected water. Thus it is no surprise that the city of Cambridge, which had confidently opted not to join the new metropolitan system in 1895, felt the need for dramatic action in the early years of the new century, to improve both the scale and the quality of its own supplies. Its activities reveal the optimistic, early twentieth-century view of science as being able to solve any problem: filtration and other treatments would ensure the purity of the water supply and thus supersede the protective role of the carefully cleared landscape.

Throughout the city, increasingly squeezed into its six square miles, space was at a premium. Sites needed to be found for various new municipal functions and the water board was content to see the land abutting the pond assigned several such roles, some of them significantly affecting its appearance. Thus, by the middle of the twentieth century, the landscape had ceased to be a unified park and had become home to a number of separate facilities that happened to share the borders of the pond, managed by a variety of municipal and state agencies. The parkland became simply the residual areas where no development had taken place. Similar development pressures elsewhere in the city meant that by the time of the Second World War, all the other large, seemingly natural areas in Cambridge had disappeared (see figure 1.5).

One of the demands on the landscape arose from a new focus on the benefits of active recreation. By the turn of the twentieth century, the need for playgrounds had joined the need for decent housing "at the forefront of the social reformers' agenda."[2] It was believed that exposure to outdoor play would encourage the creative, cooperative instincts crushed by congested housing and other negative impacts of industrialization. This was not simply about making more space available. It meant the introduction of structured, often supervised, activities through the provision of tennis courts, baseball fields, metal swings, and gymnastic apparatus. Campaigners issued leaflets that set out the perceived impact of playgrounds on working class children very starkly, asking, "Shall We Provide a Playground? Or Enlarge the Jail?"[3] Attitudes had come a long way since the early settlers' puritan concerns about the potentially corrupting influence of enjoyable recreation (such as skating) on the morals of the young.

Cambridge's first partisan mayor, Democrat John H. H. McNamee, was elected in 1902. He lost no time in persuading his parks department to move its focus from pastoral parks to active recreational facilities. The city's residents voted overwhelmingly in favor of implementing the 1908 Massachusetts law that required every large town to provide and maintain playgrounds for the "recreation and physical education of minors."[4] The first annual report of the city's new playground commission in 1911 duly recommended for Fresh Pond a "children's corner" and (reflecting the game's growing popularity) a golf links.[5]

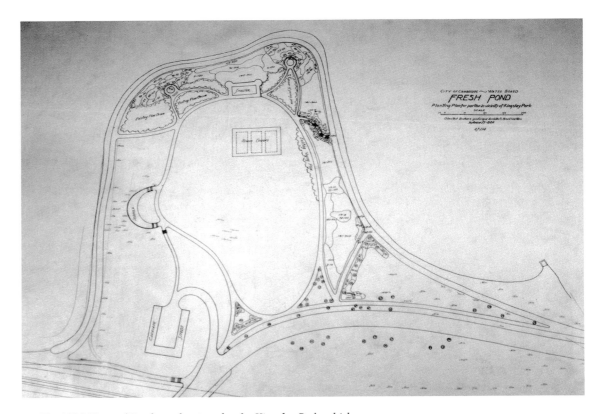

6.2 The 1904 Olmsted Brothers planting plan for Kingsley Park, which shows three tennis courts proposed at the heart of what the firm had so long envisaged as a pastoral, naturalistic park. There is no evidence that the courts were ever installed, but they reveal the redirected attention of the social reform movement, from passive enjoyment of nature to active recreation, and the change of focus from Cambridge's first partisan mayor. Courtesy of the National Park Service, Frederick Law Olmsted National Historic Site.

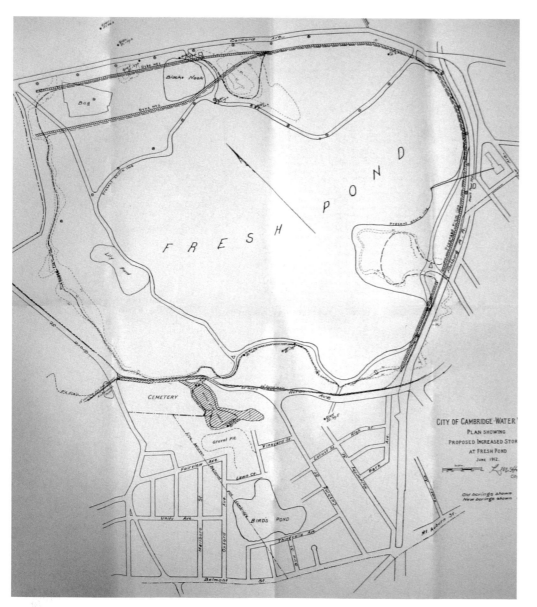

Plans to Flood the Reservation

In 1912 a small team of experts (which included Frederic Stearns, one of the creators of the metropolitan system) produced three reports advising the Cambridge Water Board how to improve the quantity and purity of its water supply. One strong recommendation was that, given Cambridge's source of supply in eastern Massachusetts, the water board should begin filtering its water, to improve its quality and reduce the risk of typhoid and other diseases. Instead of increasing capacity, the board was urged to introduce ways of reducing waste, principally by bringing in water meters for all customers. Two of the experts also proposed that Cambridge should join the metropolitan system, at least as a reserve.

The experts, seemingly at the suggestion of the board itself, also debated the idea of increasing the capacity of Fresh Pond by raising its banks and enlarging the basin. All advised against the idea, arguing that other solutions were preferable, that it would be prohibitively expensive, and that it "would interfere seriously with the present use as a park of the ground

6.3 Draft plans issued in 1912 considered raising the level of Fresh Pond by fifteen feet, to increase capacity. The dark lines show two options for installing dykes to retain the newly enlarged basin: either would have meant flooding almost all of the reservation. City of Cambridge Water Department.

surrounding the pond."[6] It was a notion, however, that the board did not abandon. For another fifteen years, it seriously considered enlarging the basin. Making use of the parkland that it already owned probably seemed more attractive than the controversial and slow process of acquiring more land outside of the city. It even took serious steps to implement this change, whatever its experts' advice. Thus, within three years of the departure of the Olmsted firm, the importance of the landscape as a public park seems to have diminished significantly; it was now simply another resource available to the board in its management of the water supply.

The New Filtration Plant

In 1915 the board took action to implement one of the key recommendations from its experts' reports, when it commenced plans for a filtration plant at Fresh Pond, although America joining the First World War in 1917 meant that construction did not start until 1921.

The reservation appears to have been closed to the public during construction of the new plant, presumably for safety reasons. It was sufficiently popular as a park that some citizens lobbied the city for the road to be reopened "in order that the citizens of Cambridge and their families, may have an opportunity to enjoy the use of the grounds."[7] Construction was complete and the building officially in operation by 1923. Water was pumped from Fresh Pond into the new plant, while the supply from Stony Brook, previously entering the system through the supply pipe and fountain, was diverted at a weir chamber to flow directly to the plant.[8]

6.4 and **6.5** Two images of the construction of the filtration plant, 1921. The new building was located within the reservation, facing the pond, near where Wyeth's brick icehouse had once stood. While its location was eminently reasonable for operational purposes, it was to herald many other encroachments on the land that the board had worked so hard to clear. Cambridge Engineering Department Collection, Cambridge Historical Commission.

6.6 The new filtration plant, located on the eastern shores of Fresh Pond, 1924. Designed by architect George A. Johnson in a grand Georgian style, the two-story building cost $7.5 million and was a fitting partner to the "palace" of a pumping station, another example of civic pride.
City of Cambridge Water Board Annual Documents, 1924, Cambridge Historical Commission.

In building the new plant, the board also saw an opportunity to implement the idea of raising the level of Fresh Pond. It included in the contract a specification that the spoil from the construction should remain the property of the city and should be dumped by the contractor close to the point of excavation.[9] Its plans were to use the surplus material to increase the height of the banks by eight feet, which would reportedly allow Fresh Pond to hold 600 million more gallons of water. By 1924, when the building had been completed, there were "earth dykes" along part of the shoreline, ready for a time when the board could afford the major engineering work involved. It was still being seriously considered as a project three years later: indeed it is the only issue about Fresh Pond mentioned in the board's annual report of 1926/27. Not everyone was happy with the way the spoil had been dumped: one city councilor was to complain that it had been done largely to save the contractor (and therefore the water board) money, and as a result "a beautiful driveway was destroyed."[10]

The new plant was enlarged in the 1930s and, to increase supply, new intakes were installed in 1932, which allowed the board to lower the water in Fresh Pond and thus reduce the wastage of water over the spillway at Stony Brook. The board also implemented the advice of its experts' report from 1912, when it installed water meters for almost all its customers between 1930 and 1932.

No More Hay

Hay had been cut around Fresh Pond over the centuries, from early colonial times. Frederic Tudor and others continued the practice well into the nineteenth century. For many years the water board did the same, using some of the cut grass itself and selling the remainder, either cut or standing. Areas at Kingsley Park, in Tudor Park, on the former Fresh Pond Farm, and along the Concord Avenue boundary were all managed in this way. The annual activity seems to have ceased when America joined the First World War (its last mention is in the board's annual report for 1916/17). Although seemingly unimportant, this change gradually led to a significant shift in the landscape, as volunteer trees and brushwood took over areas that had previously been open meadow. Combined with the reduction in maintenance work at the pond in the third quarter of the twentieth century, it arguably has been one of the most important changes in the overall appearance and feel of Fresh Pond in the last century.

From Park Land to Battleground

The entry of the United States into World War I on April 6, 1917, had another impact on Fresh Pond. It is just a small footnote now in the history of the reservation, but it serves as another example of how attitudes to the landscape had changed so dramatically since the turn of the century.

With the declaration of war on Germany, the Harvard president, A. Lawrence Lowell, took a personal interest in the Reserve Officer Training Corps (ROTC) that had hastily

6.7 This 1986 aerial view shows how far the northern borders of Fresh Pond became wooded after the city stopped cutting hay and reduced its maintenance work. This contrasts with the much more open landscape of earlier years, as seen for instance in figure 6.11.
City of Cambridge Annual Documents, 1986, Cambridge Historical Commission.

6.8 The French officers ran an innovative training program for the Reserve Officer Training Corps (ROTC) cadets, who learned from their French counterparts in the field how to make trenches (as here at Fresh Pond in 1917) and machine gun emplacements, and how to attack and defend them; and techniques for such activities as throwing grenades and night signaling.
Harvard University Archives, Call # HUP-SF ROTC (17).

formed at Harvard, and he looked for ways to extend its members' preparation for the fighting. His letter to the French ambassador in Washington led to six French officers (wounded in the war and so out of commission) traveling to the United States, to train members of the ROTC in modern warfare. One was sent to Yale and the other five arrived in Boston. They apparently "carried all before them with the student body of Harvard, and with the ladies of Boston society."[11]

President Lowell made Harvard Stadium and Soldiers Field available for practice sessions. When it quickly became clear that more land was needed for camps and trench practice, he sought permission to use other local sites. One of these was Fresh Pond reservation. The water board had no objection, provided that any activities would "in no way endanger the purity of our water supply."[12] The board had closed all roads and land inside the reservation to the public (to counter a possible enemy attack on the water supply) and so granted the ROTC a special permit to use an area bordering on Concord Avenue. It was the former site of Fresh Pond Farm, where the Olmsted firm had planned its grand refectory.

The ROTC was soon staging mock battles on the site. Hundreds of men, organized into platoons, carried out major combat exercises attacking and defending the area, complete with machine guns, listening posts, and all the paraphernalia of trench warfare.[13]

A flavor of the ROTC experience can be gained from the letters of one of its members. In 1917 Norbert Wiener was twenty-two years old and teaching mathematics at the University of Maine. He was something of a prodigy, having gained his PhD from Harvard at the age of eighteen. In later life he

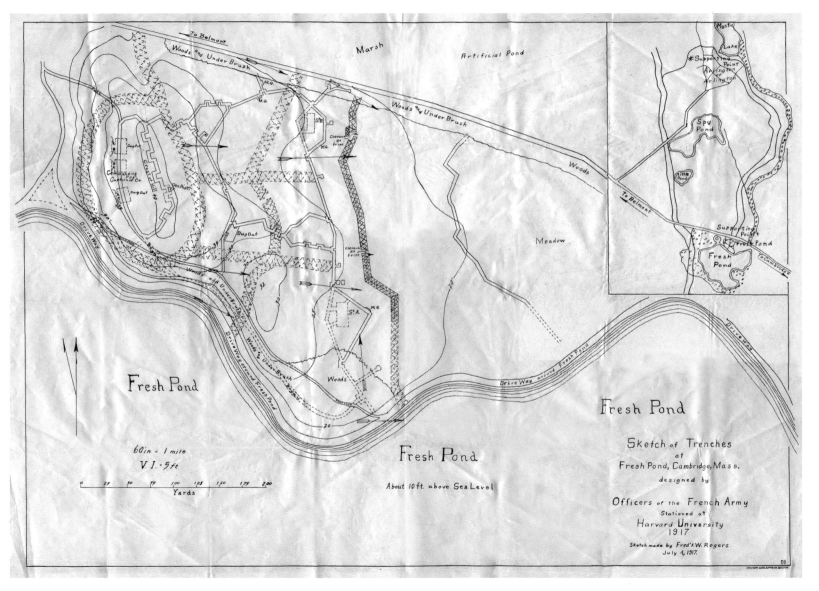

Within the map:

To Belmont

Woods and Under Brush

Marsh

Artificial Pond

M.G.

M.G.

St.B.

Chemin de frise

M.G.

Woods and Under Brush

Woods

Dugout

Commanding Captain of Co.

Dugout No.

Out Post

Dug Out

Chemin de frise

Meadow

St.A.

M.G.

Woods

Drive Way around Fresh Pond

Drive Way

Woods and Under Brush

Woods and Under Brush

20

20

Fresh Pond

Fresh Pond

Fresh Pond

About 10 ft. above Sea Level

60 in = 1 mile
V.I. = 5 ft

0 25 50 75 100 125 150 175 200
Yards

Sketch of Trenches
at
Fresh Pond, Cambridge, Mass.
designed by
Officers of the French Army
Stationed at
Harvard University
1917
Sketch made by Fred'k W. Rogers.
July 4, 1917.

Inset map:

Mystic Lake

Supporting Point Arlington

Spy Pond

Little Pond

To Belmont

Supporting Point Fresh Pond

To Cambridge

Fresh Pond

6.9 This sketch shows the trenches designed at Fresh Pond by officers of the French army, 1917. Members of the ROTC dug the trenches and boyaux (covered passages linking the trenches), created shelters, dug-outs, and gun emplacements, and set up sanitation systems. The work covered a large part of the northeastern section of the reservation.
Harvard University Archives, Records of President A. Lawrence Lowell, UA I 5.160, 1917–1919, folder 1654.

6.10 Some of the extensive trenches being dug at Fresh Pond, 1917. Harvard University Archives, Call # HUP-SF ROTC (18).

was to become a distinguished professor of mathematics at MIT and, among many accomplishments, coiner of the term *cybernetics*. Like many students and former students in 1917, he rushed to support the war effort by joining the Harvard University ROTC. On July 2 he wrote to his mother: "Excuse my writing so seldom, but we are very hard worked at trenching, map making and the like."[14]

Two weeks later, Wiener gave more information: "I am here in tent now, having a grand time, after a fair to middling day's work. It is all an old story, the drill and the exercise. . . . So far the camp is very restful and perhaps might be boresome were it not for the good swimming. My tent-mates are interesting fellows, all except one coarse old Irishman, and we have good times. They comprise an Italian lawer [sic], a son of a missionary to Burma who has been there himself, a news-editor of the New York World, and three other fellows. I bathe often in the lake (there are no sharks here)."[15]

Clearly, an admonition to ROTC members to abstain from using the waters of the pond "for any purpose whatsoever"[16] was not strictly followed. Nor was the warning from the water board that the use of the land should be "confined to daylight hours."[17] Wiener had to cancel a planned evening meeting with his father: "I am awfully sorry but all Wednesday afternoon and evening we are to be in the trenches, until almost midnight, so I cannot see dad, unless he cares to come down . . . to fresh pond, to see the trenches."[18]

The experimental training program was repeated the following summer. Harvard's undergraduate newspaper carried a number of articles describing military activities at the reservation: "This afternoon the University R. O. T. C. . . . will carry out

a combat exercise at Fresh Pond. . . . At the appointed time the two companies of infantry will be drawn up in reserve on the road west of the Fresh Pond Reservation. . . . They will move up on the system of trenches above Command Post Ridge, . . . where they will relieve a battalion, occupy the first line and attack at once in two waves in a direction west-east. . . . The work at Fresh Pond this afternoon will take precedence over all other academic engagements."[19]

The battle practice was clearly a regular event at the reservation. Two weeks later, the newspaper was reporting further planned exercises by the ROTC companies, including "put[ting] into practice the latest methods of advancing from shell-hole to shell hole under fire as explained recently by Colonel Azan."[20]

With the end of the war in November 1918 came the end of this episode in the life of Fresh Pond. Paul Azan, the French officer in charge of the mission, apparently "failed in

6.11 The two ROTC companies of infantry passing Black's Nook on their way to a combat exercise carried out before the university overseers, May 1918. Harvard University Archives, Call # HUP-SF ROTC (4).

his endeavor to marry an American heiress"[21] but returned to the French army with distinction. Another of the officers, André Morize, stayed in America and became a distinguished professor of French literature at Harvard, retiring in 1952.[22] In line with a request by the water board, Harvard duly spent $1570.05 "restoring grounds at Fresh Pond after use by Military Units."[23] Nevertheless those who know the reservation well today claim that you can still find swathes of soft soil around Neville Place, where the trenches were filled in, a remnant of its forgotten wartime use.[24]

The Shift to Active Recreation

In 1925 the state gave authorization for a large playground to be installed at Fresh Pond, replacing the small "children's corner" created some fourteen years previously. (The legislature's approval was needed for any significant change of use at Fresh Pond, as the city had acquired the land under the 1888 act for water supply purposes.) The new playground was to be on the high bluffs to the south, thus replacing the Olmsted firm's planned carriageway and concourse.

There were various additions to the playground over the years, especially during the 1940s when the WPA added permanent bleachers, several tennis courts, a wading pool, a double handball court, and a horseshoe court. By the late 1940s, the playground had become known as Glacken Field, named after Francis X. Glacken, of the U.S. Army Air Corps, who had been shot down over Tokyo Bay in 1945. In 1946 a new practice field for high school athletic teams was also laid out, near Black's Nook.

6.12 In 1911/12 the city graded and fenced a two-acre plot to create a small playground on the southwest side of the reservation. The equipment may have been similar to this metal jungle gym at Rindge Field in northwest Cambridge, 1909.
The Schlesinger Library, Radcliffe Institute, Harvard University.

6.13 A municipal toboggan slide was installed by the parks department at its new Fresh Pond playground in 1926, when this photograph was taken, and was in use for many years.
Cambridge Recreation Department Collection, Cambridge Historical Commission.

Other, longer-established methods of recreation were not altogether lost at the reservation. Fishing was allowed by permit until 1917 (when it was prohibited on safety grounds as America joined the First World War). In the 1930s, the water board considered adding a bridle path[25] (apparently, even during the Great Depression, the board thought that horseback riding for pleasure would be popular with visitors to Fresh Pond) and revisited the idea of a separate bicycle path. But the board decided against both, partly because water board regulations at that time forbade other modes of transport around the pond.[26] Boating was still allowed at this time: at least, two rowboats were purchased by the Harvard Graduate School of Engineering for "biological studies on Fresh Pond."[27]

In 1947 the pond was still being illicitly used for sport: one morning, between 100 and 300 boys and girls were found skating on Fresh Pond "and the police were powerless to prevent it."[28] The board's concerns over such activity were more about its liability in case of accidents than about the risks to the water supply.

The Golf Course

The golf links at Fresh Pond, first proposed in 1910, were long in the gestation. In 1920 planner Arthur C. Comey produced a study for the city planning board and subsequently published articles seeking to persuade both local inhabitants and design professionals of the merits of the proposals for a course.[29]

Comey argued that the world had changed since the time of the Olmsted firm's general plan. Instead of the landscape architects' vision of the public taking leisurely drives in a carriage around the water, many visitors were at most driving around in an automobile, which took only a few minutes. Comey put forward the idea that the two hours it took to play a round of golf was a good modern equivalent to a carriage drive. The course would encourage people to come to Fresh Pond and give them a reason to stay. Having analyzed the current nature of the land, Comey concluded that there were eighty-eight acres available for the course and proposed a full eighteen-hole links, arguing that "9 holes are not considered sufficient for a course open to the public."

It is clear that Comey did not regard the Olmsted firm's work as being complete or as having been officially brought to an end. He wrote as if it were simply in abeyance, so that, for instance, if it were not for the proposed golf course, perhaps one day the roadway may have been relocated away from the shore. He was explicitly pressing, on behalf of the planning board, for the Olmsted firm's plan to be changed, to allow for the introduction of the course. But he did also argue that this new development should be accompanied by further implementation of as much of the original plan as possible, "particularly the modification of the present stiff shoreline."

Comey stated that the introduction of a golf course would be popular with Cambridge citizens and that it had the approval of Frederick Law Olmsted Jr. There is no corroborating evidence of Olmsted's view. It is surprising that, given the effort that had been put into planning, grading, and planting the reservation, Olmsted would have liked the idea of most of his firm's work being replaced. But, if he really did indicate his approval, maybe he was attracted by the idea of some of the remainder of the plan being implemented, especially as

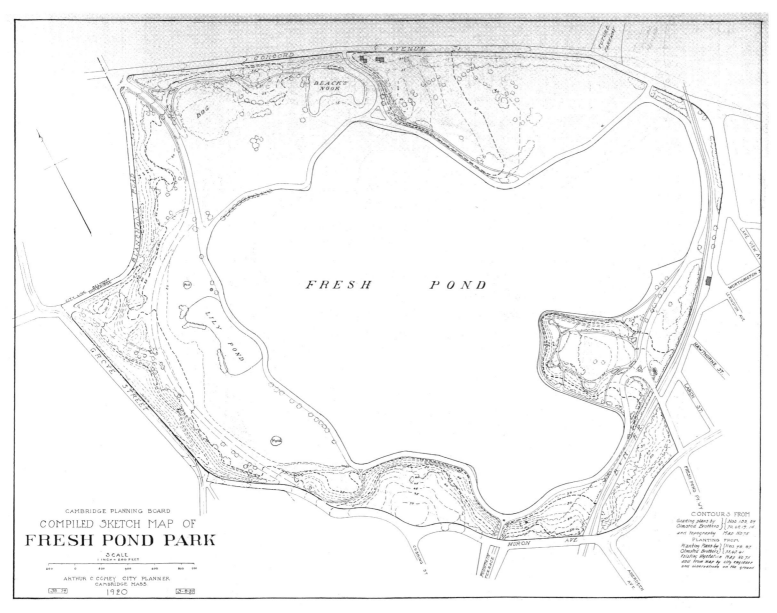

CAMBRIDGE PLANNING BOARD
COMPILED SKETCH MAP OF
FRESH POND PARK

SCALE
1 INCH = 200 FEET

ARTHUR C COMEY CITY PLANNER
CAMBRIDGE MASS
1920

CONTOURS FROM
Grading plans by } Nos 133. 84
Olmsted Brothers } 70. 68 19. 15
and topography   Map No 75
PLANTING FROM
Planting Plans by } Nos 76 67
Olmsted Brothers } 72. 67. 41
Existing Vegetation Map No 75
and from map by city engineer
and observations on the ground

6.14 Arthur Comey's compiled sketch plan of Fresh Pond, labeled "the park as it is today," 1920. It is useful to compare this sketch with the Olmsted firm's general plan (figure 5.7) to see how much of the firm's roadways, paths, and topographical changes had in fact been implemented. Comey argued that only the southeastern side of the reservation, at Kingsley Park, had been fully developed according to the Olmsted firm's plan and was increasingly popular as a recreational site. In contrast, he stated (perhaps a little disingenuously) that the vision for the northwestern part of the reservation had not been fully realized.
Courtesy of the National Park Service, Frederick Law Olmsted National Historic Site.

6.15 The proposed layout of the golf links at Fresh Pond, 1920. Comey's planned course stretched from the bluffs to the south, right around the western and northern borders, past Black's Nook, and across the former site of Fresh Pond Farm, as far as Alewife Brook. Only the eastern edge, from Fountain Terrace up through Kingsley Park and the narrow strip of Tudor Park, would be untouched (and Comey would presumably have known of the imminent plans to build the filtration plant on this shore).
Cambridge Tribune, March 5, 1921.

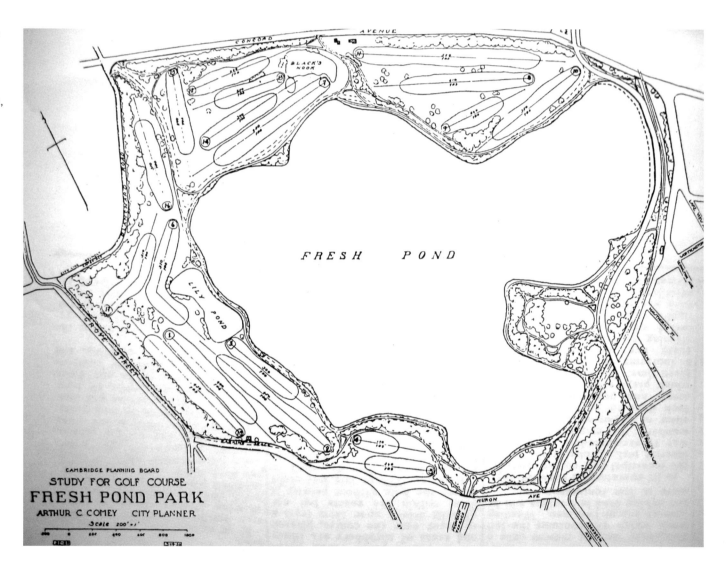

Comey promised that "I shall stand ready to recommend that the actual planning and construction supervision be done by your firm, so long associated with landscape work around the pond."[30] Perhaps Comey thought Olmsted shared the belief that well-planned and maintained golf courses, with their "distant views across rolling meadowlike greenswards fringed with trees" were not dissimilar to some of the best Olmstedian landscapes.[31]

No immediate action was taken to implement Comey's proposals: the idea rumbled on for another ten years or so. Busy with further plans to improve the purity of the supply, the water board simply noted the ongoing discussions.

It was the Great Depression that finally led to the construction of the golf course. As the water board reported, the "long-considered question" of whether or not to have a golf links at Fresh Pond was resolved by the necessity of finding work for the unemployed.[32] In 1931, the board indicated that it would authorize the use of the land by the city's park and recreation department for a golf course, subject to a few conditions. In the following year, the state legislature also gave its formal authorization. The required funds for the course were raised by private subscription and members of the Cambridge Unemployment Bureau were given the job of constructing the course. It was designed by Walter Irving Johnson Jr., who spent much of his career as the construction superintendent for well-known course designer Donald Ross.[33] Like the men employed later in the decade by the WPA to construct municipal golf courses throughout the country, the builders probably moved soil and sculpted the ground according to Johnson's

6.16 The golf course in 1945. By the time of its construction in the 1930s, the building of the city home on the former site of Fresh Pond Farm, described below, had ruled out the scope for a full eighteen holes, and so a nine-hole course was built on the western borders of the reservation.
Cambridge Planning Board Collection, Cambridge Historical Commission.

6.17 The municipal golf course, viewed over Little Fresh Pond, 2004. Jill Sinclair.

plan using hand tools and wheelbarrows rather than heavy earth-moving equipment.[34]

It was here, on the Fresh Pond golf course, that the spoil from the filtration plant, dumped along the roadway a decade earlier, finally found a home. It was used to fill in the low places and to level out the ground for the construction of the tees, fairways, and greens. Comey's proposal about implementing the Olmsted firm's plan to modify the shoreline came to nothing, but some of the landscape architects' existing work was preserved. The new fairways were laid out around the pattern of paths and driveways at least partially installed by the Olmsted firm three decades earlier (see figure 5.19). Traces of the northwestern entrance road remain today, but the footpaths appear lost under volunteer trees and later redevelopments of the course.

The golf course was officially opened by Mayor Richard M. Russell on June 13, 1934. Among its earliest visitors were some of the female students from Radcliffe College. The director of physical education reported the "real innovation" of students having golf lessons as a regular activity: apparently "over forty girls took lessons in the Spring."[35]

Later, in 1941, the city added a new, permanent clubhouse, the Edwin H. Hall Recreation Center, which was funded by the WPA, as well as working to improve the grounds and add a parking area.[36] In 1967 the course was completely reconstructed, with redesigned greens and tees, and a new watering system was installed. More trees and shrubs were added in 1974. Further work was carried out in the early 1990s and, in 1996, it was renamed the Thomas P. O'Neill Jr. Municipal Golf Course, in honor of the late Speaker of the House, who learned to play there.[37]

The City Home for the Aged and Infirm

In 1927 public arguments erupted between city councilors about a proposed new use for part of the reservation. The city had sold, and was about to vacate, the property used as a city home (commonly known as the "Poor Farm") in North Cambridge, and found itself under some pressure to find a suitable replacement. The city intended the new facility to be for the elderly and incurable, rather than just for the poor, which reflects the shifting demographics of the time. The plans also reveal an important change in attitude: previously such municipal facilities had been designed almost as prisons, using the traditional Victorian approach to almshouses. Now the Cambridge Board of Public Welfare was proposing a new home more on the infirmary model, located in "cheerful and pleasant" surroundings.[38] It therefore recommended that the new city home should be located at Fresh Pond.

The original suggestion was to build in Clinker Park, which seems to have been an informal, rather pejorative, name used for a part of Fresh Pond reservation (clinker is the stony residue from coal fires, which was often crushed to fill low-lying land or make rudimentary level surfaces). It is not clear from contemporary maps exactly where this was. By 1927, the chosen location had become the northern shores of the pond, on the former site of Fresh Pond Farm. Very much in favor, Mayor Edward D. Quinn proposed an appropriation of $425,000 for the construction. The state board of health indicated that it was content with the proposed location, meaning it did not have concerns about possible pollution of the water supply from the new building. The legislature duly authorized the building of the city home at Fresh Pond.[39] Also raising no objection, the water board was happy to transfer the land to the board of public welfare.

It all seemed to be moving forward successfully. Then the appropriation was discussed at a series of city council meetings, and strong opposition to the proposal emerged, both from councilors and from the local residents who spoke at public meetings. So strong were the feelings that local newspapers reported the discussions in some detail, often as the lead story in that week's edition. The objections varied widely. Some people were opposed to spending such a large sum of taxpayers' money (from the income of "self-supporting citizens"[40]) on the indigent. Some queried whether a home was really necessary at all, or whether it needed to be as large as proposed. While some councilors "did not begrudge having the inmates enjoy the beautiful surroundings of Fresh Pond,"[41] others challenged whether it was really appropriate to dedicate "one of the most valuable locations in the city"[42] to such a purpose.

There were objections because building a city home on the site would halt other schemes, including the enlargement of the basin, still apparently being considered, and the construction of the eighteen-hole golf course. Some members of the public still hoped to see the site developed for recreation, as proposed by the Olmsted firm, with a relocated driveway and refectory area. One councilor questioned the legality of the change of use, arguing that the land had been acquired by the city specifically to protect the water supply, and that it would need to revert to its original owners if that usage ceased. Others countered that the last owner, Dr. John E. Somers, had intended to leave the land to the Holy Ghost Hospital for Incurables,

and that the hospital would not object to a city home on the site.[43]

The language became heated. One councilor claimed that allowing the grand new building would set an unfortunate precedent, and that it was being considered mainly for reasons of personal aggrandizement: members of the board of public welfare just wanted to see "their names emblazoned on brass."[44] The superintendent's support had been bought by promising him new housing for him and his family. The whole exercise was portrayed as having been conducted largely in secret and there were allegations of "mistakes" and even "deception."[45]

Finally the city council, bolstered by advice from the city solicitor that there was no possibility of the land needing to revert to its former owner, voted thirteen to two in favor of the appropriation for the new home. The two councilors who voted against were vitriolic in defeat, calling the plans "unfortunate," "unbusinesslike," "extravagant," and "unwarranted."[46]

The water board duly transferred the land to the public welfare board to build and manage the new city home. It was low, solid, and Georgian in style, echoing the design of

6.18 The City Home for the Aged and Infirm was designed by architect Charles Greco in a W shape, to maximize the exposure of the residents to sun, air and views of Fresh Pond. Built close to the site of the former Fresh Pond Farm, the building was complete by 1929, with a new superintendent's house and large boiler house constructed just to its west. The municipal greenhouses visible in this 1948 photograph were added in the mid-1940s, their location probably not far from the original Olmsted firm plant nursery.
City of Cambridge Annual Documents, 1948, Cambridge Historical Commission.

the new filtration plant just across the water. Apparently the board wanted a design "for the middle class, who are but a step away from the home, as well as the poor."[47] At the dedication ceremony, it was described as "a monument of civic pride . . . a noble building for a noble purpose." Members of the board of public welfare felt it demonstrated how great progress had been made since officials used to use offensive terms like *pauper*, *almshouse*, and *overseers of the poor*. They also derided those who saw building as too beautiful and the location too desirable, arguing that it was not too good for those who had sacrificed all for their children, or been abandoned or robbed or crippled, or were victims of modern business.[48]

By the 1940s the home was known as the city infirmary and had acquired vegetable gardens for the residents' use. In 1954 it took on a new role as an approved medical institution and, in 1974, a new $2.5 million wing was added, and the facility renamed the Mayor Michael J. Neville Manor. In 1999 it was developed further into a public-private facility for the elderly, comprising the Neville Center for Nursing and Rehabilitation, and Neville Place, which contained seventy-one assisted living apartments.

The Hydrology of Fresh Pond

Where does the water in Fresh Pond come from? This seemingly simple question remained long unanswered and was at the heart of a major dispute between the Commonwealth and the city of Cambridge in the middle of the twentieth century. Confusion started as soon as the European settlers arrived: the 1633 map of the Massachusetts Bay Colony (see figure 2.2)

clearly and inexplicably marks Fresh Pond as being "40 fathoms" (240 feet) deep; it is actually perhaps a third of that.

In the 1850s, in an attempt to assess the source of Fresh Pond's supply, the private Cambridge Water Works company commissioned various tests and decided that the watershed could not alone provide the water in the pond. The civil engineer who reported the results was clearly surprised and rather baffled by what he had found. He decided that Fresh Pond "must be fed by copious and unfailing springs in the bottom, which are scarcely at all effected by the variable supplies of rain."[49]

A few years later, in 1870, the water board also investigated Fresh Pond to see if it was large enough to supply the fast-growing city: the board concluded it had "an imperfect idea" of the real capacity of the pond and believed it was "fed from a fountain independent of the rainfall and watershed for any given time, defying all our powers of computation."[50]

During its disputes over water quality with Belmont later that decade, the water board tried again to establish the source of the water in Fresh Pond. Engineers put down sixty-foot borings to try to calculate where the watershed was and how much water came from where. The borings revealed a complex mix of slate, gravel, clay, and sand, as might be expected in this typically glacial landscape. They identified some areas where water was flowing through gravel into the pond, but they were left with considerable uncertainty about how far the underground connections went. They also reported that changes in the level of the pond would affect the flow of water: with so much swampland around, if the pond level sank significantly, the marsh would simply drain into it. The subsequent 1879 report concluded, rather vaguely, that much of the water came from underground sources.[51]

A number of stories exist about the inexplicable hydrology of Black's Nook, but the details are often sketchy and the sources unofficial. A letter to a local newspaper[52] claimed that the writer had been one of a WPA team instructed to fill in the nook in 1934. Street department trucks collected material from all over the city, including old cars, hot top paving, cement, bricks and gravel, hundreds of old tree trunks, indeed anything of a heavy nature that would sink. This was all dumped in the nook, but it was "hopeless": everything just disappeared. The writer recalled advice allegedly given by "old timers" that even locomotives and old freight cars had ended up in the nook and that everything sank into the ground at the bottom and just dispersed into the surrounding soil.

A subsequent correspondent, who had spent her childhood living in the John Barker house just north of Black's Nook, denied ever having seen such activity there.[53] There is certainly no official record of such endeavors (although another writer to the paper referred to the legend of railroad cars sinking overnight into the mud). The water board minutes of the time do refer to work by the employment relief teams of the EPA on roads and fences at Fresh Pond in 1934 (the WPA was not created until the following year), but there is no mention of Black's Nook. Yet the story has much resonance with the earlier unsuccessful attempts by the water board to fill the "bottomless pit"[54] of this nook. Certainly following the 1938 hurricane, which destroyed thousands of trees at Fresh Pond (as well as parts of the road, 600 feet of fencing, and part of the roof of the pumping station[55]), the water board hauled much of the debris into the nook,[56] presumably confident that it, too, would disappear.

Soon after, the city was embroiled in a landmark judicial hearing, where all the evidence hinged on the hydrology of Fresh Pond. It is clear from this that, even in the middle of the twentieth century, there was no consensus on the source of its water. The hearing was a consequence of the water board's 1939 plans to augment its filtration plant and to build a new pumping station. Fearing raised water rates, some citizens pressed the city to reconsider its decision not to join the metropolitan system. The board duly investigated and decided that the cost of joining was simply too high. It seemed an end to the matter. But the Commonwealth had other ideas. With the copious and pure supply of water from the vast Quabbin reservoir about to come on line, it believed that it did not make sense, in economic or health terms, for towns all over Massachusetts to continue investing in their own local supplies. So in 1943 the legislature passed an act that required cities without sufficient safe supplies to join the metropolitan water supply system. To keep its own supply, a city had to prove that it could readily supply at least 10 percent in excess of its average annual consumption.

Tests were carried out on the Cambridge system. The Metropolitan District Commission (MDC, the state agency then responsible for metropolitan water) decided that Cambridge had a safe yield of only 8 percent more than current consumption. Consequently it ordered the city to abandon local supplies and take its water from the metropolitan system. Arguably the Commonwealth's actions, in earlier authorizing Cambridge to acquire land for water supply purposes and now attempting to force the city to join the metropolitan system, reveal a political judgment that Cambridge was more important than the smaller, more rural towns from which land was acquired, but less important than Boston, for which the metropolitan system was largely designed.

Cambridge appealed against the ruling. The transcript of the subsequent judicial hearing[57] makes fascinating reading. With the instigation of legal proceedings, a long-standing animosity between Cambridge and the MDC had come to the fore.[58] It is impossible in this brief summary of the hearing to give any sense of how expert witnesses for both sides were disparaged and derided over the evidence they gave. The city of Cambridge argued that, with its glacial origins, Fresh Pond was like a large well, with water flowing in from the surrounding gravel and sand when levels were low, and out when levels reached a certain height. Thus the city could significantly increase the quantity of water available simply by lowering the level in the pond and letting it refill (a rather ironic argument, given the previous plans to increase the quantity of water by raising the levels).

In addition, one expert testified that, before the last ice age, water had run through New England in canyons and deep valleys several hundred feet below current sea level. One such canyon had run under Winchester, the Mystic lakes, and Fresh Pond to Allston, through the South End and out to Dorchester Bay. At Fresh Pond the valley had been perhaps 160 feet below sea level. During the ice age, the canyon had filled with sand, providing an excellent, porous channel for water to flow into Fresh Pond. The sand was buried under layers of peat and clay, and so it was impossible to tell exactly where it was, despite

6.19 A view of the much-loved Black's Nook, to the north of Fresh Pond, n.d. Its mysterious hydrology has led to a number of splendid "urban myths."
Reprinted by permission of the Cambridge Public Library.

6.20 Costing $50.3 million, the Quabbin reservoir became the new source of water for the metropolitan system. This image shows a view of the valley partially submerged, in November 1940. It was to be six more years before the vast reservoir had completely filled. As a result of its construction, Cambridge came under pressure to abandon Fresh Pond and join the metropolitan system.
Courtesy the DCR Archives at the Quabbin Reservoir Visitors Center, Belchertown, Mass.

the many borings that had been carried out both by the city and more recently by the MDC. But there was some strong evidence that the area to the north and northwest of the pond was one major source of such underground water.

The state expert witnesses told a different story. One argued that Fresh Pond was in fact surrounded by an impervious bowl of clay, and so lowering the levels in the pond would have no appreciable impact in drawing in water from surrounding soils. Others challenged the idea of large amounts of water being available to the north, disparagingly calling it a "mysterious" or even "mythical" source of supply. In an effort to ensure it had the winning argument both ways, the state also produced witnesses who testified that any supply from the north would be highly polluted. They cited horrific reports from earlier in the century about the nature of the pollution in Alewife Brook, and so argued that water drawn in from there would not be safe, even if it was sufficient, under the terms of the 1943 act.

Ultimately the supreme judicial court had to decide which side was more likely to be right and, on balance, it found in favor of the city, ruling that Cambridge did have a "continuous, safe and dependable supply" in excess of what was required.[59] And so Fresh Pond was allowed to remain at the heart of the city's water system.

Experts continued to explore and debate its hydrology. One of the city's witnesses, Professor Camp of Harvard University, was engaged after the court battle to do further work to ascertain the amount of groundwater available at Fresh Pond. Then in 1949 a U.S. Geological Survey concluded that much of the groundwater flowed through sand and gravel from the main catchment areas to the west and northwest of the pond. Lesser amounts of water also came from smaller sandy areas to the north and southwest. The survey team also carried out tests that seemed to confirm there was capacity to secure "a large amount of water from the underground storage around the pond."[60]

Ten years later another study corroborated the evidence about an underground valley or canyon, as outlined during the court case. This research suggested that such a valley, with an inner gorge some eighty feet below sea level, ran from Wilmington, passed under Fresh Pond, and, about a mile southeast of there, joined with the buried valley of the Charles River, which then ran under Brighton and Brookline to Boston Harbor. The research identified where clay, gravel, and sand were likely to have been deposited by the last ice age and concluded that the sand and gravel to the northwest were probably yielding the greatest amount of groundwater for Fresh Pond.[61] It seems that the city's concerns about run-off from the Belmont slaughter house, some seventy-five years earlier, may have been fully justified.

More Development

The legislature passed an act in 1945 that made it easier and cheaper for cities to join the metropolitan system or to use its water supply in an emergency. The city of Cambridge, unsurprisingly, decided to keep its own supply but paid $150,000 over ten years to link with the MDC for emergency and possible future supplies. It was formally accepted into the metropolitan water system on that basis on December 19, 1946.

Bolstered by the court decision about the dependable nature of its Fresh Pond supply, the water board then set about a

6.21 The proposed layout for the integrated Water Works, 1950. All the construction was clustered around the existing filtration plant on the eastern shores of the pond.
City of Cambridge Annual Documents, 1950.

UNDERGROUND

ROAD

FRESH POND

PARKING

FILTER BUILDING
(EXISTING)

PUMPING STATION
(UNDER CONSTRUCTION)

UTILITY BUILDING
(PROPOSED)

VALVE CHAMBER

FLOCCULATION CHAMBERS
(UNDER CONSTRUCTION)

SEDIMENTATION BASINS
(EXISTING)

FRESH POND PARKWAY

LEXINGTON AVE.

PUMPING STATION
(EXISTING)
(TO BE REMOVED)

CAMBRIDGE WATER WORKS
TREATMENT PLANT & PUMPING STATION

6.22 and **6.23** In the early 1950s the water board added a new pumping station (under construction, left), designed by Camp, Dresser and McKee. With its three electric pumps, this replaced the steam-driven "palace" of the 1870s. The board also built a new maintenance or utility plant, just north of the new pumping station, and a boiler room with chimney, to double as a fire tower for fire department training. In addition it added underground flocculation chambers (under construction, right), to allow for a process that improves water purification.
City of Cambridge Annual Documents, 1950, Cambridge Historical Commission.

6.24 The tall chain-link fencing in place near the northwest corner of Fresh Pond, 2004, designed to prevent access to the water. Similar fencing appears to have been first installed around the reservoir just after the Second World War, replacing the 1880s post-and-rail fence. Jill Sinclair.

program of improvements to its own system (see figures 6.22 and 6.23), rationalizing its estate, and replacing and coordinating its "widely scattered and inadequate" facilities.[62]

It was around this time that the board also decided to change the fencing that surrounded Fresh Pond. The whole question of fencing had originally been reviewed when America joined the Second World War in 1942. The superintendent, considering the possibility of some sort of "defense fence," took advice from two representatives of the U.S. Army. They recommended that, to safeguard the water supply, both the pumping station and the filtration plant be protected with seven-foot-high fencing topped with barbed wire, and that all watchmen and guards be given Winchester rifles. It was a recommendation accepted promptly by the board.[63] After the war ended, the board agreed to a major contract to install fencing "around the Fresh Pond area."[64] Further new fencing was installed at the reservation in 1970.

Relinquishing the Land

With its continued investment in the infrastructure at Fresh Pond, the board judged that some of the land it had fought so hard to acquire was now unnecessary for water quality purposes, and could sensibly be relinquished. The first wave of selling took place in the 1920s, when the board explicitly stated that it believed the new filtration plant removed the risk of pollution entering the water supply.[65] It duly sold parcels of land, acquired under the 1888 act, abutting Vassal Lane, Lake View Avenue, and Worthington Street, just outside the reservation to the east. It later also sold two large lots on Huron Avenue.

In 1933 it granted to the city a twelve-foot-wide strip of the reservation south of Concord Avenue, for street widening. Then in 1948 the board released three small parcels of land abutting Fresh Pond Parkway to the MDC.

The most controversial activity came in the 1950s. The board decided (and gained the legislature's approval) to sell off four separate parcels of land along the golf course boundary, on Grove Street and Blanchard Road, for housing development. The sales, and the thinking behind them, do not feature at all in the water board's annual reports of the time. They must have been, at least in part, designed to raise revenue. One newspaper later reported a persistent story that a city council order "designated veteran's preference" for the lots, to provide housing for soldiers returning from the Korean War, but that instead every one of them somehow ended up in the hands of a "well-connected citizen of Cambridge." It alleged that the selling price ($4,000 for a typical 10,000-foot lot) was less than half the true market value, and that they were further revalued down after purchase.[66]

It is difficult to work out what actually happened. Although nothing in the legislation specified the land was for veterans' housing,[67] city council minutes certainly show that councilors voted unanimously to make at least some of the lots available first only to Cambridge veterans. Any left after ninety days would be offered at public auction to all Cambridge residents and then finally made available to members of the general public.[68] On the other hand, the marketing materials put out by the city do not seem to be pitched at veteran purchasers, but perhaps they were produced once the ninety-day period for veterans' preference had expired. To add to the

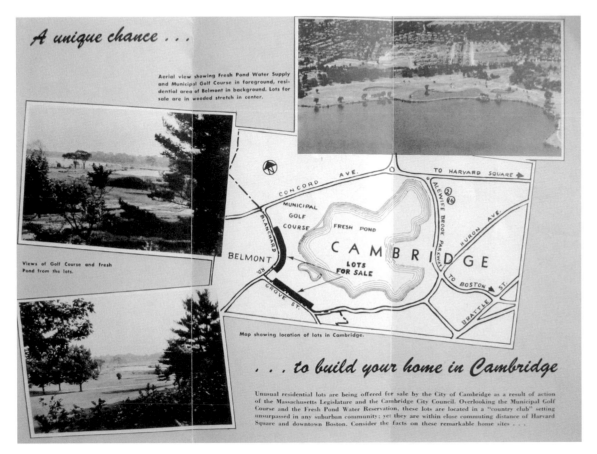

A unique chance . . .

Aerial view showing Fresh Pond Water Supply and Municipal Golf Course in foreground, residential area of Belmont in background. Lots for sale are in wooded stretch in center.

Views of Golf Course and Fresh Pond from the lots.

Map showing location of lots in Cambridge.

. . . to build your home in Cambridge

Unusual residential lots are being offered for sale by the City of Cambridge as a result of action of the Massachusetts Legislature and the Cambridge City Council. Overlooking the Municipal Golf Course and the Fresh Pond Water Reservation, these lots are located in a "country club" setting unsurpassed in any suburban community; yet they are within close commuting distance of Harvard Square and downtown Boston. Consider the facts on these remarkable home sites . . .

6.25 A publicity leaflet produced in the 1950s advertising the housing lots for sale along the golf course boundary. It describes the development as a "country club" setting with single-family residential zoning and beautiful views of Fresh Pond. City of Cambridge Water Department.

confusion, one source says that veterans' housing was in fact planned along Concord Avenue and never carried out.[69]

The newspaper reported that "the list of residents of the strip literally reads like a who's who of Cambridge's political elite," with houses owned by mayors and former mayors, commissioners, city solicitors, and attorneys.[70] The strip became part of what one writer has described as "the finest array of 1950s suburban architecture in Cambridge," and, even today, it is sometimes called "politicians' row."[71]

An "Urban Fringe"

A massive project undertaken between 1909 and 1912 had dredged and straightened Alewife Brook, to remove the risk of water-borne diseases and free up more of the Great Swamp for development. During the First World War this work, plus the

presence of good transport links, and the area's location on the edge of the city, brought a new influx of industry. Oil companies, battery manufacturers, steel fabricators, and others moved in to the north of Fresh Pond. In 1928 two Lexington developers filled in Tudor's Glacialis and set out an industrial subdivision around Moulton and Fawcett Streets (named after the developers). Gasoline filling stations and automobile dealerships appeared along Concord Avenue, which was a main thoroughfare by the 1920s.

In 1929/30 the Commonwealth extended Fresh Pond Parkway northward from its Kingsley Park terminus, as far as Concord Avenue, and added a new segment to Alewife Brook Parkway from Massachusetts Avenue to Concord Avenue. Four years later, in 1934, the state added Route 2 (the new Concord Turnpike), which meant that the newly extended Fresh Pond Parkway, now running alongside the reservation's eastern edge, would become part of a major arterial route linking the city of Boston to its northwestern suburbs.[72] The resulting escalation in traffic volume increased further when Gerry's Landing Road and the Eliot Bridge over the Charles River were built in 1950, providing easier access to Route 2 from Boston via Fresh Pond.

The Metropolitan District Commission (state custodians of the reservations and parkways championed by Charles Eliot and others in the 1890s) found itself under pressure to release lands for the developing highway network and to support the growth of new suburban areas. In the 1940s and 1950s, it relinquished parcels of land throughout many of the metropolitan park reservations, including, between 1948 and 1951, about thirty acres of land around Alewife Brook Parkway. This was sold to private groups, much of it for industrial development.[73]

There followed a whole wave of new industry finding its way to the area, steel fabricators and then small manufacturing, industrial, and warehousing companies locating on the new industrial park to the north, between the pond and Route 2. In 1952 Arthur D. Little, the research and consulting firm, relocated there, and over the next fifteen years it continued to develop its Acorn Park campus, with new buildings and parking lots being added to the forty-acre site.

With the disappearance of much of the brick industry around the early 1950s, as the supply of clay finally dried up, the old clay pits and brickyards were ready for redevelopment. One clay pit, immediately to the northeast of Fresh Pond (see figure 3.9), became the fifty-acre city dump in 1952, used as a municipal solid waste landfill. It was closed in the 1970s and capped with rock excavated from the new tunnel of the Red Line subway, brought by rail from Porter Square (see below). By 1990 the former dump had been recycled into the innovative Mayor Thomas W. Danehy Park.

Some of the other developments took advantage of the good transport links, to create venues for popular activities and entertainment. An open air ("drive-in") movie theater was built in 1950. Bowling alleys and casual family restaurants

6.27 This 1952 aerial image of the pond shows the developments to the north and east of the site. The 350-car Fresh Pond "drive in" movie theater had been built two years earlier on part of the former Glacialis; to its east is the site that would become the shopping center and, beyond that, the new city dump, now home to Danehy Park. Courtesy DCR Archives.

6.28 The $84-million Alewife T Station and Garage, built to the northeast of Fresh Pond in 1985, n.d. With its 2,600-car parking garage, the new station was designed principally to encourage commuters driving in from the north and west of Boston to use the mass transit system for the final part of their journey. Courtesy of Ellenzweig, Architect. Copyright Alex S. MacLean/Landslides.

sprang up along Alewife Brook Parkway and Fresh Pond Parkway. In 1962 the old Union Carbide dump just northeast of the reservation was turned into the strip mall–style Fresh Pond Shopping Center. The $3-million development of this "blighted area" was seen by the city as a way of both reversing the trend for residents to leave Cambridge to shop and of increasing tax revenue through the appreciation of property values. The developers, Wasserman Development Corporation, described it as the beginning of the "conversion of low value wastelands . . . to choice, high-value business properties."[74] A cinema was added two years later, replacing the drive-in. Federally sponsored public housing appeared in 1968 at the twin Rindge Towers, with a third tower added in 1970. In the mid-1980s the Red Line of the MBTA public transportation system was extended from Harvard Square through Porter and Davis Squares to its new $84-million terminus at Alewife, located just across Alewife Brook Parkway from Rindge Towers.

One writer concluded (even before the controversial Red Line extension) that with all this development, Fresh Pond had become the new "urban fringe" of Boston, just as it had been in the 1880s. The "necessary but unpleasant" ice and brick industries, railroads, tanneries, glue factories, and slaughterhouses had been replaced with their modern equivalents: arterial roadways, a large public transport center, places of popular entertainment, industrial parks, and housing projects.[75]

7 Citizen Involvement and the Green Agenda

The overall program is extensive and it is planned to continue the work for years to come. It is encouraging to receive co-operation by people who are interested in the development of this beautiful area. . . . It is definitely a relaxing area of natural beauty.

City of Cambridge Annual Report, 1963, describing the improvement work at Fresh Pond carried out in partnership between the city and members of local horticultural clubs.

The late twentieth-century attitude to landscape was characterized by an increasing belief that the natural world was being irreparably damaged by human activities. People came to question the benefits of technological advances and, more fundamentally, the subservient role that humanity had assigned to nature. Rachel Carson's 1962 book *Silent Spring* was instrumental in raising awareness of threats to the environment. She was arguably the first to warn of the potential dangers of the poisonous chemicals widely used by the agricultural industry, and she suggested a complicity between government, big business, and scientists not to investigate or warn the public of the damage being done.

The issues raised strong emotions, with a growing environmental movement lobbying against parts of industry and government. Heated arguments focused on the kind of world humanity should be bequeathing to future generations: one supported by all modern technological advancements, or one free of the risk of contamination and pollution.[1] As the environmental movement became more and more mainstream, those designing and managing landscapes increasingly began to talk in terms of improving biological diversity, sustaining an ecological balance, and the preservation of natural habitats.

The increasing interest in protecting what became known as natural ecosystems led to a new focus on wetlands (areas where "saturation with water is the dominant factor determining the nature of soil development and the types of plant and animal communities living in the soil and on its surface"[2]). Having been seen previously as worthless swamp, wetlands were now understood to play an important role in maintaining watershed ecosystems: filtering excess nutrients, pollutants, and sediment from run-off; regulating the flow of water in times of drought and flood; and protecting against shoreline erosion.[3]

7.1 Part of the large forested wetland at Fresh Pond, near the Concord Avenue boundary, 2005. These areas, which the water board and the Olmsted firm tried so hard to fill, are now safeguarded by wetlands protection legislation. All of Fresh Pond and the land surrounding it comes under the jurisdiction of the Cambridge Conservation Commission, a part of city government that acts as guardian of the municipality's wetland protection responsibilities.
Jill Sinclair.

7.2 The building of the Walter J. Sullivan Water Treatment Facility confirmed the pond's continuing place at the heart of the city's water supply system. It was also the catalyst for the environmentally driven master plan for the reservation, produced in 2000 through a partnership between the city and local residents. Participants found it an exhausting, cumbersome, sometimes infuriating process of community-based planning, but it led to the production and implementation of the first reservation-wide plan for Fresh Pond since the Olmsted firm's 1897 general plan. Jill Sinclair, 2004.

Inspired by a wish to protect landscapes from destructive human activities, citizens in the 1960s and 1970s increasingly took action themselves to improve or reclaim dilapidated landscapes, a frequent problem at that time as a lack of appropriate funding and skills meant that many publicly owned sites were being poorly maintained. Such citizen involvement stemmed sometimes from growing environmental awareness, sometimes from a desire to protect examples of America's history from development or neglect. These two movements did not always sit easily together: environmental activists tended to discourage any human intervention in a landscape, believing that "nature knows best." Preservationists, on the other hand, often wanted to celebrate and restore specific signs of that intervention, such as engineering works or historic landscape designs.

Toward the end of the century, whenever the managers of a public landscape embarked on plans for its preservation or development, the process would increasingly include consultation with local residents. Such public involvement had emerged as a reaction to the approach in the mid-twentieth century when urban renewal projects were led by powerful individuals, such as Robert Moses in New York, who imposed on communities visions of Corbusier-inspired high-rise buildings surrounded by greensward and interconnected highways. This turned out to be a flawed model, with unsightly, unhealthy results and a high human cost. As a result, cities and states turned to a new approach of community-based planning, where local citizens had a clear voice in the design of public buildings and public space. At its worst, the approach could lead to bland, compromised designs that everyone could accept and no-one would love. But it meant that citizens had a chance to influence public works and therefore gained an important sense of ownership in the results.[4]

An Example of Citizen Intervention

It was in the early 1960s when pressure began to save Fresh Pond as the last seemingly natural space in the city. The main instigator was a group of local women, members of the Cambridge Plant Club (founded in 1889 for women with an interest in "the serious study of horticulture") and the related Garden Club, established around fifty years later. With a mass of experience of community planting and landscaping projects in Cambridge, the two clubs often worked together, and merged into the Cambridge Plant & Garden Club in 1966.[5]

The women became interested in the early 1960s in Fresh Pond as the "only sizeable tract" of open land remaining in Cambridge.[6] A former club president remembers that while the planting around the perimeter path (the old carriage road) was in fair shape, everywhere else was in poor condition, especially around Black's Nook. This had become an illegal dump, seemingly with the implicit acceptance of the city.[7] Apparently dumping had started once the caretaker, who had lived for thirty-five years in the John Barker house just to the north of Black's Nook, had departed.[8]

The club duly proposed reclaiming a five-acre area around Black's Nook as an informal park, with the pond to be used for skating in the winter and fishing in the summer, plus a shaded area for picnicking, and a walk passing through pines, swamp maples, and other native trees and shrubs. The plan called for some regrading to be able to plant new trees, as well as a wildflower meadow and granite rocks for sitting.

The work received favorable comment from the local press. One newspaper ran a piece describing how Black's Nook was a "gold mine of outdoor treasure" now that it had been transformed from "an unofficial dumping area into an attractive green breathing space surrounding the nicest little pond in Cambridge."[9] The same newspaper was later to report that the work at Black's Nook had won a "Civic Beautification Award" for the creation of a "new type of natural park in the city."[10] This description was supplied to the newspaper by club members. They wanted to stress that this was a place where people could study nature: they could pick flowers, catch frogs, skate, and fish. Such passive recreation in seemingly natural surroundings was explicitly seen as the true role of Fresh Pond, "rather than housing developments or public buildings."[11] Unfortunately the water department was not in a position to maintain the new meadow correctly and after eight years or so it became overgrown and was lost.[12]

7.3 Some of the rubbish that had been dumped around Black's Nook, 1963. The city apparently welcomed the approach by the Plant & Garden Club to reclaim this area, and readily agreed to start cleaning it up. City trucks duly removed some ninety tons of debris in and around the water. Dumping was officially prohibited and the road that was being used to bring in the rubbish was closed.
Barbara Paine photograph, courtesy of Patricia Ross Pratt, and The Schlesinger Library, Radcliffe Institute, Harvard University.

The Cambridge Plant & Garden Club continued to work with the city to tackle other areas of the reservation, most notably in a major program of work in the late 1970s and early 1980s. This started with work on the "windswept strip between the Water Works and Lusitania Field" in 1978. Having matched $5,000 of federal funding with the same amount privately raised, the club designed and the city planted a four hundred foot screen of trees on a new berm, to hide an "ugly, exposed commercial complex"[13] that had developed on the far side of the rotary at the northeast corner of the reservation. Reminiscent of the border mounds proposed but never fully installed by the Olmsted firm, this screen ironically excluded from view the relocated 1816 Jacob Wyeth House, once such a feature next to the Fresh Pond Hotel.

The club also designed new planting areas around Lusitania Field. A soccer field had appeared there, probably some time

7.4 Plant & Garden Club members provided designs and planting materials for the work at Black's Nook and, in return, the city agreed to supply the necessary vehicles and labor to carry out the heavy work of planting and maintenance. The club also managed to persuade the auxiliary fire department, which used Fresh Pond for pumping and fire hose drills, to dedicate some of its practice time to watering the newly planted trees. Image April 1963.
Barbara Paine photograph, The Schlesinger Library, Radcliffe Institute, Harvard University.

around 1970, near where Tudor's icehouses had once stood. According to local legend, immigrants living in East Cambridge cleared the land to make the soccer field. They were part of the Portuguese Lusitania social club and started calling the area Lusitania Field, a name that was quickly adopted by everyone who used it.[14] The new planting was intended to provide shade and attractive surroundings for families who wanted to watch the soccer being played and perhaps to picnic.

The other major project, commenced in 1980 and supported by a National Founder's Fund Award from the Garden Club of America, was on a thirty-acre site just north of Little Fresh Pond (where the city had once installed an athletic practice field), and where a wetland was now threatened by encroachment from the adjacent golf course. It was a popular picnic site and birds nested there in some numbers. In addition it was a location for school science studies for those using the Maynard Ecology Center, which had been established by the Cambridge Public Schools District at Black's Nook, to enable teachers and students to learn about ecology through scientific fieldwork. Despite the center's rather grand name, for many years it was located in a trailer near Neville Manor. Classes would visit to collect and examine specimens, analyze water samples, take guided nature walks and sketch plants. Over the next few years, the club worked to restore the wetland meadow, with plantings of tansy and other two- or three-foot-tall wildflowers, plus a few shrubs. Again, the city did not have the workforce necessary to cut the meadow by hand; it was largely taken over by volunteer trees and shrubs.[15]

The Cambridge Plant & Garden Club has undoubtedly been influential on the landscape at Fresh Pond. While some

7.5 The "windswept" land next to Fresh Pond Parkway, still sometimes known as Tudor Park, a few years before the Plant & Garden Club began work there, 1975.
City of Cambridge Water Department.

7.6 The 2005 view from the northeast corner of the reservation. The screening designed by the Plant & Garden Club in 1979 was largely lost as a result of the later installation of the bike path in this area.
Jill Sinclair.

of its individual designs for replanting have not survived, its members hope that it brought a new ethos to the reservation, which values the diversity of its different areas, from wetland meadow to hardwood forest. They believe that its approach, of using only native plantings and devising short- and long-term planting strategies, has served as a guide for the city in all its work at Fresh Pond. In the beginning, in the early sixties, members felt that city employees saw them as essentially amusing, "fluffy" women playing at large-scale landscape management.[16] But the joint venture prospered into the "largest and the longest" project in the history of the club.[17]

Studies, Plans, and False Starts

As the only large open space of its kind in Cambridge, and now completely surrounded by housing and commercial development, Fresh Pond was becoming more and more popular for both passive and active recreation: it was "a pastoral retreat in the midst of intense urban activity."[18] In 1980, the Cambridge Plant & Garden Club estimated that the reservation was being used by 7,000 people a week.[19] By 1982 the city was seriously considering whether it could restrict access just to Cambridge residents, or deter visitors from other towns by charging some sort of entrance fee.[20]

Throughout the seventies and beyond, the city commissioned a succession of reports and plans about the management of Fresh Pond. Their recommendations reflect the range of views about the appropriate use of the site, from encouraging greater public access (more paths, a new dog run, a bandstand, a garden for the blind; even the reintroduction of fishing and swimming in the reservoir); detailed horticultural advice for the management of the existing trees and new planting; to ways of improving water quality and increasing wildlife habitats.[21] Ad hoc proposals for new uses of the land continued, from affordable housing near the golf course[22] to a large shelter for the homeless near Neville Manor.[23] Some ideas (such as plans for two sets of community gardens) were put into practice, but in general little evidence exists of follow-up activity or the implementation of proposals.

The Catalyst for Change

In 1987 the city began a five-year capital program to improve its water treatment and distribution systems. Three years into the work, an audit recommended the upgrading or replacement of the existing treatment plant. The old building had passed its life expectancy and did not comply with current building codes or state regulations on water quality. It was labor-intensive to run and subject to frequent problems and system upsets. The water department considered giving up local supplies and switching to the metropolitan water system (now run by the Massachusetts Water Resources Authority [MWRA]), but it judged that such a change would lose the benefits of substantial previous investment in the system and could lead to higher water rates.[24]

By 1996, after extensive studies, the city decided to build a new treatment plant on the site of the existing buildings, but with a smaller overall footprint. A series of public meetings was held to seek views on the planned new facility. While there were few reactions to the technical issues involved in designing a new plant, strong views quickly emerged over the accompanying planting schemes proposed around the building. Some felt that they were too formal and did not fit in with the more natural feel elsewhere. People pressed for a comprehensive study of the reservation as a basis for clear decisions on its future management. Keen not to slow down the plans for the plant, the city decided to remove the landscaping element from the building design contract and instead to organize a parallel study of the landscape, in order to produce a master plan for the whole reservation.[25]

7.7 and **7.8** Two attempts to manage the public's impact on the landscape: stabilizing the soil on the Glacken Field slopes (left) and posting rules for dog owners (above), 2004. Preserving the purity of the water supply while allowing significant public access to the reservation has long been one of the challenges faced by the water department. Jill Sinclair.

Community-Based Planning in Action

The decision to create a master plan unleashed the full range of views about this much-loved, much-used landscape. Some people were passionate in their belief that this was an opportunity to restore the landscape into a wilderness: to remove signs of human intervention, discourage large-scale human access, and allow local flora and fauna to regain the upper hand. Others thought that human presence was what made Fresh Pond special: one newcomer to Cambridge wrote a newspaper article about the "wonders" of Fresh Pond. She described with affection the myriad dogs and their owners, the golfers and joggers, the range of languages accompanying the birdsong, the snippets of overheard conversation. "I know there is a park ranger who cares for the reservoir, and that it probably has a rich history, but I prefer to imagine my own stories about this magical place. I prefer to think about the lives of the people who briefly cross my path there each day."[26]

The ranger herself, Jean Rogers, who was appointed in 1994 to assist in public education and rules enforcement at Fresh Pond, also had a primary interest in the human visitors. Working to help people understand and appreciate the landscape, she described the contact with people as the best part of her job, from answering questions about wildlife to mediating altercations between cyclists and dog owners and making bird boxes with schoolchildren. "I know city people. I know them and appreciate them. I enjoy the diversity of the cultures, languages, people, and food. It's a rarified people who get to the national parks. I want to be with people where they live."[27]

Others strongly argued that the city should seize the chance to rediscover and celebrate the Olmsted park, as was happening with the Emerald Necklace, Boston's Olmsted-designed municipal park system: "We really need to make an effort to get the Cambridge community to understand that this was a planned landscape—an art form to enhance the vistas around a utilitarian yet scenic urban necessity, the reservoir. . . . This park is a critical preservation issue which needs the historic building community to come to its aid and raise a loud voice for protection."[28] Others fought strongly to retain and improve the active recreational facilities present on the landscape, arguing that they were of more practical importance in ensuring the well-being of the city's children than the creation of some kind of nature reserve: "The Fresh Pond Park should not be reserved for only golf and the 'passive recreation' pastimes enjoyed by the upper-middle-class communities located near it."[29] All the while, the water department was seeking to keep the protection of the purity of the water supply, the original purpose of the reservation, at the top of the increasingly long agenda.

Clearly battles were to be fought during the review: the process would not be easy. The city manager set up the Fresh Pond Reservation Master Plan Advisory Committee, comprising twelve local residents (chosen from those who had responded to local newspaper advertisements seeking help) and six city officials. As the city's watershed manager remembers, the main groups were "pretty well represented"[30] among the volunteers: they included walkers, joggers, dog owners, bicyclists, golfers, soccer and baseball supporters, bird watchers, teachers, cross-country skiers, photographers, writers, lawyers, and parents. The city was represented by officials from the water department, the conservation commission, the recreation division, the community development department, the housing authority, and the school department (who shared membership with an environmental consultant from the Massachusetts Audubon Society).

In retrospect, despite this lengthy list of interests, some voices may have been missing. The people using the community gardens went unrepresented. Many of them were Russian or Asian immigrants living in the Rindge Towers to the north of the reservation. While the water department felt it worked hard to involve them in discussions about the use of the land, officials accepted that they probably felt excluded from the process.[31] For whatever reason, the city also decided not to include an official historic preservation representative on the committee, and it seems that the history of the site did not establish a sufficient resonance within the group for any committee member to decide to take on that role. Although the history of the landscape was investigated, passionate views focused more on its current uses and future potential, rather than on how it had evolved over time. In any event, the staff of the Cambridge Historical Commission judged that there was no constituency for landscape restoration, and no obvious way to recapture some of the lost history.[32]

The early days of the committee were particularly fraught. These were complex community groups, sharing their citizenship of Cambridge, but sometimes little else. With the various strong-minded citizens, the city officials each with their own priorities, and a team of professional consultants, there were, as one participant remembers, "egos all over the place."

7.9 The city ordinance that allowed dogs to exercise unleashed made Fresh Pond a popular location for dog owners from Cambridge and neighboring towns, including Belmont, Watertown, Somerville, Newton, and Brookline. Managing the impact of dogs was one of many topics that caused animated debate at the master plan committee meetings.
Jill Sinclair, 2004.

Building consensus took time and patience. Committee members brought such a wide range of opinions and perspectives to the group. It took the committee three months just to agree on a short mission statement. Debates were particularly lively on issues such as dogs, signage, and fencing. One published review of the process identified how, in considering a planned inventory and stewardship plan, there were lengthy debates to agree, for example, whether cultural (that is, man-made) features should be included; to decide whether beneficial but nonnative plant species should be recommended for future use; even to agree what terminology should be used to represent the range of users of Fresh Pond.[33]

The process was further complicated by the other work underway at Fresh Pond. The city was focused more on the new treatment plant itself, a project that was proving both expensive (finally costing about $80 million) and controversial. Designed by Camp, Dresser and McKee, the building was a modern version of the neo-Georgian style of its predecessor. Some welcomed the new design, believing it had emerged well from the lengthy design process and the significant input from local residents. Its motifs paid homage to Boston's H. H. Richardson, the nineteenth-century architect, and its materials to the red brick of Harvard. It was designed to demonstrate its "civic importance"[34] just as the original "palace" of a pumping station had done over one hundred years earlier. Others liked the modern, elegant interior but felt it was trapped inside a disappointingly bland exterior, which provoked descriptions such as "historicist wallpaper . . . a bunch of boxes with cookie-cutter decorations . . . architectural elevator music."[35]

As it was built, much of the reservation became a construction zone, with the land around Lusitania Field being used as a vast staging area. The city's water was being purchased from the MWRA all the time that Fresh Pond was effectively out of commission. With so much going on, the watershed manager remembers ruefully that it was sometimes hard for city officials to see discussions about trees as a high priority.[36]

As well as the plans for the new water facility, the city was reviewing the future of Neville Manor. In the 1960s responsibility for caring for the poor shifted from cities to the state, leaving Neville Manor dependent on third-party payments. By the 1990s it was losing $2 million every year. The city produced its plan to turn the old city home into a location for assisted living and a skilled nursing facility. The proposed redevelopment was contentious, with some people pressing the city to abandon the building and return the site to parkland. Similar arguments emerged to those that were expressed when the city home was first proposed in the 1920s: whether affordable housing for the elderly was more or less valid on this landscape than public open space. Apparently members of the water board, the Cambridge Conservation Commission and some state officials were also worried about the impact of the $20-million redevelopment plans on water quality.[37]

In 1998, in an effort to address these concerns, the city manager appointed the Neville Manor Site Plan Advisory Committee (comprising officials and local residents, including three members of the master plan committee) to investigate and recommend the best location for the new facilities. Eventually it was agreed that they should remain on the northern shores of the reservation, but with a smaller overall footprint and with about four acres of land being returned to the water department to become vegetated open space. The yard used by the city's Department of Public Works was to be removed, the ancillary buildings demolished (with the Maynard Ecology Center relocated into the basement of Neville Place), and Lusitania Field in the northeastern section of the reservation returned to a more natural state.

That seemed to be a good compromise, but then another fierce argument broke out, reflecting yet again the many tensions and colliding viewpoints over Fresh Pond. Soccer coaches, players, and their families felt that they had not been given the chance to influence the decision about Lusitania Field, already temporarily lost to them under a mass of construction materials. The local press reported the fury of those who felt that a dishonorable bargain had been made when people "whose overriding concern is something other than soccer purported to give away a soccer field."[38] One coach described the decision as "madness." The organizer of a local soccer program recognized the attractions of increasing the city's areas of "pristine environment" but argued that, "weighed against the loss of playing fields that are irreplaceable, it just doesn't balance against the needs of the city's children." Those in favor of the plan included two members of the master plan committee: one explained that "Lusitania joins into a wild, wooded area. . . . The combined area will be very good for wildlife." Another stressed the increased opportunities for children to learn about local flora and fauna: "We all know that soccer is great, but it's not the only game in town."[39]

Another project already underway was the new bike path planned by the MDC on land it owned along Fresh Pond Park-

7.10 The bike path, seen here in 2005, was designed as part of the reconstruction of the parkway undertaken at the same time as the new water treatment plant was being built. Running from the Alewife Brook Parkway/Concord Avenue rotary to the junction with Huron Avenue, it was controversial for a number of reasons.
Jill Sinclair.

7.11 Views collided over a proposed piece of public art. "Acoustic Weir" by Mags Harries and Lajos Héder was an abstracted representation of the largely invisible water system. Some local residents argued that the artwork should be made to blend in with its surroundings, essentially to appear natural. After much controversy, it was abandoned in favor of an installation located mainly inside the new treatment plant. Harries/Héder.

way, with federal funds meeting some of the cost. Some cyclists criticized the design, as it confusingly followed state guidelines for bike paths rather than municipal ones, and some sections were considered badly designed and dangerous.[40] The water department worried that the bike path would simply bring more people to the reservation while it was attempting to limit access, for instance through allowing only those with Cambridge resident permits to park there. Members of the master plan committee were also unhappy, as the bike path was explicitly excluded from their deliberations even though it would encroach onto an already narrow strip of land, at Tudor Park, and bring nonporous hard surfaces ever closer to the water's edge.[41]

Even the design and location of the public artwork proposed for the weir meadow evoked strong feelings. At a packed public meeting to discuss the proposals, some people spoke in favor of the proposed installation, while others argued that "the art itself is not the point. Maintaining the natural, undeveloped space is the point." The deputy city manager was clearly surprised at the depth and range of the reactions: "There have been over 100 public art projects and I've never seen the city engage in a debate like this over the placement of public art."[42]

Somehow the master plan committee members persevered. They felt a strong sense of ownership of the landscape and took seriously the opportunity presented to them to bring about change. It still took three years to produce the final version of the master plan, with a considerable amount of time invested at the end in drafting and printing the 150-page report. One participant remembers its production as "a nightmare." But there was also a sense of profound satisfaction that all the tensions and disagreements had finally been resolved and a way forward agreed on. Patricia Pratt, who represented the Cambridge Plant & Garden Club on the committee and who had been part of the club's efforts at Fresh Pond since the early 1960s, clearly saw it as "the most important thing since I've been involved."[43]

The Master Plan Realized

The final report was produced in May 2000. With its cover photograph of a quiet nook enclosed by vegetation, it began with a "vision statement" that attempted to capture the main purpose of the group's work: "The Fresh Pond Master Plan expresses the vital importance of protecting and enhancing both the water quality of the Fresh Pond Reservation and its open space and naturalistic character. The Plan embodies a vision and sets a framework for the preservation of water quality, recreational open spaces, natural green spaces, wildlife habitat, and a refuge from hectic urban life."[44] It included five goals, which focused on improving water quality, wildlife habitats, and educational opportunities; preserving natural character; and ensuring amicable mixed recreational use.[45]

A major priority was the need to restore and improve the ecological balance of the landscape, especially its shorelines and wetlands. Specimen trees and patches of important or unique vegetation were to be protected by the removal of invasive vines and careful pruning and feeding. The plan also proposed improving (and sometimes limiting or redirecting) human access in a number of areas.

In addition, a series of policies was proposed about how the reservation should be used. These recommended, among other things, that any future development of the land should be subject to public scrutiny and that generally such development was to be discouraged. The executive summary of the master plan particularly stressed a recommendation that, whenever possible, land currently under hard surfaces should be returned to green open space. The recreation policy proposed retaining Glacken Field, the golf course, and the perimeter path for active recreation (with a major redesign recommended for Glacken Field), plus creating a new youth soccer

7.12 The new swale at the edge of the weir meadow, installed as part of the master plan implementation. The plan proposed the use of "bioengineering" techniques, which included the removal of invasive plant species, the use of natural materials to stabilize shorelines and slopes, and the planting of diverse, native woody plants and ground cover. Vegetated swales (shallow depressions planted with native species), such as this one, help filter storm water runoff before it enters the reservoir. Jill Sinclair, 2004.

field to replace the one lost. In addition, it recommended a permit system for all large gatherings and sports events and a medallion program to reduce and better manage the number of dogs allowed to run unleashed. Proposals about signage were also made, especially that all signs and information should have a consistent design, to help reestablish the reservation as a single, unified landscape.

The master plan was accepted by the city of Cambridge and, at the time of writing, is part way through implementation. Now that there is a way forward agreed with local residents, the city is prepared to invest both people and funds in significant changes to the landscape. Money is also forthcoming under the new Community Preservation Act, passed by the Massachusetts legislature in 2000 and designed, among other things, to allow local people to preserve their open spaces. There is much evidence of activity and much enthusiasm from both city officials and many members of the public. Projects are underway to improve the soil and drainage on Kingsley Park; to restore the shoreline at Little Fresh Pond; and to develop a master plan for the Black's Nook area. Pilot projects have tested porous path materials and tried out different heights of fencing around the reservoir, with new four-foot fences in well-protected areas allowing unimpeded views of the water. A major redesign project in the northeast sector includes restoring a wetland meadow on the old soccer field, creating a butterfly meadow, building a new youth soccer field, and relocating the perimeter path to allow better views across the water. With such extensive and evident improvement work underway, the reservation has become even more popular as a place for passive and active recreation, so much so that the water department, perhaps ironically, began to urge Cambridge residents to visit other local parks and green spaces instead of Fresh Pond.[46]

It is perhaps too soon to tell how significant an impact the plan will have in the long term. It has, at the very least, allowed members of the local community and the city of Cambridge together to consider anew the significance of Fresh Pond, and to plan for the future of this precious, irreplaceable landscape.

Afterword

It is debatable how much physical evidence of its history remains at Fresh Pond. Certainly an application to add the reservation to the National Register of Historic Places (the nation's official list of cultural resources worthy of preservation) was rejected by the Massachusetts Historical Commission in 1982. An internal note at the commission states simply: "Lost integrity. Not enough there."[1]

Some continuing strands of the landscape's past do emerge, however, evidence of the site's history that is still present and celebrated by those who use the land today. Fresh Pond has certainly retained its sense of being rural, that deceptive feeling that it is somehow natural or untouched by human intervention. Present for a long time when the landscape lay outside the centers of population, its rural character arguably disappeared with the city's stark engineering works in the 1880s. But people now feel that it has returned: despite its role as a reservoir, and its new situation subsumed within Cambridge's residential and commercial districts, Fresh Pond is now widely seen again as undeveloped, an urban wild, a wilderness.

There is also a long-standing tradition of using this landscape for educational purposes. Catholic schoolgirls and volunteer soldiers have learned lessons along its shores. Birdwatchers, even before Brewster, saw Fresh Pond as a place to study and document waterfowl and other avian residents and visitors. Such activity continues today. Harvard students did not just play here: they also saw it as an opportunity to further their learning, for instance with the biological studies conducted from rowboats in the 1930s. The Maynard Ecology Center, set up in the 1960s, allows school children to explore nature and conduct scientific fieldwork. In the last decade, the water department has appointed rangers to work with the public and provide a variety of educational opportunities for visitors. The 2000 master plan suggests an extended educational outreach program.

8.1 The Friends of Fresh Pond Reservation produce educational materials and arrange events to involve members of the local community at the pond. Here a group on a summer "nesting birds and fledglings walk" is helped to spot a warbling vireo, 2007. Elizabeth Wylde photograph.

Recreation runs throughout the history of Fresh Pond. From the seventeenth-century Harvard skaters to the bowling alleys and boats of the hotels, it has offered many opportunities for people to get together and play. Picnicking, sleigh riding, enjoying a quiet stroll or a noisy fair, jogging or bicycling, walking a dog, or kicking a ball: all have been done on the shores of Fresh Pond. It was one of the early municipal sites for a playground and remains an important location for organized sports in the city.

On a smaller scale, sections of the reservation have long been cultivated, from the probable seasonal plantings of indigenous peoples and the early settlers' farms and orchards, to the ice traders' fruit trees, the Olmsted nursery on the northern shores, the vegetable garden run by residents of the city home, and the municipal greenhouses, to today's two sets of popular community gardens.

Some of the names also commemorate the pond's history: Kingsley Park in memory of the first water board president, Lusitania Meadow for the Portuguese soccer players, Black's Nook recalling the local family whose icehouse once stood there.

Other strands of history have not survived so clearly. It is not just the Great Pond rights that have been surrendered. Apart from the water treatment plant, there is little evidence of the intensive industry that once crowded around the shores. A lonely historical plaque at the entrance to Neville Center is the only official mark of the ice industry, and its location means it is rarely seen by those who visit the reservation. There may be archaeological traces of some of the icehouse foundations and of Frederic Tudor's boathouse on the northern shore,[2] but they are not marked or obviously discernable.

8.2 The Cambridge Historical Commission plaque at the entrance to Neville Center, 2005. Its slightly cryptic inscription reads: "Tudor Ice Company. The seasonal industry of Fresh Pond supplied Frederic Tudor's company with ice for the Caribbean, India South America and Europe. 1826–1892."
Jill Sinclair.

Although still there, the railroad gives no clues about its origins. Even the term Tudor Park, to describe the strip of land donated to the city by Tudor's heirs, seems to have fallen into disuse. The English author of a recent book on the ice trade visited Fresh Pond as part of his research. Describing the trip as a "pilgrimage" to the place that was the center of the extraordinary industry he was investigating, the writer was astonished and saddened to find that there was no obvious memorial or mention of the business, or its Ice King.[3]

Other elements of the reservation's history are also arguably uncelebrated. Little commemorates the early years of the water industry, with its "palace" of a pumping station and two nearby reservoirs (although part of the walls remain on Reservoir Street, for those who know where to look). The old Payson Park gatehouse near the treatment plant stands unexplained and in need of repair. Similarly the site of the temporary Civil War barracks is unmarked, lost under subsequent developments. Nothing recalls the trenches dug and mock battles fought during the First World War on the northern shores of the pond. Even the relocated Fresh Pond Hotel, despite its inclusion on the National Register of Historic Places, is not really commemorated.

In addition, much of the Olmsted firm's work has not been clearly identified and is little known or celebrated. Some of the firm's topographical changes, plantings, roads, and pathways definitely remain, but parts of the design are irretrievably lost as a result of later developments, and none of it is safeguarded. New planting has sometimes been in keeping with the pastoral, naturalistic style of the firm, but some of it has not: the most public section of the reservation, as it borders Fresh Pond Parkway, has recently been laid out in an unsympathetic, suburban style dotted with individual trees.

There are no easy answers to the issues about preserving and celebrating the rich and diverse history of Fresh Pond. Indeed, there is no consensus for even attempting to do so.

Few would argue for the slavish preservation or restoration of all historical aspects of a landscape. Time moves on; public expectations shift; landscapes are living creations that have a habit of growing and changing, sometimes in surprising ways. But knowledge of the history is important, so that decisions can be made in the light of the landscape's past. Perhaps the bike path and community gardens would have been located anyway over the site of the Civil War barracks; but it was probably done without knowledge of that part of the reservation's history. Encouraging students, citizens, local historical organizations, and others to explore and share the history would help the city make informed decisions about its future. Including archaeological work in the implementation of the master plan (particularly on Kingsley Park) would uncover new information about the landscape's past. In addition, keeping important city records and establishing a Fresh Pond archive would mean that today's decisions and activities are preserved for future generations as a basis for their planning.

Recent guidance on National Register properties emphasizes that history is not just about the "great men" whose deeds fill the pages of traditional history textbooks. We need to find ways to celebrate and remember the range of history and stories about a landscape. Properties on the register "can help the nation see history not only as great national events in which only a few participated, but as a cavalcade of events,

8.3 and **8.4** Only mysterious remnants are left of many of the nineteenth-century features at the pond. By the early 1940s the bridge under Huron Avenue was in such a poor state of repair that the city engineer decided, with the water board's agreement, to replace it with fill. Thus the curious gully (left, 2005) just east of Glacken Field is all that remains of the Fountain Terrace entrance. Nearby, the fountain itself, which celebrated the arrival of the Stony Brook supply, is reduced to a mysterious piece of metal just visible in the water (right, 2005).
Both Jill Sinclair.

trends, and patterns that still affect our lives today, including many ethnic and cultural groups as participants. The public is drawn to history that relates to their everyday lives, and that can give their own lives meaning."[4]

Whether or not it is time to reconsider if Fresh Pond has a place on the National Register of Historic Places, it must be helpful to find ways to explore and celebrate its vibrant, varied past. People like water board president Chester Kingsley and landscape architect Charles Eliot are undoubtedly important. So too are the carousing picnickers, the women's horticultural club, the Catholic schoolgirls, the Russian immigrant gardeners, the Irish laborers, the volunteer soldiers. It has been a place of industry, education, and production, a political battlefield, and a practice battlefield, and it is richer—and we are richer—as a result.

8.5 The Historic Cambridge Collaborative ran a "Walk through the History of Fresh Pond," led by Harvard historian Don Ostrowski, as part of its 2007 Discovery Days.
Elizabeth Wylde photograph.

Notes

Chapter One

1. Cambridge Water Department Chief Ranger Jean Rogers, quoted in Colleen Walsh, "Fresh Pond Balancing Act: Recreation Vs. Preservation," *Boston Globe*, January 9, 2005.
2. Charles Eliot to Henry D. Yerxa, president of the Cambridge Park Commission, October 16, 1893, Records of the Olmsted Associates, Manuscripts Division, Library of Congress (hereafter Olmsted Records).
3. Clifford Geertz, "Thick Description: Toward an Interpretive Theory of Culture," in *The Interpretation of Cultures* (Basic Books, 2000), 23.
4. Neil Evernden, "The Social Use of Nature" and "Nature and Norm" in *The Social Creation of Nature* (Baltimore: Johns Hopkins University Press, 1992), 3–17 and 18–36.

Chapter Two

1. Massachusetts Historical Commission, *Reconnaissance Survey Town Report: Cambridge* (1980), 4–5. A 1999 archaeological survey confirmed a Native American "find spot" on the north shores: Neville Manor (Cambridge Home for the Aged and Infirm) National Register of Historic Places (NR) nomination form, 2002, Massachusetts Historical Commission, Boston, Mass.
2. Around 1912, Harvard's Peabody Museum was given a Native American skull and other parts of a skeleton, supposedly from "an Indian grave near Fresh Pond." Harvard University, "The Peabody Museum of American Archaeology and Ethnology," in *Report of the President and the Treasurer of Harvard College, 1912–13*, 229. Courtesy of the Harvard University Archives.
3. Cambridge Historical Commission, *Survey of Architectural History in Cambridge, Report Five: Northwest Cambridge*, ed. Arthur J. Krim (Cambridge, Mass.: MIT Press, 1977), 8.
4. Christopher Coli McMahon, "To Have and Have Not—Nantucket, Martha's Vineyard, and the Public Trust Doctrine," *Boston College Environmental Affairs Law Review* 31, no. 2 (2004), http://www.bc.edu/schools/law/law-reviews/meta-elements/journals/bcealr/31_2/09_TXT.htm.
5. CHC, *Northwest Cambridge*, 13.
6. Charles W. Elliott, *The New England History*, vol. 1 (Michigan Historical Reprint Series, 2005), 300–301.
7. Francis Knapp, "A New England Pond," in *Poetical Quotations from Chaucer to Tennyson*, ed. S. Austin Allibone (Michigan Historical Reprint Series, 2005).
8. Lincoln Diamant, ed., *Revolutionary Women in the War for American Independence: A One-Volume Revised Edition of Elizabeth Ellet's 1848 Landmark Series* (Westport, Conn.: Greenwood Publishing Group, 1998), 49.
9. Elizabeth A. Fenn, *Pox Americana: The Great Smallpox Epidemic of 1775–82* (New York: Hill and Wang, 2002), 47–48.
10. Jacques Pierre Brissot de Warville, quoted in Alan Emmet, *Cambridge, Massachusetts: Changing of a Landscape* (Cambridge, Mass.: Harvard University Press, 1978), 13.
11. CHC, *Northwest Cambridge*, 17.
12. Ellen Susan Bulfinch, "The Tudor House at Fresh Pond," in *Proceedings of the Cambridge Historical Society*, vol. 3 (Cambridge, Mass.: Cambridge Historical Society, 1908), 100.
13. *Boston Gazette*, May 30, 1816.
14. *Columbian Centinel*, June 29, 1816.
15. Bulfinch, "Tudor House at Fresh Pond," 100.
16. Frederic Tudor, diary entry, April 3, 1838, Tudor Ice Company Records, 1752–1902, MSS 766, Baker Library Historical Collections, Harvard Business School, Boston (hereafter cited as Tudor Records, Harvard).
17. The Storers, Apthorps, Bulfinches, and Fosters were all closely related by marriage. John Apthorp was married to Grace Foster and then her twin, Mary; his sister Hannah married her cousin Charles Bulfinch, the architect; Charles's sister was Anna, George Storer's wife; Ellen Susan Bulfinch (the writer of the "Tudor House" article) was Anna and George's granddaughter.
18. Bulfinch, "Tudor House at Fresh Pond," 101.
19. Hannah Bulfinch, letter, June 18, 1830, quoted in Bulfinch, "Tudor House at Fresh Pond," 107.

20. Hannah Bulfinch, letter, September 26, 1830, quoted in Bulfinch, "Tudor House at Fresh Pond," 107.

21. Charles W. Eliot, *Charles Eliot, Landscape Architect* (Boston: Houghton, Mifflin & Co., 1903), 248.

22. Alan Emmet, *So Fine a Prospect* (Hanover, N.H.: University of New England Press, 1996), 57–68.

23. Dr. Benjamin Waterhouse, quoted in Roger Gilman, "Wyeth Background," *Proceedings, Cambridge Historical Society*, vol. 28 (1942), 43.

24. Lucius R. Paige, *History of Cambridge, Massachusetts 1630–1877* (Boston: H. O. Houghton & Co., 1877), 641. Paige sites the hotel near the 1877 division line between Cambridge and Belmont, which was formed by the Alewife Brook, but its exact location is no longer known.

25. Judith Sargent Murray, letter, to Sarah Sargent Ellery, August 25, 1795, transcribed by Bonnie Hurd Smith. The writer does not specify the name or owner of the house she visited, but it was most likely the dwelling house at Fresh Pond Farm, rented from Henry Prentiss by the Burkes.

26. *Columbian Centinel*, May 25, 1811. It seems that, like the Burkes before him, Wrightson was renting the dwelling house at Fresh Pond Farm (he advertised his hotel as "the House formerly occupied by Col. Apthorp"), rather than relaunching Richardson's failed hotel.

27. Gilman, "Wyeth Background," 31.

28. The source of this information (Joseph Palmer, *Necrology of Alumni of Harvard College 1851–52 to 1862–63* [Boston: John Wilson & Son, 1864], 107–108) does not explain the nature of the mortgage on the hotel, but presumably it was more a promissory note than the arrangements we understand by this term today.

29. Palmer, *Necrology of Alumni*, 108.

30. Charles Francis Adams quoted in Emmet, *Changing of a Landscape*, 15.

31. Sam'l May, Jr., "Class of 1829—Commencement," in *Proceedings, Cambridge Historical Society*, vol. 12 (1829), 14.

32. Paige, *History of Cambridge*, 705.

33. "Fresh Pond Hotel," *Cambridge Chronicle*, May 8, 1947.

34. William Callahan owned it in 1848 and William G. Fischer from 1875, according to Chauncey Depew Steele Jr., "A History of Inns and Hotels in Cambridge," *Proceedings, Cambridge Historical Society*, vol. 37 (1957), 34. Steele speculated that there might have been a gap in the hotel's operations between 1848 and 1875, as he found some diary entries that bemoaned the lack of dining facilities and public houses in Cambridge between those dates.

35. David Pulsifer, *Guide to Boston and Vicinity* (Boston: A. Williams & Co., 1868), 213.

36. David Hackett Fischer, *Four British Folkways in America* (New York: Oxford University Press, 1989), 139.

37. F.O. Vaille and H.A. Clark, *The Harvard Book: A Series of Historical, Biographical, and Descriptive Sketches* (Cambridge, Mass.: Welch, Bigelow and Co., 1875), 188. This book makes it clear that, by the 1870s, boats had become available for hire on the Charles River, even though it was still tidal and presumably not entirely odor free.

38. Mary Daughtry, *Gray Cavalier: The Life and Wars of General William H. F. "Rooney" Lee* (Cambridge, Mass.: Da Capo Press, 2002), 21.

39. William Tucker Washburn, *Fair Harvard: A Story of American College Life* (New York: G. I. Putnam & Son, 1869), 161.

40. Moorfield Storey, quoted in Harvard College, "Class of 1864 Class Book: an inventory," *OASIS*, http://oasis.lib.harvard.edu/oasis/deliver/~hua30004. Courtesy of the Harvard University Archives.

41. Richard S. Kennedy, *Dreams in the Mirror: A Biography of E. E. Cummings* (New York: Liveright, 1994), 87.

42. Thomas Russell Sullivan, "A Poetical Record or a 'Feast of Reason': For the Boys' Sleigh Party to Fresh Pond Hotel, January 9, 1850," Houghton Library, Harvard University.

43. Nathan Haskell Dole, introduction to *The Poems of James Russell Lowell*, by James Russell Lowell (New York: Thomas Y. Crowell & Co., 1898), xiii.

44. William Brewster, *The Birds of the Cambridge Region of Massachusetts* (Cambridge, Mass.: Nuttall Ornithological Club, 1906), 37.

45. Rufus Dawes, *Nix's Mate: An Historical Romance of America* (New York: Samuel Colman, 1839), 122–130.

46. "Annual Picnic of the Printers of Cambridge, at Fresh Pond Grove, August 8, 1868," pamphlet, Houghton Library, Harvard University.

47. "Fresh Pond Hotel," *Cambridge Chronicle*, May 8, 1947.

48. *Report of the Massachusetts State Board of Health, 1878*, quoted in *Fresh Pond Water: Measures Proposed for the Protection of the Purity of the Water-Supply of the City of Cambridge* (Boston: Franklin Press: Rand, Avery & Co., 1878).

49. "Pollution—1878," Belmont Historical Society Newsletter, Fall 1970, Belmont Historical Society, Belmont, Mass., 16.

50. Roy Rosenzweig, *Eight Hours for What We Will* (Cambridge: Cambridge University Press, 1985), 36–45.

51. Richard M. Thomas, "A Glimpse into Fresh Pond's History," *townonline* (December 12, 2001), www.issues2000.org/spectrum/32892352.htm. There are similar descriptions in "Fresh Pond Hotel," *Cambridge Chronicle*, May 8, 1947; and CHC, *Northwest Cambridge*, 136.

52. Steele, "History of Inns and Hotels," 34. The link became so widely quoted that by 1984 even the sisters who had bought the hotel were telling the tale ("Centenary Program," Fall 1984, Boston Congregation of the Sisters of St. Joseph Archives, Brighton, Mass., hereafter CSJ Archives).

53. Gilman, "Wyeth Background," 31.

54. Citizens' Committee, *Ten No-License Years in Cambridge 1887–1897, A Jubilee Volume* (Cambridge, Mass.: The Citizens' Committee, 1898), 93–112.

55. Undated, untitled file note, CSJ Archives.

56. Sister M. John McLaughlin, "History of the Sisters of St. Joseph, Boston, Mass" (unpublished paper, c. 1939), CSJ Archives.

57. Sister Cecilia Agnes, letter [c. 1910], quoted in "The Development of the Community in Cambridge and Brighton" (undated note), CSJ Archives.

Chapter Three

1. Susan E. Maycock and Charles M. Sullivan, *Building Old Cambridge* (Cambridge, Mass.: MIT Press, under contract), draft copy, June 2006.

2. *Boston Gazette,* quoted in Gavin Weightman, *The Frozen Water Trade* (New York: Hyperion, 2003), 37.

3. *Pittsfield Sun*, January 17, 1856.

4. Weightman, *Frozen Water Trade*, 45. See also F. H. Forbes, "Ice," *Scribners Monthly* 10, no. 4 (August 1875), which reported that "the cutting of ice for commercial purposes first commenced" at Fresh Pond.

5. Richard O. Cummings, *The American Ice Harvest, A Historical Study in Technology* (Berkeley: University of California Press, 1949), 21–25.

6. Nathaniel Wyeth to his wife, March 31, 1834, "Selected Letters of Nathaniel J. Wyeth," Library of Western Fur Trade Historical Source Documents, http://www.xmission.com/~drudy/mtman/html/wyethltr.html.

7. Thoreau was told that some of the supply in the icehouses at Fresh Pond was five years old and "as good as ever." Henry David Thoreau, *Walden & Civil Disobedience* (East Rutherford, N.J.: Viking Penguin, 1983), 247.

8. Gilman, "Wyeth Background," 37, states that Wyeth had never before been outside Cambridge; but Carl Seaburg and Stanley Paterson, *The Ice King: Frederic Tudor and His Circle,* ed. Alan Seaburg (Boston: Massachusetts Historical Society, 2003), 136, find evidence in Tudor's diaries that he sent his young protégé to New York, Philadelphia and Baltimore to sell ice in 1828.

9. Tudor's diaries record that Wyeth wished to be apart from his wife because of "her habit of drinking. He had been a long while greatly distressed by this domestic trouble" (September 19, 1831). On January 6, 1832, Tudor notes that Wyeth's "domestic inquietude" was the main reason why he was determined to go (Tudor Records, Harvard).

10. John B. Wyeth, *Oregon; or a Short History of a Long Journey from the Atlantic Ocean to the Region of the Pacific, by Land* (Cambridge, Mass., 1833), http://www.xmission.com/~drudy/mtman/html/jwyeth.html.

11. *Boston Transcript*, August 1856, quoted in Stephen P. Sharples, "Nathaniel Jarvis Wyeth," in *Proceedings, Cambridge Historical Society*, vol. 2 (1907), 37.

12. Dr. Benjamin Waterhouse, quoted in Weightman, *Frozen Water Trade*, 154.

13. Weightman, *Frozen Water Trade*, 154–155.

14. Tudor, diary entry, April 3, 1838, Tudor Records, Harvard.

15. Tudor's Journal D, 1858–1864, Tudor Records, Harvard. The journal also includes references to income from the rent of a "Tavern at Fresh Pond" to Charles H. Blanchard around 1860, but the author could find no other information on this.

16. CHC, *Northwest Cambridge*, 178.

17. Tudor, diary entry, December 31, 1838, Tudor Records, Harvard.

18. Weightman, *Frozen Water Trade*, 175.

19. Justin A. Jacobs, *Opinion Concerning the Rights of the City of Cambridge in and to the Waters of Fresh Pond* (Cambridge, Mass.: Metcalf & Co., 1856); legal opinion of Judge Curtis, January 20, 1858, quoted in *Cambridge Water Reports, 1867–79* (Cambridge, Mass.: John Ford & Co., c. 1879).

20. Cummings, *American Ice Harvest*, 25.

21. Hittinger, quoted in Forbes, "Ice," 469.

22. Sources vary on when the Glacialis was dug. *Pittsfield Sun,* October 6, 1842 reported the creation of a "very large" shallow reservoir at Fresh Pond, to manufacture ice, which most obviously would be a reference to the Glacialis. Brewster, *Birds of the Cambridge Region*, 44, quotes Hittinger as saying it was dug around 1850 and the spoil deposited in the northeast tip of Cambridge Nook. CHC, *Northwest Cambridge*, 25, erroneously reports that it was not created until the early 1860s.

23. Nathaniel Wyeth et al., "Brief Statement of Facts," 1840, quoted in Weightman, *Frozen Water Trade*, 161.

24. *Pittsfield Sun*, January 13, 1842.

25. Thoreau, *Walden*, 343–347.

26. Becky M. Nicolaides and Andrew Wiese, eds., *The Suburb Reader* (New York: Routledge, 2006), 88.

27. Alan Seaburg, Thomas Dahill, and Carol Rose, *Cambridge on the Charles* (Cambridge, Mass.: Anne Miniver Press, 2001), 115.

28. "Ice," *New York Sun*, reprinted in *Pittsfield Sun*, January 18, 1844.

29. Tudor, various diary entries, October 1859, Tudor Records, Harvard.

30. Cambridge Water Works, "Report to Stockholders, 1855–1861," in *Cambridge Water Reports*.

31. Ibid., 17.

32. Legal opinion, Judge Curtis.

33. For instance, Tudor paid his lawyers, Butler & Green, $50 for "Legal Services in Case v. Cambridge Water Works," Tudor's Journal D, 1858–1864, May 20, 1861, Tudor Records, Harvard.

34. For more on the workers' housing around Fresh Pond see CHC, *Northwest Cambridge*, 68–73.

35. Brewster, *Birds of the Cambridge Region*, quoted in Wilfred Osgood, "In Memoriam: Ruthven Deane, 1851–1934," *The Auk* 52, no. 1 (January 1935), 4.

36. Philip Van Doren Stern, *Soldier Life in the Union and Confederate Armies* (Bloomington: Indiana University Press, 1961), 22.

37. *Boston Post*, June 3, 1861.

38. Ibid.

39. *Roxbury City Gazette*, June 6, 1861.

40. *Boston Post*, June 3, 1861. The article mentions a "merchant of this city" who boarded up several nearby houses rather than allow the soldiers to use them. Given the location of the regiment, the merchant may have been Frederic Tudor.

41. Allen Alonzo Kingsbury, letter to his parents, June 5, 1861, from his posthumous memoirs, *Hero of Medfield* (Boston: J. M. Hewes, 1862), http://letterscivilwar.org/6-5-61b.html. Kingsbury was killed at Yorktown, April 26, 1862.

42. *Roxbury City Gazette*, June 6, 1861.

43. Stern, *Soldier Life*, 22.

44. *Roxbury City Gazette*, May 5, 1864.

45. *Pittsfield Sun*, January 17, 1856.

46. Charles Louis Flint et al., *One Hundred Years' Progress of the United States* (Ann Arbor: University of Michigan Library, 2005), 388.

47. Lady Emmeline Stuart Wortley, *Travels in the United States etc. during 1849 and 1850* (New York: Harper & Brothers, 1851), 143.

48. Elizabeth Barlow Rogers, *Landscape Design: A Cultural and Architectural History* (New York: Harry N. Abrams, 2001), 311–312.

49. James Elliott Cabot, quoted in Emmet, *Changing of a Landscape*, 29. A piece that included similar language appeared as "Sedge-Birds" in *Atlantic Monthly* 23, no. 137 (March 1869): 384–386. The "Sedge-Birds" author complains how at Fresh Pond the present time has its "far-reaching schemes, its cosmopolitan interests, and must live on the street, and has no time to think of the sunshine or the want of it."

50. Bulfinch, "Tudor House at Fresh Pond," 108.

Chapter Four

1. David Schuyler, *The New Urban Landscape: The Redefinition of City Form in Nineteenth Century America* (Baltimore: Johns Hopkins University Press, 1986), 2.
2. Ibid.
3. Michael Rawson, "The Nature of Water: Reform and the Antebellum Crusade for Municipal Water in Boston," *Environmental History* (July 2004), http://www.historycooperative.org/journals/eh/9.3/rawson.html.
4. Eliot, *Charles Eliot, Landscape Architect*, 340. Eliot (or his source) may be mis-quoting the year: Fairmont Park was the site for a major centennial celebration in 1876, which over 10 million people attended (then about a quarter of the population of America).
5. George Cook, Superintendent of Cambridge Parks, quoted in Albert Fein, "Frederick Law Olmsted and the City of Cambridge—A Note on the Career of an Environmental Gardener" (paper presented to the Cambridge Plant & Garden Club, Massachusetts, April 2, 1974).
6. CHC, *Northwest Cambridge*, 18.
7. For instance, the board hoped that Fresh Pond would become to Cambridge "what Chestnut Hill Reservoir is to the City of Boston," *City of Cambridge Water Board Annual Report (CWB AR) 1885*, 8.
8. Kingsley is usually given much of the credit for the city's intervention at Fresh Pond: "His zeal and foresight as president of the Board that inaugurated the present magnificent water system of the city caused him to be known as 'father of the Cambridge Water Works.'" (Samuel Atkins Eliot, *A History of Cambridge, Massachusetts, 1630–1913* [Cambridge, Mass.: Cambridge Tribune, 1913], 218). He was also a life-long prohibitionist, which must have left him uncomfortable with the liquor licenses being granted to the Fresh Pond Hotel.
9. Chester W. Kingsley, "Cambridge Water Works," in *The Cambridge of Eighteen Hundred and Ninety-six: A Picture of the City and Its Industries Fifty Years After Its Incorporation*, ed. Arthur Gilman (Cambridge, Mass.: Riverside Press, 1896), 114.
10. Ibid., 115.

11. Just two years earlier Boston's water board had created a triumphal entrance arch and three elaborate, Renaissance Revival gatehouses at the new Chestnut Hill reservoir.
12. Henry W. Muzzey, quoted in *Fresh Pond Water*, 24. In 1896 Fresh Pond gained a pumping engine designed by Edward D. Leavitt, a Cambridge resident who was one of the most prominent steam engineers in America. A similar one at Chestnut Hill reservoir, apparently the only one still in existence, has been designated a National Mechanical Engineering Landmark by the American Society of Mechanical Engineers.
13. City of Cambridge, *Report of a Special Committee of the Water Board in Relation to Leakage and Waste of Water* (Cambridge, Mass.: Welch, Bigelow & Co., University Press, 1876), 7.
14. *Fresh Pond Water*, 15.
15. *The Petition of the Mayor of Cambridge for Annexation of a Part of Belmont, Closing Argument of Hon. Henry W Muzzey, March 9, 1880* (Boston: 1880), 5.
16. *Fresh Pond Water*, 17. The speaker, Henry W. Muzzey, refers to the paper by Dr. Cogswell in the *Report of the State Board of Health 1878*.
17. "Pollution—1878," Belmont Historical Society, 13.
18. *Petition of Mayor of Cambridge*, 6.
19. "Pollution—1878," Belmont Historical Society, 13–15.
20. *CWB AR 1884*. Because of uncertainty over whether Fresh Pond would be the long-term water supply for Cambridge, the city had originally decided not to take the land when the 1875 act was passed.
21. Commonwealth of Massachusetts, 1888 Acts Chapter 137, section 3.
22. *Cambridge Chronicle*, January 26, 1889.
23. "For Sultry Days," *Cambridge Tribune*, April 2, 1892.
24. Boston Ice Journal B 1880–92, Tudor Records, Harvard.
25. *Cambridge Chronicle*, c. July 23, 1892 (photocopy at the Cambridge Historical Commission: the date on the copy is difficult to decipher).
26. "New City Home Appropriation Postponed for Another Week," *Cambridge Chronicle*, May 13, 1927.
27. *CWB AR 1893*.
28. The practice became less common with the arrival of overhead wires, which impeded removal. Nowadays the main impediments are the lack

of vacant lots and the fact that old houses become subject to building codes once they are moved. Even so, a handful are still sold and relocated each year in Cambridge. (Charles Sullivan, executive director, Cambridge Historical Commission, interview with author, May 5, 2005.)

29. Richard Betts of the Belmont Historical Society kindly provided newspaper articles and photographs of this house, owned for many years by Timothy J. Mannix Sr., and located at 126 Blanchard Road. It appeared to be a nineteenth century property, with a substantial mansard roof, but could conceivably have been remodeled from an earlier colonial structure.

30. *Cambridge Chronicle*, June 15, 1889.

31. *CWB AR 1890*.

32. "Fresh Pond Days, 1885–91," undated photocopy of selected entries from the CSJ Annals, CSJ Archives.

33. *Boston Daily Globe*, October 6, 1890.

34. *CWB AR 1889*.

35. "What's to Be Done?" *Cambridge Chronicle*, October 28, 1893.

36. *CWB AR 1897*. The act gave the city the right to "take and hold by purchase or otherwise, all the rights, privileges, property and easements" of the Fitchburg Rail Road on "any land, real estate and locations" around Fresh Pond. The city then granted the railroad company a perpetual easement to maintain the tracks and operate trains over the land.

37. Commonwealth of Massachusetts, 1888 Acts, chapter 137, section 3.

38. Brewster, *Birds of the Cambridge Region*, 191.

39. *CWB AR 1895*.

40. *The Crimson*, February 5, 1889.

41. Frederick Law Olmsted Jr., "The Relation of Reservoirs to Parks," paper 32 in *American Park and Outdoor Art Association, 1899* (Boston: Rockwell & Churchill Press, 1899), 4–32.

42. *City of Cambridge Superintendent of the Water Board Annual Report 1892*, 345.

43. *CWB AR 1894*.

44. Entry, August 31, 1894, Minutes of the City of Cambridge Water Board, 1865–1947, City of Cambridge Water Department (hereafter Minutes, Water Board). At the time of writing, the original books containing the hand-written minutes were located in two "Rubbermaid" tubs near the office of the department's managing director.

45. *CWB AR 1886*, 9.

46. *CWB AR 1892*, 328.

47. *CWB AR 1884*, 192.

48. *CWB AR 1888*, 261.

49. For more information on the construction of roads and bridges around the Pond in the early 1890s, see Kingsley, "Cambridge Water Works," 117, and *CWB AR 1891*.

50. *CWB AR 1891*, 320.

Chapter Five

1. Schuyler, *New Urban Landscape*, 5.

2. Ibid., 7.

3. Anne Whiston Spirn, "Constructing Nature: The Legacy of Frederick Law Olmsted," in *Uncommon Ground: Toward Reinventing Nature,* ed. William Cronon (New York: W. W. Norton & Co., 1995), 91–113.

4. Eliot, *Charles Eliot, Landscape Architect*, 340.

5. Ibid., 342.

6. Arleyn Levee, "John Charles Olmsted," in *Pioneers of American Landscape Design*, ed. Charles Birnbaum and Robin Karson (New York: McGraw-Hill, 2000), 282–285.

7. Susan L. Kraus, "Frederick Law Olmsted Jr.," in *Pioneers,* ed. Birnbaum and Karson, 273–277.

8. "A High Compliment," *Cambridge Chronicle*, October 14, 1893.

9. Charles Eliot to Henry D. Yerxa, President of the Cambridge Park Commission, October 16, 1893, Olmsted Records.

10. *Second Annual Report of the Board of Park Commissioners of the City of Cambridge 1894*.

11. Olmsted Jr., "Relation Reservoirs to Parks."

12. Eliot, *Charles Eliot, Landscape Architect*, 554.

13. Charles Eliot, letter to the Cambridge Water Board, April 3, 1894, in Eliot, *Charles Eliot, Landscape Architect*, 476–478.

14. Minutes, Water Board, January 16, 1895.

15. Ironically, eighty years later, one observer was to blame the Olmsted firm for the appearance of the shoreline, claiming that the Pond's edges were "rationalized" as part of a plan by Olmsted Sr. that "never went further than straightening the borders" (Jean Tibbils, "Natural High: Answering the Call of the Wild at Fresh Pond," *Cambridge Chronicle*, August 2, 1984).

16. Charles Eliot, letter to the Cambridge Water Board, April 3, 1894, in Eliot, *Charles Eliot, Landscape Architect*, 477.

17. Stillman Kelley to Olmsted, Olmsted and Eliot, July 11, 1896, Olmsted Records.

18. Minutes, Water Board, March 19, 1895.

19. John Charles Olmsted to Stillman Kelley, October 31, 1902, Olmsted Records.

20. John Charles Olmsted to Stillman Kelley, October 23, 1902, Olmsted Records.

21. Stillman Kelley to Olmsted Brothers, January 24, 1901, Olmsted Records.

22. Minutes, Water Board, May 23, 1898.

23. Stillman Kelley to Olmsted, Olmsted and Eliot, June 12, 1895, Olmsted Records.

24. John Charles Olmsted, file note, May 4, 1901, Olmsted Records.

25. Karl Haglund, *Inventing the Charles River* (Cambridge, Mass.: MIT Press, 2003), 162–164.

26. Minutes, Water Board, July 5, 1895.

27. Frederick Law Olmsted Jr., file note, October 15, 1898, Olmsted Records.

28. John Charles Olmsted to Stillman Kelley, October 31, 1902, Olmsted Records.

29. H. J. Kellaway file note, May 18, 1901, Olmsted Records.

30. John Charles Olmsted, file note, May 4, 1901, Olmsted Records.

31. Olmsted Jr., "Relation Reservoir to Parks," 24.

32. H. J. Kellaway, file note, August 13, 1902, Olmsted Records.

33. *CWB AR 1896*.

34. G. Gibbs Jr., "Planting Report and Plan," April 6, 1906, Olmsted Records.

35. H. J. Kellaway, file note, August 13, 1902, Olmsted Records.

36. *CWB AR 1896*.

37. Rizzo Associates, Inc., *Fresh Pond Reservation Natural Resource Inventory* (Rizzo Associates, 1998).

38. A. Phelps Wyman, file note, June 11, 1901, Olmsted Records.

39. *CWB AR 1907*.

40. Henry D. Yerxa, "Cambridge Parks," in Gilman, *Cambridge*, 124.

41. Fresh Pond Parkway, Metropolitan Park System of Greater Boston National Historic Register nomination form, October 2004, photocopy, Cambridge Historical Commission.

42. Dorothy Elia Howells, *A Century to Celebrate: Radcliffe College, 1879–1979,* Harvard / Radcliffe Online Historical Reference Shelf, http://pds.lib.harvard.edu/pds/view/2573612?n=105. Courtesy of the Harvard University Archives.

43. Irving Howe, introduction to Henry James, *The American Scene* (New York: Horizon Press, 1967), v–vi.

44. Henry James, *The American Scene,* 71.

45. Brewster, *Birds of the Cambridge Region*, 36.

46. Frederick Law Olmsted Jr., file note, May 10, 1909, Olmsted Records.

47. *CWB AR 1901*, 220.

48. *CWB AR 1910/11*, 215.

Chapter Six

1. City of Cambridge, *Expert Reports upon the Development of the Water Supply of Cambridge, Mass.* (Cambridge, Mass., 1912).

2. Rogers, *Landscape Design*, 427.

3. Playground Association of America leaflet number 2, 1909, quoted in Rosenzweig, *Eight Hours*, 147.

4. Sarah Jo Peterson, "Voting for Play: The Democratic Potential of Progressive Era Playgrounds," *Journal of the Gilded Age and Progressive Era,* 3.2 (2004), http://www.historycooperative.org/journals/jga/3.2/peterson.html.

5. *City of Cambridge Playground Commission Annual Report 1910/11*.

6. City of Cambridge, *Expert Reports*, 17.

7. Letter to Mayor Quinn, quoted in Minutes, Water Board, June 8, 1922.

Another reference in the board minutes (on June 16, 1922), to a request to allow horseback riding, describes the carriageway, of which the board was once so proud, simply as the "dirt roadway skirting Fresh Pond."

8. Fred. E. Smith, "Filter-Plant Operation at Cambridge, Massachusetts," *Journal of the New England Water Works Association* (March 18, 1948), 220.

9. Minutes, Water Board, April 20, 1921.

10. "Plan for New City Home Strikes a Snag," *Cambridge Chronicle*, April 29, 1927.

11. Julian Lowell Coolidge, "Lawrence Lowell, President," in *Proceedings, Cambridge Historical Society*, vol. 34 (1951–1952), 11.

12. James Scully, letter to Lawrence Lowell, May 21, 1917, Norbert Wiener Papers (MC 22), Institute Archives and Special Collections, MIT Libraries, Cambridge, Massachusetts (hereafter Wiener Papers, MIT).

13. "Plan of Defense of the Fresh Pond Supporting-Points," instruction leaflet, folder 1654, Abbott Lawrence Lowell Papers, Harvard University Archives (hereafter Lowell Papers, Harvard). Courtesy of the Harvard University Archives.

14. Norbert Wiener, letter to his mother, July 2, 1917, Wiener Papers, MIT.

15. Norbert Wiener, letter to his mother, July 15, 1917, Wiener Papers, MIT.

16. U.S. Army Captain C. Cordier, memo to ROTC members, May 29, 1917, folder 724a, Lowell Papers, Harvard.

17. Scully, letter to Lowell, May 21, 1917.

18. Norbert Wiener, letter to his mother, July 15, 1917, Wiener Papers, MIT. Despite these experiences and his undoubted enthusiasm, Wiener was subsequently turned down for Officers' Training Camp and did not see the active service for which he had practiced at Fresh Pond.

19. "Overseers to Review Maneuvers of Corps—Fall In at 2.30," *The Crimson*, May 13, 1918.

20. "Combat Maneuver And Review Today Close R. O. T. C. Activities For Year," *The Crimson*, May 28, 1918.

21. Coolidge, "Lawrence Lowell," 12.

22. "Goodbye, Messrs. Chips," *Time Magazine* (June 25, 1951), http://www.time.com/time/magazine/article/0,9171,806040-1,00.html.

23. Harvard University, *Report of the Treasurer of Harvard College, 1919–20*, 179. Courtesy of the Harvard University Archives.

24. Jean Rogers, interview with the author, October 25, 2004.

25. *CWB AR 1930/31*.

26. Minutes, Water Board, May 22, 1939.

27. Harvard University, *Report of the President of Harvard College, 1936/37*, 200. Courtesy of the Harvard University Archives.

28. Minutes, Water Board, January 9, 1947.

29. Arthur C. Comey, "Fresh Pond Golf Links Proposed," *Cambridge Tribune*, March 5, 1921, and "Adapting a Park to Modern Needs," *Landscape Architecture* 11 (July 1921): 176–179.

30. Arthur C. Comey, letter to Gallagher, April 8, 1920, Olmsted Records.

31. Rogers, *Landscape Design*, 493.

32. *CWB AR 1931*.

33. Paul Harber, "A Tip of the Cap to These Nine Holes," *Boston Globe*, May 9, 1996.

34. Rogers, *Landscape Design*, 494.

35. Radcliffe College, *Reports of College Officers, 1934–1935*, 58–59. Courtesy of the Harvard University Archives.

36. *City of Cambridge Park Commissioners Report 1941*.

37. Harber, "Tip of the Cap."

38. Neville Manor NR nomination form.

39. Commonwealth of Massachusetts, 1925 Acts, chapter 225, section 1.

40. "Pertinent Points about City Home," *Cambridge Chronicle*, June 3, 1927.

41. "Plan for New City Home."

42. "Pertinent Points."

43. "New City Home Appropriation Postponed for Another Week," *Cambridge Chronicle*, May 13, 1927.

44. "Proposal for New City Home Stirs Vigorous Opposition at Hearing," *Cambridge Chronicle*, May 6, 1927.

45. "New City Home Appropriation."

46. "New City Home Order Passed," *Cambridge Chronicle*, May 27, 1927.

47. "Proposal for New City Home."

48. *City of Cambridge Board of Public Welfare Annual Report 1928/29*.

49. Civil engineer's report, November 12, 1855 in *Cambridge Water Works Records,* May 31, 1853–June 16, 1865, manuscript document, City of Cambridge Water Department.

50. Howard M. Turner, "Recent Additions to the Cambridge Water Supply," *Journal of the New England Water Works Association* 66, no 2 (1952): 6–7.

51. City of Cambridge, *Report of the Special Committee on the Water Supply of the City* (Cambridge, Mass.: John Wilson & Co., 1879).

52. Henry R. Snell, letter to the editor, "Black's Nook Pond 'Unfillable,'" *Cambridge Chronicle*, May 9, 1963.

53. Eleanor and John Beck, letter to the editor, *Cambridge Chronicle*, May 23, 1963.

54. *CWB AR 1895,* 504.

55. *CWB AR 1938.*

56. File note, box 13, Cambridge Plant & Garden Club Records, 1889–1991, MC 419, Schlesinger Library, Radcliffe Institute, Harvard University (hereafter Plant & Garden Club Records, Harvard).

57. *Hearing in the Matter of Water Supply of City of Cambridge before Board of Assessment Commissioners*, stenographic record by Ella M. Foster (Barristers Hall, Boston, 1944).

58. *Hearing, Water Supply*, 1014.

59. Minutes, Water Board, April 17, 1944.

60. Quoted in Turner, "Recent Additions," 6.

61. Newton Earl Chute, "Glacial Geology of the Mystic Lakes-Fresh Pond Area, Massachusetts," *U. S. Geological Survey Bulletin*, Report: B 1061-F (1959).

62. Turner, "Recent Additions," 19.

63. Minutes, Water Board, October 5, 1942.

64. Minutes, Water Board, July 12, 1945.

65. *CWB AR 1928/29.*

66. "Cambridge Report I: Real Estate Racketeers," *Boston Phoenix*, October 12, 1971.

67. Commonwealth of Massachusetts, 1951 Acts, chapter 255, section 1 (April 20, 1951). Later enactments allowed the sale of further plots: see chapter 302, section 1 of the 1955 Acts and chapter 112, section 1 & 2 of the 1961 Acts.

68. Minutes, City of Cambridge Council, September 24, 1951.

69. Sheila G. Cook, *The Great Swamp of Arlington, Belmont, and Cambridge: an Historic Perspective of its Development, 1630–2001* (Cambridge, Mass.: S. Cook, 2002), 37.

70. "Real Estate Racketeers."

71. CHC, *Northwest Cambridge*, 177.

72. Maycock and Sullivan, *Building Old Cambridge,* draft, May 2005.

73. Almost no official records survive of the MDC's land sales in the 1940s and 1950s, but I am grateful to Sean Fisher, the DCR archivist, who managed to unearth one typewritten document that lists ninety-six parcels of MDC land sold between 1945 and 1953. Nine of them relate to Alewife Brook Parkway, although exact locations are not recorded. By 1956 a report produced for the MDC (*Study and Recommended Program of Development of Parks and Reservations and Recreational Facilities of the Metropolitan Parks District*, 1956, iii) was ruefully recording that land was being sold without an overall strategy for the future of the metropolitan parklands, and in the face of considerable economic and social pressures: "Glowing pictures have been presented of the tax advantages and other economic benefits to local communities of the transfer of large and apparently idle public areas to private ownership for industrial or residential development."

74. "Shopping Center," *Magazine of Cambridge*, April 1962, 8–10.

75. CHC, *Northwest Cambridge*, 18.

Chapter Seven

1. Evernden, "Social Use of Nature," 4–5.

2. This definition is from the 1979 system devised by Lewis M. Cowardin et al, for the U.S. Department of the Interior, which has been adopted as the national classification standard for wetlands.

3. Environmental Protection Agency, *America's Wetlands, Our Vital Link between Land and Water,* pamphlet.

4. Charles Sullivan, interview with author, February 3, 2005.

5. Finding aid, Plant & Garden Club Records, Harvard. I am also grateful to Annette LaMond for information on the club's history.

6. Undated file note [c. 1973], box 13, Plant & Garden Club Records, Harvard.

7. Patricia Pratt (former president, Cambridge Plant & Garden Club), telephone interview with author, January 2005.

8. *Cambridge Chronicle*, May 2, 1963. After the caretaker left, the little brick house was boarded up and later demolished.

9. Ibid.

10. *Cambridge Chronicle*, June 1, 1967.

11. Undated file note [c. 1966], box 13, Plant & Garden Club Records, Harvard.

12. Pratt, interview.

13. Undated file notes [c. 1979], box 14, Plant & Garden Club Records, Harvard.

14. Sarah Boyer (oral historian, Cambridge Historical Commission) in discussion with the author, May 2005; see also Catherine Ivey, "Soccer Zealots Hoping to Sink Lusitania Plan," *Boston Globe*, January 24, 1999.

15. Pratt, interview.

16. Ibid.

17. File note [c. 1987], box 14, Plant & Garden Club Records, Harvard.

18. Roy Mann Associates Inc., *Fresh Pond Reservation Master Plan* (1978), 9.

19. File note, 1980, box 14, Plant & Garden Club Records, Harvard.

20. *Cambridge Chronicle*, April 8, 1982.

21. The studies included: John B. Hepting, *A Land and Water Use Study of Fresh Pond Reservation* (1971); Council on Environmental Quality, *Recreation on Water Supply Reservoirs—A Handbook for Increased Use* (September 1975); the Cambridge Plant & Garden Club's 1978 *Horticultural Review and Recommendations for Planting at Fresh Pond Reservation*; and the 1978 Roy Mann Associates' *Fresh Pond Reservation Master Plan*.

22. Fresh Pond Reservation Master Plan Advisory Committee, *Fresh Pond Reservation Master Plan* (Cambridge, Mass.: City of Cambridge, May 2000), 32.

23. City of Cambridge, City Council Order, January 12, 1987.

24. City of Cambridge, *Water Treatment and Supply Improvement Program* pamphlet, n.d. [prior to 1997].

25. Chip Norton (Watershed Manager, City of Cambridge Water Department), interview with author, February 8, 2005.

26. Judy F. Kugel, "Reservoir Is Quite an Attraction," *Boston Globe*, March 26, 2000.

27. Morgan Baker, "Her Class Meets at Fresh Pond," *Boston Globe*, June 7, 1998.

28. Arleyn Levee, letter to Charles Sullivan, May 9, 1998, Fresh Pond folder, Cambridge Historical Commission.

29. Kathleen M. Genova, "Soccer Players Take Offense to Healy's Comments on Lusitania," letter in an uncredited local newspaper, February 25, 1999, Fresh Pond folder, Cambridge Historical Commission.

30. Norton, interview.

31. Ibid.

32. Sullivan, interview.

33. Thomas S. Benjamin, "Fresh Pond Reservation: Building Consensus for Natural Resource and Water Quality Preservation at the Fresh Pond Reservation," *Erosion Control* (September/October 1999), http://www.forester.net/ec_9909_pond.html.

34. Robert Campbell, "New Waterworks Excels at 'Rhetorical' Design," *Boston Globe*, October 21, 2001.

35. David Eisen, "Cookie-cutter Design Dampens Cambridge's New Waterworks," *Boston Herald*, March 4, 2001.

36. Norton, interview.

37. *Cambridge Chronicle*, July 12, 1998.

38. Genova, "Soccer Players Take Offense."

39. Ivey, "Soccer Zealots."

40. Kristen Lombardi, "Uneasy Riders," *Boston Phoenix*, May 30, 2002, and John S. Allen, "Sidepath between Concord Avenue Rotaries, Cambridge, Massachusetts," Bike Expert, http://www.bikexprt.com/massfacil/cambridge/freshpond/sidepath.htm.

41. Norton, interview.

42. Christopher Muther, "New Plans for Water Sculpture Don't Satisfy Foes," *Boston Globe*, December 14, 1997.

43. Pratt, interview.

44. Advisory Committee, *Fresh Pond Master Plan*, 1.

45. Ibid., 17.

46. Walsh, "Fresh Pond Balancing Act."

Afterword

1. The application put forward by the Cambridge Historical Commission briefly outlined Fresh Pond's history, with mentions of the ice trade and the Olmsted firm's work. It implicitly placed its period of significance during the creation of the public park and rather harshly concluded that, with the later "intrusions," the only remaining feature from that time was a cast iron railroad bridge on Huron Avenue. The application form was endorsed with the commission's rejection on May 20, 1982. Fresh Pond District National Register of Historic Places survey form, 1964[?], Massachusetts Historical Commission, Boston, Mass. Ironically, the only part of the reservation on the register is one of the later "intrusions": in 2002 Neville Manor was added for its significance in the development of municipal support to the elderly indigent. This nomination was made principally to enable Neville Manor's developers to apply for the investment tax credit on approved historic rehabilitations.

2. Rizzo Associates, *Fresh Pond Inventory*. See also "Ice Cutting on Fresh Pond," *Belmont Historical Society Newsletter,* December 1972, which reported that the piles of the icehouses could still be seen when the water in the Pond was low.

3. Weightman, *Frozen Water Trade*, 246.

4. Ron Thomson and Marilyn Harper, "Telling the Stories: Planning Effective Interpretive Programs for Properties Listed in the National Register of Historic Places," *National Register Bulletin* (2000), U.S. Department of the Interior, National Park Service, http://www.nps.gov/history/nr/publications/bulletins/interp/.

Index

Page numbers in italics refer to figures.

Abbott, Almon, 46
Acorn park, 137
African-Americans, 51
Alcohol, 22, 28, 30, 38, 165n9, 165n15
Alewife Brook, 91
   clearing of, 95
   floodgates, 61
   footpaths and, 12
   hydrology studies and, 131
   ice industry and, 39, 41–42
   pollution and, 64, 131
   straightening of, 136
   suburban development and, 136–137
Alewife Brook Parkway, 136, 139, 171n73
Alewife T station, *138*, 138–139
Alewives, 14
Algonquian tribes, 12. *See also* Native Americans
Annexations, 5, 64, *65, 67*
   eminent domain and, 66, 68–71
   municipal expansion and, 107
Apthorp, John, 16–17, 163n17
Architecture, 48, 81. *See also* Design; Olmsted, Olmsted and Eliot
   American Association of Landscape Architects (ASLA), 83
   Bulfinch and, 18, 163n17
   Fresh Pond Hotel and, 21
   Georgian style, 126–127
   Greek Revival, 22
Arlington, 62, 64, 66, 107
Arthur D. Little, 137
Artists, 26–27, 152

Asian immigrants, 149
Auburn (subdivision), 51
Automobiles, 5, 104, 120, 136. *See also* Transportation
Azan, Paul, 117–118

Barker, John, 39
   John Barker House, *69*, 128, 143
Barracks, 52–53, 159
Baxter, Sylvester, 83
Bellmont estate, 18, 62
Belmont, 5, 41, 62, *63*
   annexation of, 64, 66, 107
   loss of Great Pond rights and, 72
   reputation of, 64, 66
Berms, 143
Bicycling, 120, 158
   bike path, *151*, 151–152, 159
   Olmsted firm plans for, *87*, 88, 99
   speedways, 92–94
Birds, 1, 144, 148, 157
   hunting of, 27, 54, 71–72 (*see also* Fowling)
Black, Mary, 73–74
Black's Nook, 1, *86, 117*
   Cambridge Plant & Garden Club and, 143, *143, 144*
   Civic Beautification Award and, 143
   Community Preservation Act and, 154
   decorative plantings and, 98, 143, *144*
   filling and regrading, 6, 73, *76*, 92, 96, 128
   hydrology of, 128, *129*
   ice industry and, *44*, 74, 158
   neglect of, 143
   Olmsted firm and, 92, 96, 98
   pleasure drive and, *74, 77*
   pollution and, 62, 66, 73
   recreation at, 118, *122*, 143

Blanchard Road, 69, 134–136
Boarding houses, 50–51
Boathouse Nook, 72–73, 77
Boating
    banning of, 72
    Belmont residents and, 64
    Harvard students and, 22, 25, 120, 157
    hotels and, 19, 22, 23, 158
    Storer estate and, 17–18
    tranquility of, 25–28
Boston, 83
    Emerald Necklace and, 59, 148
    public parks and, 59
    reputation of, 26
    urban fringe of, 60, 136–139
    water supply and, 57
    West Boston Bridge and, 5, 16
Boston & Lowell Railroad, 43. *See also* Railroads
Boston Ice Company, *42*, 68–69, 72, 75
Bowling alleys, 18, 22, 137, 158
Bradford, Isaac, 62
Brattle Street, 23, 26
Brewster, William, 27, 51, 102, 157, 166n22
Brick industry, 1, 66, 137
    rise of, 46–48
    urban fringe and, *48*, 60
    worker housing and, 47, 50–51
Bridle paths, 120
Bright, Joseph, 70
Bright, Josiah, 70
Brighton, 70, 83, 131
Bright's Nook, *44*, 70, *73*. *See also* Little Fresh Pond
Brookline, 16, 131
Bulfinch, Anna, 17, 163n17
Bulfinch, Charles, 18, 163n17

Bulfinch, Hannah, 18, 163n17
Burke, John, 19–21
Burke, Mary, 19–21

Cabot brothers, 54
Cambridge
    annexation and, 5, 64, 66, 68–71, 107
    attitude over parks investment and, 83
    City Home for the Aged and Infirm and, 125–126
    civic expansion and, 60–63
    Community Preservation Act and, 1H54
    cramped conditions in, 3–4, *5*
    eminent domain and, 66, 68–71
    geologic history of, 1, 5, 11–12, 129, 131
    loss of Great Pond rights and, 71–72
    municipal expansion and, 7, 107–139 (*see also* Municipal expansion)
    as Newtowne, 12
    parkland design and, 59
    plans to flood Fresh Pond, 110–111
    population growth and, 107–108
    prohibition and, 30
    railroads and, 45–46
    Revolutionary War and, 16
    summer homes and, 16–18
    taxes and, 92
    water supply and, 48–50, 60–66, 131 (*see also* Water supply)
Cambridge Conservation Commission, 141, 150. *See also* Wetlands
Cambridge Historical Commission, 149, 158, 173n1
Cambridge Nook, 39, 41–42, *44*
Cambridge Parks Commission, 83–84, 92, 100–101
Cambridge Plant & Garden Club, 142–146, 152, 161, 172n21
Cambridgeport Aqueduct Company, 48–49, 50
Cambridge Public Schools District, 144
Cambridge Unemployment Bureau, 123
Cambridge Water Board, 2, 57, 60

eminent domain and, 66, 68–71
funding issues and, 91–92
hydrology studies and, 127–131
increased development and, 131–133
Kelley and, 91–92, 104
labor supply issues and, 94–95
loss of Great Pond rights and, 71–72
Olmsted, Olmsted and Eliot and, 83–104
pleasure drive and, 77–79
popular opinion and, 92, 94
project difficulties and, 90–95
relinquished land of, 133–136
shoreline clearing and, 66–71
Cambridge Water Works, 49, *49*, 52, 60–61, 127
Cameron Avenue, 53
Camp, Dresser and McKee, 132, 150
Camp Cameron, 53
Camp Ellsworth, 52
Camp (Harvard professor), 131
Carriage roads, 170n7
automobiles and, 104
Chestnut Hill reservoir and, *58*
creation by Water Board, 6, 31, *59*, 60, 74, 76, *78*
Olmsted, Olmsted and Eliot plan and, 86–90, *87, 88, 90, 97*
pleasure drive and, *77*, 77–79
relocation of, *89*, 91, 93, 99–100, *103*
safety and, 99
speedways and, 92–94
Tudor Park and, 86, 88
Carson, Rachel, 141
Catholic school girls, 2, 30, 157, 161. *See also* Sisters of St. Joseph
Central Park, 59, 81
Charles I, King of England, 14
Charles River, 12, 131
boating on, 25, *29*, 164n37

roads to, 101, 136
speedway, 92–94
Charlestown, 43, 83
Charlestown Branch Railroad, 43, 45–46. *See also* Railroads
Chestnut Hill reservoir, *58*, 59, 167n7, 167nn11–12
Child, Spencer, 69
Children, 109
Catholic school girls, 2, 30, 157, 161
Maynard Ecology Center and, 144, 151, 157
playgrounds and, 2, 109, 118–120, 158
Children's corner, 109, 118
Cider Mill Pond, 90
Citizen involvement, 159
Cambridge Plant & Garden Club and, 142–146, 152, 161
community-based planning and, 142, 148–154
Community Preservation Act and, 154
Fresh Pond Reservation Master Plan Advisory Committee and, 148–154
historical preservation and, 142, 149, 159
horticultural clubs and, 141
natural ecosystems and, 141–142
Neville Manor Site Plan Advisory Committee and, 150–151
pollution and, 141
reclaiming land and, 142
wetlands and, 141, 144
City Home for the Aged and Infirm. *See* Neville Manor
Civic Beautification Award, 143
Civil engineers, 1–2, 81, 83, 127. *See also* Design
Civil War, 5, 51–53, *52*, 57, 159
Clay, 7, 60
brick industry and, 1, 46–48
diminished supply of, 137
glaciers and, 11
hydrologic studies and, 127, 129, 131
rush, 46

Clinker Park, 125
Comey, Arthur C., 120, 123–124
Common law, 14, 41, 49
Community-based planning, 7
    citizen involvement and, 142, 148–154
    Community Preservation Act and, 154
    Fresh Pond Reservation Master Plan Advisory Committee and,
        148–154
Community gardens, 146, 149, 158, 159
Community Preservation Act, 154
Concord Avenue, *60*, *70*, 95–96, 114
    development around, 42, *50*, 51, 61, 134
Concord Turnpike, *2*, 5, 19–20, 54
Congregation of the Sisters of St. Joseph. *See* Sisters of St. Joseph
Continental Army, 16, 70
Convent. *See* Jacob Wyeth House; Sisters of St. Joseph
Coolidge, Josiah, 49
Coolidge, Susan Bulfinch (Mrs. Joseph Lyman), 17–18, 54
Coolidge homestead, 14
Council on Environmental Quality, 107, 172n21
Country seats, 16–18, 23, 39, 53–54
Crane, Edward, 136
Cromwell, Oliver, 14
Cummings, E. E., 26
Cushing, John Perkins, 18, 62
Cushing Street, *96*
Cybernetics, 116

Dancing, 22, 28
Danehy Park, 2, *47*, 137
Dawes, Rufus, 27–28
Decorative plantings. *See* Plantings
Design, 1–2, 7
    aesthetics and, 83–84
    carriage roads and, 86

Central Park and, 81
City Home for the Aged and Infirm and, 125–126
community-based planning and, 142, 148–154
control issues and, 92, 94–95
critics and, 101–102, 104
crowded cities and, 81
decorative plantings and, 88, 90–91, 94–99, 142–145, 150, 159
designer/engineer contrasts and, 83
Eliot and, 82–84
footpaths and, 88
funding issues and, 91–92
General Plan and, 86–90
golf courses and, 120–124
grading and, 92, 94, 96, 98–99, 101
harmony and, 81
Metropolitan Park Commission and, 82–84
as moral revolution, 82
natural, 82, 84–85, 88, 96
new water treatment plant, 150
Olmsted, Olmsted and Eliot firm, 83–104
parklands and, 57, 59
parkways and, 100–101
pleasure drive and, 77–79
professional status and, 81
project difficulties and, 90–95
refectories and, 92, 96, 98, 114
results of Fresh Pond project, 95–104
shoreline clearing and, 72–77
speedways and, 92–94
subdivisions and, 51
terrain challenges and, 95
viewpoints and, 86, 88
vocational training and, 81
water supply improvements and, 60–63

Dining, 19–20, 22, 25
Disease, 16, 53, 108, 110, 136
Dogs, 1, 146, *147*, 148, *149*, 150, 154, 158
Donkey races, 28
Downing, Andrew Jackson, 18
Drinking fountain, 99
Drive-in movie theater, 137, *137*, 139
Drunkenness, 28
Dykes, *59*, 66, 77, 108, 112. *See also* Carriage roads

Eames' Nook, 72, *73*
Ecology. *See* Land use
Economic issues, 152
    Cambridge Plant & Garden Club, 143
    City Home for the Aged and Infirm, 125
    Community Preservation Act, 154
    entertainment places, 19–20
    golf course construction, 123–124
    governmental growth, 107
    grading costs, 92, 94
    Great Depression, 107, 118, 123
    hotels and, 18–23
    industry and, 33 (*see also* Industry)
    liquor sellers, 28
    municipal expansion, 107–139 (*see also* Municipal expansion)
    National Founder's Fund Award, 144
    Olmsted, Olmsted and Eliot, 91–92
    publicly owned land, 142
    ROTC exercises, 118
    summer homes, 16–18
    taxes, 57, 64, 84, 92, 125, 139, 171n73
    working class activities and, 28
Education, 144, 151, 157, 161
Edwin H. Hall Recreation Center, 124. *See also* Golf

Eliot, Charles (landscape architect), 18, 22, *82*, 136, 161. *See also* Olmsted, Olmsted and Eliot
    Cambridge Water Board and, 85–86
    crowded cities and, 81
    Fresh Pond Parkway and, 100–101
    Kelley and, 91
    Kingsley Park and, 100
    methods of, 82–83
    Metropolitan Park Commission and, 83–84
    natural design and, 84–85, 88
    Trustees of Public Reservations and, 82
Eliot, Charles W. (Harvard president), 22, 82
Eliot Bridge, 136
Elliot, Charles D. (city engineer), 13
Ellsworth, Elmer, 52
Elm trees, 39, 75, 92, 98
Emerald Necklace, 59, 148
Eminent domain, 66, 68–71
Engineering, 1–2, 81, 83, 127
Engine house (1856), *49*, 60, 61. *See also* Cambridge Water Works
England, selling ice to, 41
English hay, 39
Environmental issues
    Cambridge Plant & Garden Club and, 143, 146, 152
    capitalism and, 102
    chemicals, 141
    citizen involvement and, 141–154
    decorative plantings, 88, 90–91, 94–99, 142–145, 150, 159
    ecology studies, 141–142, 144
    endangered wildlife, 4
    glaciers, 1, 5, 11–12, 129, 131
    gravel fill, 77
    illegal dumping, 2
    industry and, 54, 57, 141–142
    invasive plants, 2

lobbying and, 141
Marsh and, 54
municipal expansion and, 108–109
natural design, 82, 84–85, 88, 96 (*see also* Design)
pleasure drive and, 77–79
pollution, 66–71, 141 (*see also* Pollution)
public attitudes and, 7
sewage, 64, 66, 70
shoreline clearing, 66–71
Silent Spring and, 141
slaughter-houses and, 64
soil erosion, 2, 141
technology and, 141
Thoreau and, 54
waste reduction, 110
water quality, 7, 57, 59–64, 66 (*see also* Water quality)
wetlands, 141, 144 (*see also* Wetlands)
Erosion, 2, 141
European settlers, 12–14
Everett, Edward, 33, 53–54

Fairmount Park, 59
Family restaurants, 137, 139
Faneuil Hall, 52
Farming, 1, 18
crop failures and, 33
early settlers and, 12, 14
gentlemen farms, 16–18
industry and, 33
New England soil quality and, 33
Tudor and, 39, *69*
Fencing, 1, 17, 53, 128, 150
introduction around the pond, *31*, *60*, *71*, *84*, *88*
later changes to, 133, *133*, 154
Filtration plant (1923), *108*, 127, 128, 132, 133, 146
building of, *111*, 111–112, *112*, 124

Fishing, 1, 4, 11, 22, 26
Burkes' advertisements and, 19
Cambridge Plant & Garden Club and, 143, 146
Great Pond rights and, 14, 71–72
permits and, 120
weirs and, 12
Fitchburg Railroad, *44*, 45–46, *47*, 71. *See also* Railroads
Flocculation chambers, *132*
Footpaths, *85*, 88, *89*, 99, *100*
Foster, C. C., 17
Foster, W., 39
Fountain, 58–59, *62*, 77, 92, *93*, 111, *160*
Fountain Terrace, 77, 96, *98*, 122, *160*. *See also* Stony Brook
Fowling, 11, 14, 16, 19, 22, *23*, 71–72
French, Daniel Chester, 27
French army officers, *114*, 114–116
French Canadian immigrants, 33, 50–51, 66
Fresh Pond
artists and, 26–27
capacity of, 127
as case study, 4–5
as country seat, 16–17
as drinking water supply, 1–2, 7, 26, 48–50, 59–60 (*see also* Water supply)
early settlers and, 4, 7, 12, 14, 16
educational purposes and, 157
eminent domain and, 66, 68–71
endangered wildlife and, 4
geologic history of, 1, 11–12
glaciers and, 1, 5, 11–12, 129, 131
Great Pond rights and, 4, 7, 12, 14, 16, 35, 50, 71–72, 158
growing reputation of, 14, 16
hotels and, 18–23
housing development and, 50–51
hydrology of, 127–131

industry and, 33–55
location of, 1, 4
as lovers' lane, 26
municipal expansion and, 107–139 (*see also* Municipal expansion)
neglect of, 2
pleasure drive around, 77–79
raising level of, 110–112, 125
recreation and, 1, 7, 11–31 (*see also* Recreation)
remaining historical evidence in, 157
ROTC exercises and, 113–118
sense of attachment to, 1–4
shoreline clearing and, 66–71
size of, 1, 3–4
smallpox hospital at, 16
water source of, 127–131
working-class use of, 27–28
World War I era and, 113–118
Fresh Pond Farm, 14, *15*, 86, 92
    elm tree avenue, 39
    eminent domain and, 69
    hay cutting and, 113
    sales of, 16
    as summer home, 16–18
    Tudor and, 39
Fresh Pond Grove, 28, 30–31. *See also* Kingsley Park; Promontory
    picnickers on, 60, *99*
    trees and, 31, *85*, *86*, 98
    Water Board and *59*, 60, *86*, 92
Fresh Pond Hotel, 2, *3*, 36, *59*, 159
    as apartment building, *22*, 70
    beginnings of, 20–23, *21*, *23*, *24*, *25*, 26
    pollution from, 66
    Sisters of St. Joseph and, 30–31, 69–70
    working class and, 27–28
Fresh Pond Ice Company, 66, 68, *68*, *71*

Fresh Pond New Hotel, 20
Fresh Pond Parkway, *100,* 100–101, *101*, 134, 139, 151–152, 159
Fresh Pond Railroad station, 46, *46. See also* Railroads
Fresh Pond Reservation Master Plan Advisory Committee, 148–154
Fresh Pond Shopping Center, *47*, 137, 139
Friendship, 3, 17, 26, 102
Friends of Fresh Pond Reservation, 4, 157

Gage, Addison, 41, 69
Gage, Hittinger & Co., 41
Garden Club of America, 144
Gay, Rosella, 70
Gay, William, 70
Gay's Nook, 72
Gerry's Landing Road, 136
Glacialis, *44*, *65*
    creation of, 42, 166n22
    filling in, 136, 137
    pollution from, 64
    skating on, 43, 72
Glaciers, 1, 5, 11–12, 129, 131
Glacken, Francis X., 118
Glacken Field, 1, 89, 118, 147, 153
Glue factories, 60
Golf, 97, 109, 148
    course design and, *122, 123, 124*, 120–125
    land use and, 2, 120–125, 134, 144, 146, 153
Grading costs, 92, 94
Gravel, 11–12, 42, 73, 77, 127–131
Great Bridge, 16
Great Depression, 107, 120, 123
Great Pond rights, 7, 16
    early settlers and, 12, 14
    ice industry and, 35, 50
    loss of, 4, 71–72, 158

Great Swamp, *2*, 11, *13*, 46, *47*, 136, 171n69. *See also* Wetlands
Great War. *See* World War I era
Greek Revival style, 22
Green Agenda. *See also* Environmental issues
    Cambridge Plant & Garden Club and, 143–146, 152, 161
    community-based planning and, 142, 148–154
    Fresh Pond Reservation Master Plan Advisory Committee and,
       148–154
    natural ecosystems and, 141–142
    Silent Spring and, 141
    wetlands and, 141, 144 (*see also* Wetlands)
Greenhouses, *126*
Greenleaf, Simon, 41
Grove, 28, 30–31. *See also* Kingsley Park; Promontory
    picnickers on, 60, *99*
    trees and, 31, *85*, *86*, 98
    Water Board and *59*, 60, *86*, 92
Grove Street, *15*, 134–136, *136*

Harvard Square, 16
Harvard University, 20, 41, 150
    Eliot and, 82
    Graduate School of Engineering, 120
    Lowell and, 113–114
    Olmsted Jr., and, 83
    Peabody Museum, 163n2
    Reserve Officer Training Corps (ROTC) and, 113–118
    students, 22, 25–26, 72, 85, 157–158
Hay, 14, 113
Health issues, 53, 136
    elderly housing and, 125–127
    filtration plant and, 111–112
    playgrounds and, 109, 118–120
    smallpox, 16
    social reform and, 57, 59–60

typhoid, 108, 110
    waste reduction and, 110
    water quality and, 108 (*see also* Water quality)
Historical preservation movement, 142, 148, 149, 159, 173n1
Historic Cambridge Collaborative, 161
Hittinger, Jacob, 41, 66, 69
Hobbs Brook reservoir, 62, *63*, 91, 108
Holden, John, 70
Holden, Joseph, 19
Holden, Justinian, 14
Holy Ghost Hospital for Incurables, 69, 125–126
Homer, Winslow, 2–3, 26–27
Horse racing, 50
Horticulture
    Cambridge Plant & Garden Club and, 142–146, 152, 161
    city studies and, 146
    decorative plantings and, 88, 90–91, 94–99, 142–145, 150, 159
Hotels, 18–23, 164nn24–26. *See also* Fresh Pond Hotel
Housing, 2, *15*, 146
    Bellmont and, 18
    controversial land sales and, 134, *134–135*, 136
    for elderly, 125–127
    eminent domain and, 69–71
    estates and, 18
    federal, 139
    industry and, 57
    playgrounds and, 109
    pollution and, 64
    subdivisions and, 51
    summer homes and, 16–18, *18*
    veterans, 134, 136
    workers, *47*, *50,* 50–51, *51*, 57, 71
Howe, Estes, 49
Hubbard, Gardiner, 49
Hubbell, Peter, 46, 48

Hudson's Bay Company, 38
Hunting, 1, 12, 14, 54
Huron Avenue, 77, 96, 97, 98, 101, 133, 173n1
Hurricane, 128
Hydrology, 127–131

Ice age, 1, 5, 11–12, 129–131, 133
Icehouses, *3, 24, 37, 55,* 60, 73, 158
    above ground, 36
    as barracks, 52–53
    brick, 46, 48
    eminent domain and, 66, 68–69, *71*
    pollution and, 64
Ice industry, 1, 7, 102, 158–159
    access rights and, 39–41, *41*
    common law and, 41
    competition in, 38–39, 41
    eminent domain and, 66, 68–71
    food preservation and, 33–34
    Glacialis and, 42, *44, 43,* 64, *65,* 72, 136, 137, 166n22
    Great Pond rights and, 35, 50
    Greenleaf method and, *41*
    iced drinks and, 41
    shifting reactions to, 53–54
    shoreline methods for, 42, *42*
    technology and, 36, *37,* 38, *55*
    transportation and, 34–35, 43–46, 48
    Tudor and, 33–42, 53–54, 68–69, 72, 144
    water supply industry and, 49–50
    worker housing and, *50,* 50–51
    Wyeth and, 35–39, 41, 43, 49, 54
Ice King. *See* Tudor, Frederic
Immigrants, 66
    Asian, 149
    French Canadian, 33, 50–51, 161

Irish, 33, 50–51, 161
    Portuguese, 144, 158
    Russian, 149, 161
India, 35, 39
Indian Board of Control, 53
Indigenous peoples, 158. *See also* Native Americans
Industrial Revolution, 5, 9, 33, 57
Industry, 158–159
    agriculture, 33
    artisanal systems, 33
    brick, 1, 46–48, 50–51, 60, 66, 137
    capitalism and, 102
    drinking and, 28
    environmental issues and, 54, 57, 141–142
    housing for, 50–51, 57, 71
    ice, 1, 7 (*see also* Ice industry)
    living conditions and, 57
    migration and, 9, 33, 50–51, 57
    morality and, 7
    municipal expansion and, 136–139
    nature and, 84
    New England and, 33
    politics and, 9
    pollution and, 57 (*see also* Pollution)
    shifting reactions to, 53–54, 57
    soldier barracks and, 52–53
    steam power and, 33
    transportation and, 34–35, 43–46, 48, 136–139
    urbanism and, 57
    water supply, 48–50
    working conditions and, 57
Irish immigrants, 33, 50–51, 161

Jacob Wyeth House, 22, *23, 24*
    as convent, 30, *31*
    relocated, *70,* 143

James, Henry, 102
Jarvis, Betsey, 20
John Barker House, *69*, 128, 143
Johnson, Walter Irving, Jr., 123–124. *See also* Golf

Kelley, Stillman, 91–92, 104. *See also* Cambridge Water Board; Olmsted,
    Olmsted and Eliot
Kendall Square, 49
Kettle lakes, 11–12
Kilns, 46, 60
Kingsbury, Allen, *52, 53*
Kingsley, Chester Ward, 61, 76, 161, 167n8. *See also* Cambridge
    Water Board
Kingsley Park, *91,* 158–159. *See also* Grove; Promontory
    carriage rides and, 84
    Community Preservation Act and, 154
    hay cutting and, 113
    location of, *1, 75, 76*
    Olmsted, Olmsted and Eliot and, *89,* 94, *94,* 96, 98–99, *100,* 101,
        104, *109*
Korean War veterans' housing, 134–136

Labor
    golf course construction and, 123–124
    industry effects and, 57 (*see also* Industry)
    living conditions and, 57
    migration and, 9, 33, 50–51, 57
    New Deal and, 5, 107
    Olmsted, Olmsted and Eliot and, 94
    urbanism and, 57
    vocational training and, 81
    worker housing and, 50–51, 57, 71
    Works Progress Administration and, 107, 118, 123, 128
Lake View Avenue, 70, 133
Land use, 1, 157

annexations and, 5, 64, 66, 68–71, 107
Cambridge Plant & Garden Club and, 142–146, 152, 161
citizen involvement and, 141–154
common law and, 14, 41, 49
Community Preservation Act and, 154
decorative plantings and, 88, 90–91, 94–99, 142–145, 150, 159
design and, 57, 59, 81–104 (*see also* Design)
early settlers and, 12, 14
ecology studies and, 141–142, 144
elderly housing and, 125–127
eminent domain and, 66, 68–71
Fresh Pond Reservation Master Plan Advisory Committee and,
    148–154
golf courses and, 2, 120–125, 134, 144, 146, 153
gravel fill and, 77
Great Pond rights and, 4, 7, 12, 14, 16, 35, 50, 71–72, 158
historical preservation and, 142, 148, 149, 159, 173n1
hotels and, 18–23
housing and, 2, 16–18, 50–51, 57, 64, 69–71, 109, 125–127, 134,
    136, 139, 146
ice harvesting and, 33–46
Metropolitan Park Commission and, 82–85, 100–101
Mount Auburn Cemetery and, 23–25
municipal expansion and, 107–139 (*see also* Municipal expansion)
National Trust and, 82
parkland design and, 57, 59
playgrounds and, 2, 109, 118–120, 158
pleasure drive and, 77–79
riprap and, 74, 88
ROTC exercises and, 113–118
shoreline clearing and, 66–71
suburban development and, 5, 136–137
summer homes and, 16–18
transportation and, 136–139 (*see also* Transportation)
Trustees of Public Reservations and, 82
water quality and, 72–77 (*see also* Water quality)

Larches estate, *18*, 20, 101
Laurentide glacier, 11
Leavitt, Edward D., 61, 167n12
Lee, Robert E., 25
Lee, William H. F. "Rooney", 25
Legal issues, 146
    annexation, 64
    change of land use, 125–126
    common law, 14, 41, 49
    eminent domain, 66, 68–71
    Great Pond rights, 4, 7, 12, 14, 16, 35, 50, 71–72, 158
    Greenleaf method, 41
    hydrology studies and, 128–130
    ice industry vs. water industry, 49–50
    Massachusetts General Laws and, 14
    playgrounds and, 109
    water quality, 128–131
Lewis and Clark expedition, 38
Lexington, 62, *63*
Lexington Avenue, 46
Lily Pond, *73*, *90*, 95. *See also* Little Fresh Pond
Lincoln (town), 62, *63*
Little Fresh Pond, 6, 70, *73*, *90*, *124*, *149*, 154
Little Pond, 62
Longfellow, Charles, 26
Longfellow, Henry Wadsworth, 26
Longfellow Bridge, 16
Lovers' lane, 26
Low, John, 51
Lowell, A. Lawrence, 113–115
Lowell, James Russell, 26
Lusitania Field, 143–144, 150, 151. *See also* Soccer
Lusitania Meadow, 158
Lyman, Mrs. Joseph, 54. *See also* Coolidge, Susan Bulfinch

McNamee, John H. H., 109
Magdalena, Sister M., 30
Man and Nature (Marsh), 54
Marsh, George Perkins, 54
Marshes. *See* Wetlands
Massachusetts Audubon Society, 149
Massachusetts Bay Colony, 14, 127
Massachusetts Bay Transportation Authority (MBTA), 139
Massachusetts First Regiment of Infantry, 52–53
Massachusetts General Laws, 14
Massachusetts Historical Commission, 173n1
Massachusetts Institute of Technology (MIT), 116
Massachusetts Water Resources Authority (MWRA), 146, 150
Massachusett tribe, 12. *See also* Native Americans
Maynard Ecology Center, 144, 151, 157
Mayor Michael J. Neville Manor. *See* Neville Manor
Mayor Thomas W. Danehy Park, 2, *47*, 137
Metropolitan District Commission (MDC), 128–129, 131, 134, 136, 171n73
Metropolitan Park Commission, 82–85, 100–101
Metropolitan Water District, 107
Migration, 9, 33
    industry effects and, 57
    urbanism and, 57
    worker housing and, 50–51, 57, 71
Model T Ford, 104. *See also* Transportation
Moore, Joseph, 21
Morize, André, 118
Moses, Robert, 142
Mount Auburn Cemetery, *3*, 23, *24*, 25, *49*, 51, 60
Mount Auburn Street, 22, 46, 52, 101
Mount St. Joseph Academy, 30–31, *31*. *See also* Catholic school girls; Fresh Pond Hotel; Sisters of St. Joseph
Municipal expansion, 57
    annexation and, 107

City Home for the Aged and Infirm and, 125–127
elderly housing and, 125–127
environmental issues and, 108–109
filtration plant and, 111–112
golf courses and, 120–125, 134
governmental growth and, 107
hydrology studies and, 127–131
increased development and, 131–133
industry and, 136–139
parkland effects and, 108–109
plans to flood Fresh Pond, 110–111
playgrounds and, 109, 118–120
population growth and, 107–108
relinquishing land and, 133–136
space premium from, 108
suburban areas and, 136–137
transportation and, 136–139
urban fringe and, *48,* 60, 136–139
World War I era and, 113–118
Music, 22, 28, 150
Myopia Base Ball Club, 28
Mystic River, 1, *12,* 18, 129, 171n61

Nahant, *35,* 53
National Founder's Fund Award, 144
National Register of Historic Places, 157, 159, 161, 173n1
National Trust, 82
Native Americans, 1, *12,* 12, 38, 158, 163n1 (chap. 2)
Nature, 28. *See also* Environmental issues
    Cambridge Plant & Garden Club and, 142–146, 152, 161
    citizen involvement and, 141–154
    Civic Beautification Award and, 143
    decorative plantings, 88, 90–91, 94–99, 142–145, 150, 159
    defeating, 85
    design and, 84–85 (*see also* Design)

ecosystems and, 141–142
importance of, 7
industry and, 84
meaning of term, 85
morality and, 7, 57, 59
orchards, 1, 14, 18, 27, 39, 51, 158 (*see also* Trees)
Neville Manor (City Home for the Aged and Infirm), 144, 146, 150–151
    Creation of City Home, 125–127, *126*
    National Register nomination, 163n1, 173n1
    Neville Center for Nursing and Rehabilitation, 1, 127, 158
    Neville Manor Site Plan Advisory Committee, 150–151
    Neville Place, 1, 14, 118, 127
New Deal, 5, 107
Newtowne. *See* Cambridge
New York, 57, 59
Niles Brothers' slaughterhouse, 64, *65,* 66
Nurseries, 91, 126, 158

Olmsted, Frederick Law, Jr., 59, 83–85, 96, 102, 104
Olmsted, Frederick Law, Sr., 81–82, 100, 169n15
Olmsted, John Charles, 83, 91–92
Olmsted, Olmsted and Eliot (Olmsted firm), 173n1
    Cambridge Water Board and, 83, 85–86
    Comey and, 120, 123–124
    control issues and, 92, 94–95
    criticism of, 101–102, 104
    decorative plantings and, 88, 90–91, 94–99
    "design and build" company, 94
    Fresh Pond vision of, 86–90, *87*
    funding issues and, 91–92
    grading and, 92, 94, 96, 98–99, 101
    impact of firm, 101–102, 104
    Kelley and, 91–92, 104
    Kingsley Park and, 94, 96, 98–99, *99, 100,* 101, *103,* 104, *109*
    Metropolitan Park Commission and, 83–85

modern ignorance of, 159, 169n15
natural design and, 84–85, 88, 96
parkways and, 100–101
political issues and, 91–92
project difficulties and, 90–95
refectories and, 92, 96, 98, 114
results of Fresh Pond project, 95–104
speedways and, 93–94
terrain challenges and, 95, *96*
Olmsted Brothers, 83
Olmsted Grove, 98
O'Neill, Thomas P. "Tip", 50, 124
Orchards, 1, 14, 18, 27, 39, 51, 158

Parkways
Alewife Brook Parkway, 136, 139, 171n73
Fresh Pond Parkway, 100–101, 134, 139, 151–152, 159
municipal expansion and, 136–139
Parry (alderman), 70
Paternalism, 57
Payson Hill, 62
Payson Park reservoir, 62, *63*, 91, 108, 159
Peabody Museum, 163n2
Perimeter path, 1, 142, 153, 154. *See also* Carriage roads
Perkins, Henry, 83. *See also* Olmsted, Frederick Law, Jr.
Picnics, 1–2, 28, 60, *99*, 101–102, 143–144, 158
Piggeries, 60, 64
Plantings, 150, 159
Cambridge Plant & Garden Club and, 142–145
Olmsted, Olmsted and Eliot and, 88, 90–91, 94–99
Playgrounds, 2, 109, *118*, 118–120, 158
Pleasure drive, *60*, 77–79, *84*, 101. *See also* Carriage roads
Poetry, 14, 26
Policy
annexations, 5, 64, 66, 68–71, 107

community-based planning and, 7, 142, 148–154
Community Preservation Act and, 154
eminent domain and, 66, 68–71
Fresh Pond Reservation Master Plan and, 2, 148–154
Great Pond rights, 4, 7, 12, 14, 16, 35, 50, 71–72, 158
Politicians' Row, 134–136
Politics, 161
citizen involvement and, 141–154
City Home for the Aged and Infirm and, 125–127
controversial land sales and, 134, 136
eminent domain and, 66, 68–71
environmental movement and, 141
Everett and, 53–54
governmental growth and, 107
Great Depression and, 107
Green Agenda, 141–154, 161
industry and, 9
interventionism and, 107
Irish immigrants and, 33
McNamee and, 109
municipal expansion and, 107–139 (*see also* Municipal expansion)
New Deal and, 5, 107
Olmsted, Olmsted and Eliot and, 81, 91–92
plans to flood Fresh Pond, 110–111
slaughter-houses and, 64
social reform and, 57 (*see also* Social reform)
Sortwell and, 92
Pollution, 1, 57, 164n37
Alewife Brook and, 64, 131
Black's Nook and, 62, 66, 73
Boathouse Nook and, 72–73
Cider Mill Pond and, 90
citizen involvement and, 141
Eames' Nook and, 72
Gay's Nook and, 72

housing and, 64
identifying sources of, 64
Niles Brothers' slaughter-house and, 66
Richardson's Pond and, 90
ROTC exercises and, 114, 116
sewage and, 64, 66, 70
shoreline clearing and, 66–71
waste reduction and, 110
water quality and, 62, 64, 66 (*see also* Water quality)
Poor Farm, 125
Population growth, 107–108
Porter Square, 137
Portuguese immigrants, 144, 158
Prentiss, Henry, 15, 16
Preservationists, 142, 148, 149, 159, 173n1
Prohibition, 30, 167n8
Promontory, 2, *12*, 20–25 passim, 46. *See also* Grove; Kingsley Park
Prospect Hill, 49
Public art, 152, *152*
Pumping station (1872), 112, 128, 133, 150, 159, 167n12
    building of, *61*
    demolition, 61, 132
    location, *75*
Pumping station (1950s), *132*, 146

Quabbin reservoir, 107, 128, *130*
Quinn, Edward D., 125

Radcliffe College, 101, 124
Railroads, 5, 71, 99, 101, 128, 159
    arrival of, 33, 46–48
    brick industry and, 46–48
    fire dangers from, 46
    housing and, 51–52, 60
    ice industry and, 43–46, 48, *68*

passenger service and, 45–46
Thoreau on, 45
Tudor and, 43
Wyeth and, 43
Recreation, 7
    artists and, 26–27
    bicycling, *87*, 88, 92–94, 99, 120, 151–152, 158–159
    boating, 17–18, 19, 22, 23, 25–30, 64, 72–73, 120, 157–158
    bowling, 18, 22, 137, 158
    carriage road, 77–79, 86–90
    common law and, 14
    dancing, 22, 28
    dining, 19–20, 22, 25
    entertainment places, 19–20
    fishing, 1, 4, 11–12, 14, 19, 22, 26, 71–72, 120, 143, 146
    footpaths, 88, 99
    fowling, 11, 14, 16, 19, 22, 71–72
    golf, 2, 109, 120–125, 134, 144, 146, 148, 153
    horseback riding, 120
    horse racing, 50
    hotels, 18–23
    hunting, 1, 12, 14, 54
    increased focus upon, 109
    loss of Great Pond rights and, 72
    music, 22, 28, 150
    picnics, 1–2, 28, 60, *99*, 101–102, 143–144, 158
    playgrounds, 2, 109, 118–120, 158
    pleasure drive, 77–79
    prohibition and, 30
    refreshment facilities, 23, 25–26, 28
    sailing, 22, *23*, 25
    skating, 25–26, *71*, 72, 109, 120, 158
    sleigh parties, 26
    soccer, 143–144, 151, 153–154, 158, 161
    social reform and, 57, 59

summer homes and, 16–18
    swimming, 26, 64, 66, 72, 116, 146
    Tally Ho events, 101
    temperance movement and, 28, 30
    tennis, 1, *109*, 118
    toboggan slide, *119*
    transportation and, 137, 139
    working class activities and, 27–28
Red Line subway, 137, 139
Reed and Bartlett icehouse, *49*, 52
Refectory, 92, 96, 98, 114. *See also* Olmsted, Olmsted and Eliot
Refreshment facilities, 23, 25–26, 28. *See also* Fresh Pond Hotel
Reserve Officer Training Corps (ROTC), 113–118, *114, 116, 117*
Reservoirs, 62, 63, 77, 91, 108, 111
    on Reservoir Street, 49, *49*, 60–62, 159
Revolutionary War, 14, 16, 18, 70
Rice, Moses, 49
Richardson, H. H., 150
Richardson, Richard, 19–21
Richardson Pond, 64, 90
Rindge Avenue, 50, *51*
Rindge Towers, 139
Riprap, 9, *73*, 74, *75*, *84*, 88, *88*
Rockwood Pond, 35
Rogers, Jean, 148
Romance, 26
Roman common law, 14
Roosevelt, Franklin D., 5, 107
Roosevelt, Theodore, 26
Route 2, 137
Rowboats, 18, *23*, *25*, 26, *27*
    Harvard students and, 22, 25, 120, 157
Russell, Richard M., 124
Russian immigrants, 149, 161

Safety, 16, 104, 108, 111, 120
Sailing, 22, *23*, *25*, 25
St. Francis Xavier University, 69
Sand, 11, 127–131
Settlers
    common law and, 14
    European, 12, 14
    Great Pond rights and, 4, 7, 12, 14, 16
    land use and, 12, 14
    Native Americans and, 12
    Revolutionary War and, 14, 16
Sewage, 64, 66, 70
Shoreline issues, 169n15
    annexation, 66, *67*
    carriage roads, *86*, 86–90
    clearing, 66–71
    erosion, 73–74, 141
    footpaths, *85*, 88
    gravel fill, 77, *78*
    plantings, 88, 90
    pleasure drive, 77–79
    public works and, *60*, 72–77
    riprap and, 9, *73*, 74, *75*, *84*, 88
    transportation, 66, 77, 79
    water quality, 72–77
Signage, *60*, *93*, *147*, 150, 154, *158*
Silent Spring (Carson), 141
Sisters of St. Joseph, 30–31, 69–70. *See also* Catholic school girls
Skating, 25–26, *71*, 72, 109, 120, 158
Slaughter-houses, 60, 64, 66, 139
Sleigh parties, 26
Smallpox, 16
Soccer, 143–144, 151, 153–154, 158, 161
Social reform, 1–2, 5, 7
    annexation and, 64

automobiles and, 104
civic expansion and, 60–63
design and, 81–82 (*see also* Design)
eminent domain and, 66, 68–71
erosion issues and, 73–74
gravel fill and, 77
health issues and, 57, 59–60
interventionist approach and, 57
loss of Great Pond rights and, 71–72
marshes and, 74
New Deal and, 107
Olmsted and, 81
outdoor access issues and, 57, 59
paternalism and, 57
pleasure drive and, 77–79
pollution and, 66
prohibition and, 30
public morals and, 57, 59
shoreline clearing and, 66–71
slaughter-houses and, 60, 64, 66
taxes and, 57
temperance movement and, 28, 30
urbanism and, 57
water quality and, 72–77 (*see also* Water quality)
Soldiers, 52–53, 113–118, 161
Soldiers Field, 114
Somers, John E., 69, 125–126
Sortwell (Mayor of Cambridge), 92
Sparhawk, Nathaniel, 14
Speedways, 93–94, 99
Spy Pond, 62
Steam power, 33
Stearns, Frederic, 110
Steel industry, 137
Stone, Elizabeth Jarvis, 36, 38

Stone, Leonard, 38
Stone, Phineas, 20
Stony Brook
    fountain, *62*, 77, *93*, 111, *160*
    reservoir, 62, *63*, 77, 108, 111, 112
    supply pipe, 62, 77, 111 (*see also* Fountain Terrace)
Storer, Charles, 16
Storer, Ebenezer, 17
Storer, George, 17–18, 163n17
Strawberry Hill, 51, 64, *65*, 71
Streetcars, 5. *See also* Transportation
Students, 1, 19, 27. *See also* Harvard University: students;
    Mount St. Joseph Academy; Radcliffe College
Subdivisions, 51
Suburban development, 5, 136–137
Summer homes, 16–18
Swales, *153*
Swampland. *See* Wetlands
Swimming, 26, 64, 66, 72, 116, 146

Tally Ho events, 101
Tanneries, 60
Taxes, 57, 64, 84, 92, 125, 139, 171n73
Technology, 7
    automobiles and, 104
    chemicals and, 141
    communications and, 33
    environmental issues and, 141
    ice harvesting and, 34–36, 38
    Industrial Revolution and, 9, 33, 57
    industry and, 33 (*see also* Industry)
    manufacturing and, 33
    New England inventors and, 33
    power-driven machinery and, 33
    production and, 33
    railroads and, 33

steam power and, 33

transportation and, 33

Temperance movement, 28, 30

Tennis, 1, *109*, 118

Tepees, *12. See also* Native Americans

Textile mills, 33

Thomas P. O'Neill Jr. Municipal Golf Course, *4, 97, 124*, 124. *See also* Golf

Thoreau, Henry David, 45, 54

Toboggan slide, *119*

Tramways, 46, *47*

Transportation, 19–20

automobiles, 5, 104, 120, 136

brick industry and, 46–48

carriage roads, 77–79, 86–94, 99–100, 104

design and, 86

ice industry and, 34–35, 43–46, 48, 136–139

municipal expansion and, 136–139

parkways, 100–101, 134, 136, 139, 151–152, 159, 171n73

pleasure drive and, 77–79

railroads, 5, 33, 43–52, 71, 99, 128, 159

safety and, 99, 104

shoreline and, 66, 77, 79

speedways, 92–94, 99

streetcars, 5, 46, *47*

subways, 137, 139

West Boston Bridge, 5, 16, *17*

Trees, 31, *76, 85, 105*, 150, 153, 159

Autumn leaves and, 54

Brewster and, *44*, 51

Cambridge Plant & Garden Club and, 143–146

elms, 39, 75, 92, 98

Fresh Pond Hotel and, 22, *23*

golf courses and, *4,* 123

hurricane and, 128

Olmsted, Olmsted and Eliot and, 86, 88, 90, 95–99, *97, 98*

Olmsted Grove, 98

orchards, 1, 14, 18, 27–28, 39, *44*, 51, 158

preservation of, 71

removal of, *59*, 71, 73–74

volunteer, 113, 124

willow, *4, 44*, 73, 90, 96

Wyeth and, 36

Trolleys, 5. *See also* Transportation

Trotting Park, 50–51

Trotting Park House, 50

Trustees of Public Reservations, 82

Tudor, Euphemia, 68

Tudor, Frederic, 17, *35*, 158, 166n40

brick industry and, 48

farming and, 39

Glacialis and, 42, *43, 44*, 64, *65*, 72, 136, 137, 166n22

hay cutting and, 113

ice industry and, 33–42, *42*, 53–54, 68–69, 72, *75*, 144

railroads and, 43, 45

worker housing and, 50, *50, 69*

Tudor, William, 16, 34

Tudor Park, *75*, 86, 88, 100, 113, *145*, 159

Typhoid, 108, 110

Union Carbide dump, 139

Union Coffee House, 20

United States, 16

capitalism and, 102

Civil War and, 5, 51–53, 57, 159

Revolutionary War and, 14, 16, 18, 70

World War I and, 27, 111, 113–118, 136

World War II and, 109, 133

Urban fringe, *48*, 60, 136–139

Urbanism. *See* Municipal expansion

U.S. Army, 133

U.S. Army Air Corps, 118
U.S. Geological Survey, 131

Vassal Lane, 51, 133
Veterans' housing, 134–136

Wadsworth, Alexander, 51
Walden Pond, 45
Walter J. Sullivan Water Treatment Facility (2001), 1, 2, *142*, 146, 150, 158
Waltham, 62, *63*
Walton (Walter), John, 21
Warren Institution for Savings, 30
Washington, George, 16
Wasserman Development Corporation, 139
Water
    drinking, 1–2, 7, 26
    environmental issues and, 57
    fire fighting and, 49
    glaciers and, 1, 5, 11–12, 129, 131
    Great Pond rights and, 4, 7, 12, 14
    hydrology and, 127–131
    ice harvesting and, 33–46, 55
    private enterprise and, 48–50
    Roman common law and, 14
    storage reservoirs and, 91
    wetlands and, 141 (*see also* Wetlands)
Water board. *See* Cambridge Water Board
Water meters, 112
Water quality, 59–60, 62, 148
    battles over, 64, 66
    disease transmission and, 108, 110, 136
    filtration and, 110–112, 133
    hydrology studies and, 131
    legal issues and, 128–131

    municipal expansion and, 107
    population growth and, 107–108
    public works and, 7, 72–77
    ROTC exercises and, 114, 116
    typhoid and, 108, 110
    waste reduction and, 110
    water source and, 127–131
Water supply. *See also* Cambridge Water Board
    barracks and, 52
    civic improvements in, 60–66, *63*
    consumption levels and, 128–129
    dykes and, 112
    floodgates and, 61
    Fresh Pond Reservation Master Plan Advisory Committee and, 148–154
    Great Pond rights and, 50
    ice age and, 129, 131
    increased demand and, 107
    indoor plumbing and, 107
    Metropolitan Water District and, 107
    municipal expansion and, 107, 128–129 (*see also* Municipal expansion)
    plans to flood Fresh Pond and, *110*, 110–111
    private enterprise, 48–50 (*see also* Cambridge Water Works)
    pumping stations and, 61, 167n12 (*see also* Pumping station)
    sewage and, 64, 66
    slaughter-houses and, 64
    source of, 127–131
    Stony Brook and, 62
    supplementary sources and, 62
    system, *63*
    system improvements and, 131, 133, 146
Watertown, 1, 12, 14, 18, 23, 41
Watertown Branch railroad, *44*, 46–47, 101. *See also* Railroads
Water treatment facility (2001), 1, 2, *142*, 146, 150, 158

Wellington Brook, 62
West Boston Bridge, 5, 16, *17*
Weston, 62, *63*
Wetlands
    attempts to fill, 74, 95, 136
    Cambridge Conservation Commission and, *141*, 150
    definition of, 12, 141, 171n2
    digging clay from, 1, 2, 46, 47
    Great Swamp, *2*, 11, *13*, 46, 47, 136, 171n69
    marsh and swampland, 43, 51, 54, 64, *95*, 127
    protection of, 141, 144, 153, 154
White Swan steamboat, *29*
Wiener, Norbert, 114, 116
Willard, Lyman, 23, 25, 28
Winthrop, Hannah, 16
Woodland Street, 51
Woodlawn Avenue, 51
Working class, 27–28
Works Progress Administration, 107, 118, 123, 128
World War I era, 27, 111, 113–118, 136
World War II era, 109, 133
Worthington Street, 133
Wrightson, R., 20
Wyeth, Ebenezer, 20–21
    farmhouse, *20*
Wyeth, Jacob, 11, 20–22, 30, 36. *See also* Fresh Pond Hotel;
        Jacob Wyeth House
Wyeth, John B., 38
Wyeth, Jonas, 22–23
Wyeth, Nathaniel J., 7, 22, *36*, 165n9
    brick industry and, 46, 48
    expedition of, 38
    ice industry and, 35–39, 41, 43, 49, 54
    railroads and, 43
Wyeth Point, *86*, 99

WEST END